# Butterfly Christian Nation

Dr. Livingstone's Luminous Legacy in Zambia

## John C. Kerr

Dr. Livingstone's
Luminous Legacy in
**ZAMBIA**

# Butterfly
## Christian Nation

# John C. Kerr

# BUTTERFLY CHRISTIAN NATION
## Copyright © 2019, John C. Kerr

All Scripture quotations, unless otherwise specified, are from the HOLY BIBLE, NEW INTERNATIONAL VERSION ®. Copyright © 1973, 1978, 1984 by International Bible Society. Used by permission of Zondervan Publishing House. All rights reserved. • Scriptures marked KJV are from *The Holy Bible, King James Version*. Copyright © 1977, 1984, Thomas Nelson Inc., Publishers.

Cataloguing data available from Library and Archives Canada

ISBN: 978-1-4600-0941-3
LSI Edition: 978-1-4600-0942-0
E-book ISBN: 978-1-4600-0943-7
(E-book available from the Kindle Store, KOBO and the iBooks Store)

*Essence Publishing* is a Christian Book Publisher dedicated to furthering the work of Christ through the written word. For more information, contact: 20 Hanna Court, Belleville, Ontario, Canada K8P 5J2
Phone: 1-800-238-6376. Fax: (613) 962-3055
Email: info@essence-publishing.com
Web site: www.essence-publishing.com

PUBLISHING

*Dedicated in loving memory to*

**John Myrrl Cornelius**
(1948-2018),

best of friends and much-loved brother,
mentor, designer, builder, spreading sunshine and goodwill
wherever he went in this wide world,
from Southern Ontario to the Zambian Copperbelt.
Uplifting the downcast, encouraging the despondent,
instilling hope among the disadvantaged
with his bright optimism, irrepressible vision
and enormous skills.

# *Endorsements*

"With the imagination of a poet, the imagery of a entomologist, and the firsthand experience of a missionary, John Kerr deftly depicts the miracle of Zambia: the metamorphosis of a region defined by war and slave-trading into a self-proclaimed Christian nation. Along the way, he has even unearthed the story of an African Azusa."

—Dr. Van Johnson

"*Lesa musuma!* God is powerful!' So says J.C. Kerr in *Butterfly Christian Nation*. His lively prose will have readers shouting, '*Lesa musuma!*' The book's epilogue on the new birth alone makes it worth reading."

—Dr. Rick Ball, Richard Ball & Associates, Inc.
Professor of Apologetics, Trans-Africa Christian University

"This book opens us up to the beauty and wonder of the Christian faith. It is well researched and artistically crafted, presented by a skillful writer who is a first-hand witness of the unfolding of the seed that was planted in Africa many years ago. He reminds us that even when we don't see the results of our labour for the Lord immediately, we should not get discouraged. We need to trust the Lord to give increase. This book is aimed at inspiring our faith as we serve God."

—Victor Chanda, ThD, Vice-Chancellor,
Trans-Africa Christian University.

"Books have played a great role in shaping and influencing the direction of my life. After fifty years in pastoral ministry and denominational leadership I must say, 'Here is another such book.' Reading *Butterfly Christian Nation* left my heart and mind in a whirl of renewed desire to be part of the great story of mission."

—Dr Peter Watt
General Superintendent, Assemblies of God, South Africa

"I feel privileged to have read *Butterfly Christian Nation* by my friend and colleague, John Kerr, who provides an informative, inspirational and challenging overview of the Christian church's history within the beautiful nation of Zambia. From David Livingston to the Ngoni Pentecostal outpouring to the proclamation of Zambia as a Christian Nation John provides an overview that honours and blesses the Zambian church while asking questions that are highly relevant to the broader church globally. *Butterfly Christian Nation* educated and challenged me."

—Rev. David Wells M.A., D.D.
General Superintendent, The Pentecostal Assemblies of Canada
Vice-Chair, The Pentecostal World Fellowship
Executive member, World Assemblies of God

"My wife, Cindy, and I and our two boys moved to Zambia shortly after the President declared it a Christian nation. The times for the church were euphoric and many people were coming into a personal relationship with Christ. John Kerr beautifully captures the history of a nation that could easily have taken another course with potentially disastrous consequences, but was rescued by the nation-changing presence of men and women who dedicated their lives to proclaiming the good news of the gospel."

—D. Murray Cornelius, Director, PAOC International Missions

"'Paths are made by walking,' says the Shona Proverb. How did we get here? A 'Christian' nation doesn't just magically appear. As John Kerr describes so well, anything so noble can only be the work of God, through His many faithful servants. Moving from David Livingstone through the many emissaries of the good news who followed in his steps, *Butterfly Christian Nation* provides a winsome invitation to look at what can be realized when vision is followed by perseverance."

—Dr. Kirk Kauffeldt, GlobalEd Director,
PAOC International Missions

# *Table of Contents*

Zambia is shaped like a butterfly in the centre of Africa. And butterflies call for wonderment. But it's not just the shape of the nation that fascinates. It is its faith. And what a wonder this is! Out of the darkest of spiritual nights, a "Christian Nation" was birthed at the centre of Africa. This calls for something more than a second look.

Zambia is a fulfilment of the Parable of the Mustard Seed: tiny beginning, florid growth.

## Part 1: Livingstone, the Trailblazer

Livingstone gave three decades of his life to Africa, having smelled "the smoke of a thousand villages" and wanting to reach them with the gospel. Each decade contains a journey. Phase 1 (1841-53) is his decade of triumph, when he pushed north from Cape Town to the heart of Zambia at Victoria Falls, then criss-crossed the continent on foot from west to east. Phase 2 (1855-65) contains a miserable decade at the head of the government-sponsored Zambezi Expedition, exploring the great mouths of the Zambezi and Shire rivers from the east coast, the region where some scholars say Solomon's ships found the gold of Ophir. Phase 3 (1865-73) contains his final journey and last journals, exploring the Rovumma River, from its mouth further north along the east coast of the Indian Ocean, then the areas around both sides of Lake Tanganyika and the Zambian lake country in which he died.

Livingstone kept very descriptive records of his amazing experiences in Africa.

Nearing the end of his trail, Livingstone uttered these words of faith, gloomy as he was over all the futility that surrounded his efforts. The man looked like an utter failure. But there was much more light being shed from his life than he realized.

## Part 2: Fast Forward to Modern Zambia

In 1991 there was a phenomenon in Zambia. The second republican president declared the country a "Christian Nation." We shall examine this phenomenon in its full dimensions.

## Part 3: How Did This Wonder Emerge?

The Christian Nation is a jaw-dropping success story in modern Christian missions.

## Part 4: A Look to the Future

# *Acknowledgements*

This habitat-dependent butterfly book would not have had its own metamorphosis, much less taken flight, without the benign influence of several friends.

Sincere thanks to my esteemed colleagues, Victor Chanda Adrian Chalwe, and Gabriel Mumba, who proved a virtual compendium of information on their land, it's history, its present, its faith.

And Jacob Palo Ntuntu, theologian-son of the Mambweland chief, with his very savvy perspective on Zambia's Christian Nation Declaration, from the perspective of the "young cheetahs" to whom the future belongs.

Special thanks to Oliver Mulenga, with his lifetime of memories and experience, steeped in waves of Zambian Pentecost and the birth of the Christian Nation; and to Barry Ilunga, Zambian Missionary extraordinaire, with his storied family lineage and history of Christianity among the Lunda people, and his unclouded vision of the Zambia church as a "sending church."

I appreciate so much the contributions of David Wells, Murray Cornelius and David Hazzard, who blessed the project from the outset on behalf of the Pentecostal Assemblies of Canada. Thanks to them for their most tangible help and warm endorsement.

Thanks to ever-young Brian Stiller, for encouraging and modelling septuagenarian productivity.

Special thanks to Rick Ball for his very masterful touch as a proofreader. And to Ruth Kerr and Kathy Cantelon for the same; and to our much-loved granddaughter, Emma Jane Kerr, for livening up the project with splashes of her butterfly art.

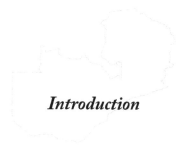

# *Introduction*

## i. The Butterfly Nation

**T**his book is about wonder. It reflects on the wonder of modern Zambia, shaped like a butterfly in the heart of Africa, the "Christian Nation." The debate about the propriety of a nation calling itself Christian, officially, we leave to others. Rather, we look at this development with just a touch of amazement. Out of the least promising of circumstances, to build a Christian nation at the centre of the "Dark Continent"? This calls for at least a second look.

Indeed, Zambia appears to be in the middle of Africa. No matter which way you attempt to advance into the African interior, the pathways are liable to converge in Zambia. It's almost as though Zambia, with its swamps, lakes, plateaus, and headwaters, acts like a magnet, always pulling migrant tribes, missionaries, empire builders, and entrepreneurs into its basin. This is the end of the pilgrimage, for all paths seem to lead here. Formerly Northern Rhodesia, Zambia has been drawn up like a butterfly, one wing enclosed by the watershed between the Congo and the Zambezi basins; the eastern wing bounded roughly by the Luapula valley and the arrangement of three great lakes: Lake Mweru, the lowest tip of Lake Tanganyika, and Lake Malawi[1]. These wings are divided up the middle by the artificial strip of the Congo Pedicle running down the butterfly's head. On the western side of the Pedicle is Ilala, where Livingstone died. On the eastern side lies the Copperbelt, one of the richest copper reserves in the world.

There are four dominant invader tribes in Zambia and a host of others. Two of the invader tribes came down from the Congo early in the eighteenth century: these were the Bemba, a matrilineal tribe of hunters and cultivators, who settled in the centre of the butterfly's eastern wing; and the Lunda, who have heavily populated the Luapula valley along the western edge of the same wing. The Bemba never traded with their neighbours, perhaps because they found their plateau soil too poor to produce any surplus; so under their paramount chief, or *chitimukulu*, they raided their neighbours instead. It is said that they enslaved their share and even sold some, in later times, to the Arab traders from Zanzibar, who had penetrated as far as their borders. The Lunda people also raided their neighbours, under their chief or *kazembe*, who held a monopoly in the ivory trade—which of course was increasingly huge, ivory being the "plastic" of the nineteenth century. Then came the Ngoni. Originating in Natal, just east of today's Cape Town, they fled the tyrant Chaka in the 1820s and struck north in a series of thrusts, one of which settled on the Rhodesian side of Lake Nyasa. The Ngoni were a patrilineal, cattle-herding people with a highly disciplined military organization. They too raided their neighbours but preferred to incorporate them into the tribe. On the west, along the fertile Zambezi valley, was the fourth of these dominant tribes, the Lozi or

Barotse. Here was another militant tribe from the south that in 1838, overran the Zambezi valley and set up a dynasty. But after twenty years, a Lozi chieftain decimated all the males of the foreign dynasty and set himself up as king. He and his successors retained the language of their invaders and the strong centralized structure they had introduced, but extended their dominance further east and inward beyond the Kafue river.

Christianity in this centre of Africa is a mustard-seed story. Today's luxuriant growth stems from the tiniest of seeds, cast upon most unpromising terrain. It is almost as though this burgeoning arm of the church has been created *ex nihilo*, a work, as Nehemiah would put it, "done by our God." How else does one explain the brilliant, high-beamed diffusion of faith across the region since David Livingstone penned his hopeful, defiant words as he lay castaway at Bambarré in 1870: "I too have shed light"? The light of the gospel was so dim, those fourteen decades back, that his words ring out like a shout of sheer defiance in the darkest of nights. Goodness, he was at the mercy of slave traders to get around! Every one of his missionary initiatives seemed destined for the ash heap of defeated visionaries. Some biographers say that he failed at everything he attempted. And yet today—this is the amazing thing—southern Africa, where the great missionary-explorer laid down his life, is part of the new centre of global Christianity!

Contemporary historian Philip Jenkins looks at the picture globally and says we are witnessing "the largest shift in religious affiliation that has ever occurred anywhere," projecting a world-wide boom for the faith in the twenty-first century, where "the vast majority of believers won't be white."[2] The 2013 report from Gordon Conwell's Center for Global Christianity affirms a Christian growth trajectory in Africa from 38.7 percent of the population (1970) to 49.3 percent (2020)—the bulk of it in the south.[3] This includes a projected African growth among "renewalist Christians," which would certainly include most of Zambia, from 18.8 million (1970) to 226.2 million by 2020.[4] Compare those astounding figures with the state of things in Livingstone's last days, and you have to believe missiologist Melvin Hodges when he says, "There is no place on earth where, if the gospel seed be properly planted, it will not produce an indigenous church."[5]

As one-time president of the Association of Evangelicals for Southern Africa (AEA) and head of Lusaka's Bread of Life Church, Zambia's Bishop Joe Imakando attempts to account for this vibrant growth: "We share a message which appeals to people," he says. "It is spiritual, but also looks after the whole person...We preach the message of Jesus Christ, but we also motivate people and tell them they can excel." This note is similar to that sounded across the border in probably the largest non-Catholic denomination in Zimbabwe, the Zimbabwe Assemblies of God Africa of Ezekiel Guti (ZAOGA), where "dominant prosperity teachings have arisen from predominantly southern African sources and are shaped by Zimbabwean concerns...self-reliance, indigenous business and black empowerment."[6]

Such expressions of the gospel deliver a very broad appeal in today's southern Africa. It is like replaying Livingstone's theme of "Commerce and Christianity" for a new age. UNISA's Tinyiko Sam Maluleke speaks of "the wave of creativity" among African Christians, "showing a remarkable knack for contextualization, dynamism, and innovation" in a "dynamic, growing, multifaceted, and dialectic movement."[7] Contrary to widespread expectations, liberation theology has not mushroomed in the region, though Christian belief and practice continue to grow out of social and economic realities among the poor. In southern Africa, liberation is holistic: it has political and economic implications, but it is primarily concerned with deliverance from supernatural evil, a combination that does not seem problematic in the least.

For Zambian leaders like Imakando, Christianity is poised to make life better across the board for the people of southern Africa. Its mission includes engaging and influencing the prevailing political process. The Association of Evangelicals for Africa, which is the umbrella body for evangelical churches, has 100 million members, making it one of the continent's largest civil society organizations. Its mission statement is "to mobilize and empower evangelical churches and agencies for total transformation of Africa through evangelization and effective discipleship." In Imakando's words, "We have a lot of clout...We can speak for Christians, for the poor, for the underprivileged...We have a big following and we make politicians aware. They need votes and they know we have votes...We educate our people on the qualities of a good leader." Imakando speaks of the growing political impact of evangelicalism on his Christian nation and predicts that "it will influence the politics of the future."[8] Whether this influence amounts to anything like a prophetic role in speaking into government abuse and corruption, something seldom seen as an evangelical strength, remains to be seen. But governments that lean towards autocracy soon hear from the church of the Christian nation. It can raise a united voice of protest.

Political influence aside, deliverance is probably the keynote for the vast majority of churches in this part of the world, expounding messages that, according to Jenkins, "appear simplistically charismatic, visionary, and apocalyptic. In this thought world, prophecy is an everyday reality, while faith healing, exorcism, and dream visions are fundamental." With all of the above, there are widespread concerns about the loss of evangelical orthodoxy in

Africa. According to Zambia's Victor Chanda, in a recent doctoral dissertation, "Word of Faith theology...has found a home in Africa." He notes the similarities between its concept of blessings and curses, built around the role of the prophet and preacher, and traditional African religion. For Chanda, "the Faith Movement is not based on sound theological and philosophical ground. It is based on unique reading of the Bible which is more esoteric than theological, more Gnostic than Christian."[9]

Still, two great defining tenets of evangelicalism are held by virtually all Christian churches in Zambia: a conversion experience and a high view of scripture. According to Jenkins, "the Bible has found a congenial home among communities who identify with the social and economic realities it portrays and read it not just as historical fact but also as relevant instruction for daily conduct...When observers complain that revivals and healing crusades make little explicit reference to evangelical theology, that is partly because pastors can...assume their hearers will already know so many of these doctrines."[10] Even religious philosopher John Mbiti, with his sympathetic assessment of traditional religions, says that "a biblical basis is all that matters for African theology...Nothing can substitute for the Bible...." Mbiti is suspicious of imported, non-biblical theological debates, "propagated without full or clear grounding." So we could say that Africa's unique approach to proclaiming the Good News is a major factor in this remarkable growth. Relevant, grassroots preaching has won the day.[11]

When Ruth and I came to Zambia in the mid-nineties, we had a feeling something special was happening, that this was a unique church to be a part of. It took Jenkins to define what we were sensing, that we are in the midst of a miraculous phenomenon in the twenty-first-century church of southern Africa, and Zambia in particular. All things considered, this is a church that has risen up out of the ashes and is something only God could put together.

As we reflect on the wonder of the Christian Nation and its churches, we might wish that it's future will be marked with the spirit of its spiritual father, David Livingstone. When the great missionary explorer penned his ironic and prophetic words, "I too have shed light," he had no way of knowing what brilliant diffusion of gospel light would break out within a few generations. Though his faith was strong, he could not have foreseen the burgeoning Christian nation that would spring from the mustard seeds he planted in the Zambian soil where he laid down his life:

"I was permitted to sow the good seed among them, and I believe that seed is not dead. It is the living word of the living God. There are few which can withstand its force, and no hatred howsoever deep can quench its power."[12]

And what of the future? Surely Dr. Livingstone lays down the primary task of those who would follow:

"The spirit of missions is the spirit of our master, the very genius of His religion. A diffusive philanthropy is Christianity itself. It requires perpetual propagation to attest its genuineness."[13]

## ii. Living in the Mustard Tree

He told them another parable: *"The kingdom of heaven is like a mustard seed, which a man took and planted in his field. Though it is the smallest of all seeds, yet when it grows, it is the largest of garden plants and becomes a tree, so that the birds come and perch in its branches"* (Matthew 13:31).

Living in Zambia is like living in the mustard tree! In Jesus' day, the mustard seed was the smallest seed farmers used. But it grew to over twelve feet tall, a very leafy tree. Small beginning, luxuriant growth! The church of Zambia's Christian Nation is like that. Infinitesimally small beginnings, astonishing growth! And all of this in a very short time.

In 1873, there was *nothing* to show for missionary labours in this part of the world, the region where modern Zambia lies. When Livingstone died at Ilala, all he had was his faith that "the seed must bring a harvest." There were very small indicators that such would be the case.

He had spent countless Sundays as he traveled sharing the word of God with "large and attentive crowds" along Africa's river banks. Often he would think it went well. But when he went to follow up his exposition of God's word with the chief a while later, he found him getting drunk with his men. "It will take time," Livingstone wrote despondently, "to enlighten minds as dark as these!"

This was a world of suspicion and intrigue. When someone was accused of a crime, they would have to drink the "mauve cup" of poison. If they survived, it meant they were innocent. Of course there were many false accusations, innuendos, tales of treachery and intrigue—and many senseless deaths.

The tribes were continually at war. The dominant Ngoni were very close to exterminating the branches of Tumbuka people, the Tonga and Senga who lived in their region. Their young men were not considered to be men until they had killed someone.

The worst of it was that the slave trade continued to poison whole societies. Slave traders would buy from tribes who would then perpetuate kidnappings and war. Late in his life, Livingstone found whole villages left desolate and abandoned because of warfare and slaving in fertile lands that had been quite prosperous. Here was a man who had given his life to breaking the curse upon the continent—now sensing that all his labours had been in vain. Warfare, illiteracy, superstition, demonic rituals—that was the heart of Africa 120 years ago!

But here is the wonder of it all: today Ruth and I work with some 200 students per year at our Trans-Africa Christian University in the Zambian Copperbelt. And who are they? These are the children of the Tumbuka people, the Tonga people, the Lunda and the Ngoni! Mambwe, Chewa, Senga, Lozi—all are represented on our campus every year. And they make it one great interactive, highly affectionate village! We are living in what the first republican president called, "One Zambia, one nation." These students of ours have been known to intermarry as early as the Student Handbook permits! As for the Ngoni warriors, they have become some of Zambia's most intrepid warriors for the gospel!

One of our students who has Ngoni roots loves to do outreach among Kamatipa soccer girls. These girls come from some of the harshest and most demanding environments in the world, the Zambian shantytowns. Cases of child defilement and forced marriages are rampant in these compounds. It would be the exception for any of these girls to emerge from the shantytowns without a child in their teens, little education, and a lot of baggage inhibiting their future development. But these girls join our Barnabas Ministries for soccer and net ball competitions. Clarissa and her team of students meet with them every week, visit in their homes, and organize discipleship and skills training. A few generations ago, Clarissa's ancestors were in conditions worse than the shantytowns, plagued by intrigue and bloodshed, living in a world of fear. Today, she and her Barnabas team are helping young women escape from such to be free and to have a chance for a much better life.

But of course our campus is a very small part of the big picture. There is the burgeoning Zambian Church, comprising some 75 percent of its Christian nation—a church distinguished by its unrelenting, vibrant ministries. This is a larger part of the mustard tree.

Then beyond that, there is the growing church of Southern Africa, the new centre of global Christianity! The statistics support what we are witnessing:

> According to the statistical tables produced by the respected Center for the Study of Global Christianity, some 2.1 billion Christians were alive in 2005, about one-third of the planetary population. The largest single bloc, some 531 million people, is still to be found in Europe. Latin America, though, is already close behind with 511 million, Africa has 389 million, and 344 million Asians profess Christianity. North America claims about 226 million believers...A large share of the Christian world is already located in Africa, Asia, and Latin America. Just as striking are the long-term trends. The number of African Christians is growing at around 2.36 percent annually, which would lead us to project a doubling of the continent's Christian population in less than thirty years.[14]

Extrapolating a bit would put Africa's Christian population at something like *800 million* by 2035! Thus Africa and Latin America would be in competition for the title of most Christian continent.

And that's why Ruth and I like to say, "We live in the mustard tree!" From these tree tops, we can see some Livingstonian truths:

1. This is pretty obvious: *We don't always see the results of our labours!* Not to worry! Livingstone reminds me of the Christian song Einer Waermo used to raise at bygone summer camps:

> "Little is much when God is in it; labour not for wealth or fame; there's a crown and you can win it, If you'll go in Jesus' name."

2.  *There is division of labour in God's kingdom: "one plants, another waters...but God gives the increase!"* Livingstone's life is a lesson. The man was not a delegator. How much stress might have been saved if this truth about division of labour had been applied—especially on the Zambezi expedition. But looking at his life with the perspective of the following years, there is no doubt. His amazing seed-sowing was followed by more seed-planting—and then by the watering of those who came after. A bumper harvest would follow.

    Also,

3.  *"birds come and nest"* in the mustard tree. Zambia's twenty-first-century peace and democracy are inviting to people from all over the world. 180,000 Chinese are projected to settle in the Copperbelt in the next decade. The Zambian church is looking at this as an opportunity for evangelism!

    This mustard tree is in full bloom.

# Part I

## *Livingstone, the Trail Blazer*

# Chapter 1

## *Thirty Years Searching for the Heart of Africa*

I
t certainly wasn't for lack of effort that David Livingstone died with so little to show. If you divide his labours into three main thrusts, each one is distinguished by the restless heart and indefatigable energy of an apostle who does not want to build on another's foundation, who backs up his vision for expansive Christian witness with his own blood, sweat, and tears. His was not the ministry of the visionary who casts a vision and then allows others to run with it. Quite the contrary, this man's vision seemed to *unfold* on the run! And he was continually at the primary task of seed-sowing, sharing the good news of the gospel to a very lost people. Indeed, unflagging devotion is the primary characteristic of this hardened Scot to the task at hand, come hell or, literally, high water. Come slave traders or murderous tribes. Come malarial fever or the internal hemorrhaging that ultimately claimed his life. Come the lag of bureaucrats or quirks of fate. Come grounded boats or walls of Kebrabasa granite. Onward he trekked. As he said in his famous lines, "I will go anywhere, provided it be forward."

David Livingstone's investment in Africa falls naturally into divisions of three decades:

1.  First (1841 to 1851), Livingstone's imprint begins in the shape of a tee, when he journeyed northward from Africa's southernmost tip to the heart of the continent at Zambia's Zambezi river, Cape Town to Victoria Falls. Today, that would be a comfortable three-day road trip of about 3,000 kilometres (or 1,800 miles) climbing up through gorgeous wine country and across South Africa's Transvaal to the Limpopo river, then through Botswana on a pretty good road. Just watch out for the elephants if you are driving at night! But for young Livingstone, with much time for living along the way, it took a decade. He then tacked on two years criss-crossing the continent from west to east, first leading a group of Makololo men through Angola to the western coast at Loanda, then—after recovering!—returning to the Victoria Falls region again, centre of the continent, before trekking eastward along the Zambezi to the east coast of Mozambique. With good roads today—something that we still patiently await—the transcontinental journey would take another three days. For Livingstone, with plenty of stops along the way, it took just over two years.

    And that was the first phase of the doctor's imprint upon Africa. You could say that he stamped the sign of the cross upon unexplored Africa at that time, the shape of a tee: running up the centre of the continent to Victoria Falls, which still raises its mighty "smoke that thunders" at the heart of the continent; then criss-crossing Africa from west to east. It was a towering feat, something that Cecil Northcott calls Livingstone's "triumph," catapulting him to fame as a missionary explorer and discoverer.[1]

2. Phase two of Livingstone's travels (1855 to 1865) began where he left off, on the east coast of Africa at the mouth of the great Zambezi, in the shape of a probe—with a V-shaped instrument! His vision and commission was to sail the broad Zambezi from the Indian Ocean coast, back to Victoria Falls and the heart of the continent and open a "highway for commerce and Christianity." Unfortunately, the Zambezi was not broad or deep enough for such a venture. He had not reckoned with the great wall of the Kebrabasa rapids that stood in his way. After doing his best to scale or circumvent the granite walls, he backed up, reassessed, and turned his team northward, up the Shire river into modern Malawi—where more rapids awaited! After traversing many a gruelling impediment, he led the expedition into beautiful Lake Nyasa. While not exactly an east to west highway for "commerce and Christianity," this Zambezi expedition opened up strategic new terrain. The Shire highlands would prove a launching point for future missionary inroads into Zambia and the heart of Africa. It did not have the expansiveness of his first journeys, but it was more like an infusion of light into dark regions of Africa from the east coast, opening up virtually unexplored areas to the eyes of the world.

3. Finally in a third phase (1867 to 1873), Livingstone penetrated still further from the east, more in the shape of a lariat, with some twists and turns. Once again he followed an African river into the interior; the Rovumma, which today flows down from the interior of Tanzania into the Indian Ocean, delineating the border between Mozambique and her northern neighbour. The environment was hostile in every respect; impediments were at times overwhelming. But the aging explorer, with his vision fixed on the headwaters of the Nile, weakening by the day, pressed westward, travelling

largely on foot with a cluster of native followers, pushing into the heart of the continent around Lake Tanganyika, where he was eventually to meet the newspaper envoy in search of him, Henry Morton Stanley. He would cross and circumvent that great lake in the years that remained him, the regions of modern Tanzania and Congo, before he gave his final days to Zambia, where he died in an African hut in 1873. Northcott calls this phase his "tragedy." For James McNair, it was his "martyrdom."[2] However you label it, this final infusion into Africa was filled with discoveries, both beautiful and horrific, which opened up further the heart of the continent to the eyes of the world. Livingstone paved the way, so to speak, for the "beautiful feet" that would follow.

Thirty years given to Africa! When you think of that three-fold, life-blood investment, you are impressed with how fundamentally solitary it was, as befitting the rugged individualist, David Livingstone. He had none of the support networks that we gladly make use of today. Although he came out from the mission societies that were springing up across the British Isles in the nineteenth century and he left a long paper trail of correspondence with various geographical and mission organizations and although he had those miserable years as team leader on the ill-fated Zambezi expedition, still, Livingstone was a very free spirit. He had this admirable quality of being true to a personal vision, come what may. In that sense of calling to penetrate Africa, he invested his solitary life.

Indeed, David Livingstone's life speaks of the one candle that we all hold up and the power of the same—like that "lone candle" of Hungarian Reformed Church pastor László Tőkés in 1989, which inspired the city of Timisoara to seek revolution and throw off a most oppressive regime in Romania. Livingstone tells us that your voice matters, that being true to your vision is the best contribution you can make. As Thoreau put it, "If one advances confidently in the direction of his dreams and endeavours to live the life which he has imagined, he will meet with a success unexpected in common hours."[3] Or that great spokesperson for individualism, Ralph Waldo Emerson: "Insist on yourself. Never imitate."[4] This is the stuff of Livingstone. "I mean to go up" was his famous line, when others sought to dissuade him from his early ventures northward. "I'm going up." And all along the way he holds to that rigid determinism, "moving not a hairsbreadth" from his vision, come boat foundering, drenching, constant fever, burying friends and family. This is David Livingstone, the individualist. He was least effective when working with others, leading expeditions, assigned to be part of a missionary community. At his best, he travelled solo, following his instincts into a lifetime of innumerable serendipities and discoveries. Fortunately for us, his constant companion was his journal. And he wrote copious letters along the way. While he was pretty much a solitary, he certainly was not incommunicative!

A second thing that comes to mind out this tripartite investment of a life: the man *kept coming back*. "I must finish my task," he kept saying, when offers of something like "being flown out" came his way. Any "normal" person would have taken those two-year furlough years in England (1855-1857 and 1862-1864) to enjoy domesticities and recovery time, get some rest—maybe never return! Livingstone did all the above to an extent, but Africa was deep in this man's heart and soul. As many have observed, he was never happy away from Africa. And so we find him turning up again and again, even in a very weakened condition, which surely called for as good medical treatment as was available in Victorian England. Marching on, onward and upward, pursuing visions of highways for civilization, for the headwaters of the Nile, for a world of peace and prosperity for all—there is something Pauline about this persistence, this coming back to the continent where many of his co-workers and friends had paid the ultimate price and lay buried beneath the soil. "Forgetting the things that are behind" sounds like a Livingstone motto. "By all means Christ is preached." Such apostolic language seems prescribed for the lips of Livingstone, and he trekked through Africa with his sunny confidence.

And vision? What was Livingstone if not a *visionary?* "The glorious kingdom is coming," he wrote, while the world around him seemed to be descending into hell. "The knowledge of the Lord will fill the earth!" How admirable, that quality of vision in the face of the most hopeless scenes of human depravity! Livingstone saw "the big picture." He saw "things yet unseen," like the great heroes of faith. Whether it was fuelled by his early years in the environment of missionary zeal or by his constant reading of scripture, he carried a glorious vision wherever he went. In that sense, his life brought to Africa hope. At a time when the continent seemed to be under a curse, he brought his blessing and the vision of a better day.

At times his vision reads like a chimera and his dreams illusive. He appears at times like a Don Quixote figure tilting at windmills. In fact, one thinks of Livingstone when reading Rob Peters, founder of StandardOfTrust.com, who extols Cervantes' hero as a source of leadership principles:

> We live in a world that emphasizes realistic expectations and clear successes. Quixote had neither. But through failure after failure, he persists in his vision and his commitment. He persists because he knows who he is.[5]

This sounds like David Livingstone on his last journey, pursuing the illusive sources of the Nile. For Rob Peters, such heroes teach us "that life is to be challenged:

> ...that passion and discipline of a determined soul are a foundational element of being a leader; that the leader does not accept current reality, but rather forces his creative imagery, his commitment, and his happiness onto it, creating a world of beauty and meaning; that like a flamenco dancer, the leader communicates his passion within a dance of great discipline, expressing his passion with a defined self-identity of passion and discipline.

Peters seems to sum up the man of the Rovumma as much as the man of La Mancha in his reflections on the bedrock convictions of a leader:

> Quixote also faces hopes and disappointments. But his answer is different. As he walked the plains of La Mancha, he had illusions, of course. But his illusions were for the most part not the illusions of action or inaction. They were illusions that reminded him of the obligations to adhere to his principled identity. His imagination saw inns as castles. He saw windmills as giants...Quixote is not driven by the consequences of his actions, at least not in a meaningful way. Rather he asks: What kind of person am I? What circumstance do I find myself in? What does an individual such as myself do in my current situation?
> 
> Quixote says, "I know who I am." He is not driven by traditional notions of success, but rather in "fulfilling his sense of himself." He is disciplined not by incentives, but by his identity of purpose. Quixote knows who he is and what is demanded of him by his purpose. He states, "Knight I am and knight I will die if it pleases almighty God."

Indeed, Quixote's self-endorsement might well be Livingstone's:

Foolish men might take me for a fool It is one of the hardships I have to bear. For I follow the narrow road of night, air, and tree. I despise riches, but not honour...My intention is to do wrong to no man, but good to all the world.

These and many more outstanding qualities stand out in the amazing life of David Livingstone. Peter Birkinshaw talks about "the Livingstone touch" in his book by the same title. "One shares in his books the outer life of an observant, enterprising, simple, compassionate man:"

As I sat in the rain a little tree-frog, about half an inch long, leaped on to a grassy leaf, and began a tune as loud as that of many birds, and very sweet; it was surprising to hear so much music out of so small a musician.[6]

Livingstone continued to reel off his "basic English prose," even when his heart was breaking near the grave of his wife, Mary, beneath the baobab tree on the shores of Lake Nyasa:

Being now within three miles of the...Lake we could see the whole plainly...There we first saw the Shire emerge, and there all of us gazed down on the broad waters of Nyasa. Many hopes have been diverted here. Far down on the right bank of the Zambezi lies the dust of she whose death changed all my future prospects; and now, instead of a conclusion being given to the slave trade by lawful commerce on the Lake, slave traders prosper...It is impossible not to regret.[7]

Trying to sleep on the ground through an African storm, he writes,

This, with great volumes of sheet lightning, enabled us at times to see the whole country. The intervals between the flashes were so densely dark, as to convey the idea of stone-blindness. The horses trembled, cried out, and turned round, as if searching for each other, and every new flash revealed the men taking different directions, laughing and stumbling against each other...My clothing having gone on, I lay down on the cold ground expecting to spend a miserable night, but Sekeletu kindly covered me with his own blanket and lay uncovered himself. I was much affected by this little act of genuine kindness (MT, 342).

Through Livingstone's prolific letters and journals, one is immersed in the world of nineteenth-century Africa. Birkinshaw is no doubt right. This Livingstone touch is something special.

Ultimately, we would have to say that Livingstone was a *trail-blazer*—a missionary trailblazer. He stands at the middle of the continent, the centre of Zambia's butterfly nation, and looks to the west and to the east, in 1854, about to launch his great transcontinental trek:

I had fully made up my mind as to the path of duty before starting. I wrote to my brother-in-law, Robert Moffat: "I shall open up a path into the interior or perish." I have never had the shadow of a shade of a doubt as to the propriety of my course, and wish only that my exertions may be honoured so far that the gospel may be preached and believed in all this dark region.[8]

For him, the arduous path ahead was a high calling:

Viewed in relation to my calling, the end of the geographical feat is only the beginning of the enterprise...I will place no value on anything I have or may possess except in relation to the kingdom of Christ...to whom I owe all my hopes in time or eternity" (Northcott, 39).

What joy keeps breaking out in Livingstone, the missionary-explorer, with this new, arduous assignment of his!

In traveling in Africa, with the specific object in view of ameliorating the benighted condition of the country, every act is ennobled...The mere animal pleasure of travelling is very great. The elastic muscles have been exercised. Fresh and healthy blood circulates in the veins, the eye is clear, the step firm, but the day's exertion has been enough to make rest thoroughly enjoyable...The effect of travel on my mind has been to make it more self-reliant, confident of resources and presence of mind (WGB, 16).

This man was a trailblazer. Three years after his death, Livingstone's life was commemorated in such terms by Sir Bartle Frere in the Glasgow Chamber of Commerce:

The object of Dr. Livingstone's geographical and scientific explorations was to lead his countrymen to the great work of Christianizing and civilizing the millions of Central Africa. You will recollect how when first he came back from his wonderful journey, though they were all greatly startled by his achievement and by what he told us, people really did not lay up what he said much to heart. They were stimulated to take up the cause of African discovery again, and other travellers went out and did excellent service; but the great fact which was from the very first upon Livingstone's mind, and which he used to impress upon you, did not make the impression he wished...It was not until his third and last journey, when he was no more to return among us that the descriptions which he gave of the horrors of the slave trade in the interior really took hold upon the mind of the people of this country, and made them determine [to take up] the great work which this country had undertaken, to free the African races, and to abolish, to the first place, the slave-trade by sea, and then, as we hope, the slaving by land (WGB, 55).

William Blaikie quotes another eulogist's speech:

Of his primary work the record is on high and its imperishable fruits remain on earth. The seeds of the Word of Life implanted lovingly, with pains and labour and above all with faith—the outdoors scenes of the simple sabbath services; the testimony of Him to whom the worship was paid, given in terms of such simplicity...These seeds will not have been scattered by him in vain. Nor have they been sown by words alone, but in deeds...teaching by good deeds as well as by the words of truth and love, the successor who treads in the steps of Livingstone...will assuredly reap the benefit (WGB, 390).

As for his tombstone, Livingstone had penned the words one year before his death that would be inscribed on the stone to his memory in Westminster Abbey:

All I can add in my loneliness is, may Heaven's rich blessing come down on everyone—American, English, or Turk—who will help to heal the open sore of the world (LJ, 182).

Amid the universal darkness around him, the universal ignorance of God and of the grace and love of Jesus Christ, it was hard to believe that Africa should ever be redeemed. Livingstone's sights were set not just on the trail, stimulating as it was, but on the prize:

He will keep his word—the gracious One, full of grace and truth; no doubt of it. He said, "Him that cometh unto me, I will in no wise cast out" and "Whatsoever ye ask in my name I will give it." He *will* keep his word; then I can come and humbly present my petition and it will be all right. Doubt is here inadmissible, surely (LJ, 186).

*Livingstone attacked by lion, 1857*

## Escaping from the Lion's Mouth (and Other Highlights)

### 1. In the Jaws of the Lion!

One of the best ways to get a feel for Livingstone is just to enjoy his writing. His description of the world of African nature have been compared to some of the great nature writers of his day. As I follow him through some most uncivilized territory, I get the feeling that Dafoe's *Robinson Crusoe* must have been found in Livingstone's early reading. His journal entries often carry so much delightful detail and depth of feeling that he can rise to the level of some of the best of his contemporaries. Philip Birkinshaw loves the texture of Livingstone's prose and what the prose reveals about Livingstone's values, flowing voluminously over the years and preserved miraculously in his journals, letters, and records: "Basic English prose...in which only eight percent of words have over two syllables...plain words, short sentences, unpretentious, easy rhythms, quick apt similes." Livingstone writes with "a perfect ear."[1]

Mabotswa was the family home of the newly married Livingstones, David and Mary. It was his first mission outpost on his own, among the Kgatla people, in 1844. It was the scene of many happy domesticities—that and at least one near-terminal, bone-crunching experience!

It is well known that if one in a troop of lions is killed, the others take the hint and leave that part of the country. So, the next time the herds were attacked, I went with the people in order to encourage them to rid themselves of the annoyance by destroying one of the marauders.

We found the lions on a small hill about a quarter of a mile in length, and covered with trees. Going around the end of the hill I saw one of the beasts sitting on a piece of rock with a little bush in front. Being about thirty yards off, I took a good aim at his body through the bush, and fired both barrels into it. The men then called out, "He is shot, he is shot!" Others cried, "He has been shot by another man too!" I saw the lion's tail erected in anger behind the bush and turning to the people said, "Stop a little till I load again."

When in the act of ramming down the bullets I heard a shout. Starting and looking around, I saw the lion just in the act of springing upon me. I was upon a little height; he caught my shoulder as he sprang, and we both came to the ground below together. Growling horribly close to my ear, he shook me as a terrier dog does a rat. The shock produced a stupor similar to that which seems to be felt by a mouse after the first shake of the cat. It caused a sort of dreaminess, in which there was no sense of pain nor feeling of terror, though quite conscious of all that was happening...The shake annihilated fear, and all the sense of horror in looking round at the beast. This peculiar state is what is produced in all animals killed by the carnivore; and if so, it is a merciful provision by our benevolent Creator for lessening the pain of death.

As I turned round to relieve myself of the weight, as he had one paw on the back of my head, I saw his eyes directed to Mebalwe who was trying to shoot him from a distance of ten or fifteen yards. His gun, a flint one, missed fire from both barrels; the lion immediately left me, and attacking Mebalwe, bit into him. Another man, whose life I had saved before...attempted to spear the lion while he was biting Mebalwe. The beast then left Mebalwe and caught this man by the shoulder, but at that moment the bullets he had received took effect, and he fell down dead.

They made a huge bonfire over the carcass, which was declared to be the largest lion they had ever seen. Besides crunching the bone into splinters, it left eleven teeth wounds on the upper part of my arm (MT, 12).

Livingstone lost the full use of that shoulder and could never again raise a rifle as he had. But he brought down the largest of the king of beasts in this memorable act of public service!

## 2. An Unexpected Visitor: Henry Moreland Stanley (1871)

Just two years from his deathbed, Livingstone had a most welcome visitor. Henry Moreland Stanley found him on the eastern shores of Lake Tanganyika at Ujiji—in very bad shape. The New York newspaper man had been hired to spare no expense on an African expedition and "find Livingstone," who could not have lasted much longer without some help. The aging explorer had encountered no end of misfortunes and adversities in his search for the headwaters of the Nile. Now, after two years in no-man's land, stranded for want of supplies and carriers, he was finally back at a "major centre"—and den of thieves—Ujiji, on the western shores of Lake Tanganyika, where he hoped to regather the supplies he thought were awaiting him and try to get body and soul back together.

## 23rd October—

At dawn, off and go to Ujiji. Welcomed by all the Arabs, particularly by Monyegheré. I was reduced to a skeleton, but the market being held daily, and all kinds of native food about it, I hoped that food and rest would soon restore me, but in the evening my people came and told me that Shereef had sold off all may goods, and Monyegheré confirmed it by saying, "We protested, but he did not leave a single yard of calico out of 3,000, nor a string of beads out of 700 lbs." This was distressing. I had made up my mind, if I could not get people at Ujiji, to wait till men should come from the coast, but to wait in beggary was what I never contemplated, and I now felt miserable. Shereef was evidently a moral idiot, for he came without shame to shake hands with me, and when I refused, assumed an air of displeasure, as having been badly treated. I felt in my destitution as if I were the man who went down from Jerusalem to Jericho and fell among thieves; but I could not hope for Priest, Levite or good Samaritan to came by on either side.

But one morning, Syed bin Majid said to me, "Now this is the first time we have been alone together; I have no goods, but I have ivory; let me, I pray you, sell some ivory, and give the goods to you." This was encouraging; but I said, "Not yet, but by-and-bye." I had still a few barter goods left, which I had taken the precaution to deposit with Mohamad bin Saleh before going to Manyuema, in case of returning in extreme need.

But when my spirits are at their lowest ebb, the Good Samaritan was close at hand, for one morning Susi came running at the top of his speed and gasped out, "An Englishman! I see him!" and off he darted to meet him. The American flag at the head of a caravan told of the nationality of the stranger. Bales of goods, baths of tin, huge kettles, cooking pots, tents, etc., made me think "This must be a luxurious traveller, and not one at his wits' end like me." It was Henry Moreland Stanley, the travelling correspondent of the New York Herald, sent by James Gordon Bennett, Junior, at an expense of more than 4,000£, to obtain accurate information about Dr. Livingstone if living, and if dead to bring home my bones. The news he had to tell to one who had been two full years without any tidings from Europe made my whole frame thrill. The terrible fate that had befallen France, the telegraphic cables successfully laid in the Atlantic, the election of General Grant, the death of good Lord Clarendon and many other points of interest, revived emotions that had lain dormant in Manyuema. Appetite returned, and instead of the spare, tasteless two meals a day, I ate four times daily, and in a week began to feel strong. I am not of a demonstrative turn; as cold, indeed, as we islanders are usually reputed to be, but his disinterested kindness was simply overwhelming (MT, October 28, 1871).

## 3. They Stole His Medicine Chest!

Among Livingstone's many discoveries was the use of quinine as an antidote for malaria, although the actual cause of the fever, in the mosquito-borne malaria parasite, would not be discovered until 1898. He was of course very dependent on it as his bouts of "fever" became more frequent. And he carried other medicines to treat the internal bleeding issues and haemorrhoids, which were a continual battle. Hence, one of his worst days!

### 20th January—

The two Waiyau who joined us at Kandemi deserted. Knowing the language well, they were extremely useful and though I thought that they would desert, for they were free men, their donkey had been killed by the Mazitu—and this circumstance, and their reliable conduct, made us trust them more than we should have done with men who had been slaves. But they left us in the forest, and heavy rains fell which obliterated every vestige of their footsteps. To make the matter more galling, they took what we could least spare—the medicine box, which they would only throw away as soon as they came to examine their booty…The forest was shoulder-high, there was no chance of getting a trace of the fugitives with all the dishes, a large box of powder, the flour we had purchased to take us as far as the Chambezé, the tools, two guns and a cartridge. But the medicine chest was the sorest loss of all! (LJ, 178.)

Then Livingstone, hard-pressed though he was, almost exonerated the Waiyan thieves!

These men had few advantages: sold into slavery in early life, they were in the worst possible school for learning to be honest and honourable. They behaved well for a long time; but having had hard and scanty fare in Lobisa…and misery in passing through dripping forests, hungry nights and fatiguing days, their patience must have been worn out, and they had no sentiments of honour, or at least none so strong as we ought to have; they gave way to the temptation which their good conduct had led us to put in their way (LJ, 178).

## 4. Locusts, Caterpillars, and Frogs— the Kids Loved Them!

Of course Livingstone ate all kinds of stuff on his African travels, and some say his lack of care in these matters, especially with water, may have contributed to his early demise. As for food, he ate a sample of most everything, including the rigorous fare of John the Baptist! He had a taste of this in one of his first African homes:

Locusts are strongly vegetable in taste, the flavour varying with the plants on which they feed. There is a physiological reason why locusts and honey should be eaten together. Some are roasted and pounded into meal, which eaten with a little salt is palatable. It will keep thus for months. Boiled they are disagreeable; but when they are roasted, I should much prefer locusts to shrimps, though I would avoid both if possible.

In travelling we sometimes suffered considerable from scarcity of meat, though not from absolute want of food. This was felt more especially by my children; and the natives, to show their sympathy, often gave them a large kind of caterpillar, which they seemed to relish; these insects could not be unwholesome, for the natives devoured them in large quantities themselves.

Another article of which our children partook with eagerness was a very large frog, called Matlamétlo: when cooked, they look like chickens (MT, 1850).

## 5. Cutting Up an Elephant (not for the Faint of Heart!)

The cutting up of an elephant is quite a unique spectacle. The men stand around the animal in dead silence, while the chief of the travelling party declares that, according to ancient law, the head and right-hand leg belong to them who killed the beast, that is, to him who inflicted the first wound; the left leg to him who delivered the second, or first touched the animal after it fell; the meat around the eye to the English or chief of the travellers, and different parts to the headmen for the different fires, or groups, of which the camp is composed; not forgetting to enjoin the preservation of the fat and bowels for a second distribution. This oration finished, the natives soon become excited, and scream wildly as they cut away at the carcass with a score of spears, whose long handles quiver in the air above their heads. Their excitement becomes more and more intense and reaches the culminating point when, as

denoted by a roar of gas, the huge mass is laid fairly open.
Some jump inside, and roll about there in their eagerness to
seize the precious fat, while others run off, screaming, with
pieces of the bloody meat, throw it on the grass and run back
for more: all keep talking and shouting at the utmost pitch of
their voices. Sometimes two or three, regardless of all laws,
see the same piece of meat, and have a brief fight of words
over it. Occasionally an agonized yell bursts forth, and a native
emerges out of the moving mass of dead elephant and wrig-
gling humanity, with his hand badly cut by the spear of his
excited friend and neighbour: this requires a rag and some
soothing words to prevent bad blood. In an incredibly short
time tons of meat are cut up, and placed in separate heaps
around (MT, 55).

## 6. "How is it you did not send word... sooner?"

Sechele was a famous chief among the Bakwena people, just north
of the mission stations around Kuruman. Livingstone had
befriended him early on, and he became his one lasting convert.
He grew to be a devoted Christian and expounded the faith to his
people, living until 1892. But what a question he threw at
Livingstone early on in their relationship:

Sechele married the daughters of three of his under-chiefs,
who, on account of their blood relationship, stood by him in
his adversity...The chief attaches the under-chiefs to himself
and family by marrying, as Sechele did, their daughters, or
inducing his sons to do so. They are fond of the relationship
to great families. Sechele was thus seated in his chieftain-
ship when I made his acquaintance.

On the first occasion in which I ever attempted to begin
religious service, he remarked that it was the custom of his
nation when a new subject was brought before them to put
questions on it; asking me to allow him to do the same in this

case. On expressing my willingness to answer his questions, he said, "You startle me—you make all my bones to shake—I have no more strength in me: all of my fathers were living at the same time yours were, *and how is it you did not send them word about these terrible things sooner?* They went away into darkness without knowing whither they were going...." I expressed my belief that, as Christ had said, the whole world would yet be enlightened by the gospel. Pointing to the great Kalahari desert, he said, "You never can cross that country to the tribes beyond; it is utterly impossible even for us black men, except in certain seasons, when more than the usual supply of rain falls, and an extraordinary growth of water-melons follows. Even we who know the country would certainly perish without them." Reasserting my belief in the words of Christ, we parted...(MT, 12).

"How is it you did not send word...sooner?" Were ever more plaintive words heard from a searching heart, hearing the gospel for the first time? Surely the chief speaks for all the lost people of the world, not just trembling with concern over their ancestors but fearful over their *own* lost state, present and future, "without hope and without God in the world." How his words still live, as we hear them today, reminding the church of Jesus not to take its time, not to lose its sense of urgency about world missions. Sechele would say, with the great hymn, "Oh Zion, *haste!*"

## 7. "But why not use rhinoceros whips?"

Not all cultures believe that conversion must be an individual thing. Sechele was very much of the view that it should be a group experience, which all his people should share together. And if so, why not provide some incentives to move things along?

As soon as he had an opportunity of learning, he set him-self to read with such close application that, from being comparatively thin, the effect of having been fond of the chase, he became quite corpulent from want of exercise. He was by no means an ordinary specimen of the people, for I never went to town but what I was pressed to hear him read some chapters of the Bible. Isaiah was a great favourite to him..."He was a fine man, that Isaiah; he knew how to speak." Sechele invariably offered me something to eat on every occasion of my visiting him. Seeing me anxious that his people should believe the words of Christ, he once said, *"Do you imagine these people will ever believe by our merely talking to them? I can make them do nothing except by thrashing them; and if you like, I shall call my head men, and with our litupa* [whips of rhinoceros-hide] *we will soon make them all believe together."* The idea of using entreaty and persuasion to subject people to become Christians was especially surprising to him. He considered that they ought only to be too happy to embrace Christianity at his command (MT, 13).

## 8. "We will never leave you..."

On the way to Loanda, on the first leg of his transcontinental journey, Livingstone faced a lot of incredible hardships, including hostility from tribes along the way. They demanded "hongo" payment to pass through their territory. It was enough to put his men of a mind to abandon the trek. But to lose the carriers, so essential for the missionary travels in Africa, would have been a terminal blow:

My people were now so much discouraged that some proposed to return home; the prospect of being obliged to return when just on the threshold of the Portuguese settlement distressed me exceedingly. After using all my powers of persuasion, I declared to them that if they returned, I would go on alone, and went into my little tent with the mind directed to

Him who hears the sighing of the soul; and soon followed the head of Mohorisi, saying, *"We will never leave you. Do not be disheartened. Wherever you lead we will follow. Our remarks were made only on account of the injustice of these people."* Others followed, and with the most artless simplicity of manner told me to be comforted—they were all my children; they know no one but Sekeletu and me, and they would die for me; they had not fought because I did not wish it. They had just spoken in bitterness of the spirit and when feeling that they could do nothing; but if these enemies begin, "You will see what we can do." (MT, 157.)

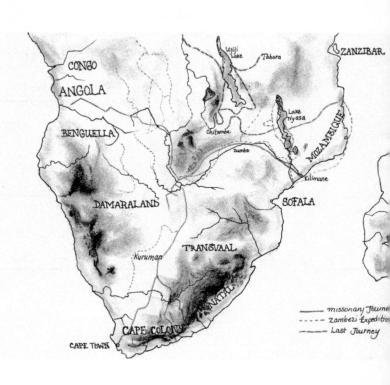

CONGO

ANGOLA

BENGUELLA

DAMARALAND

Kuruman

TRANSVAAL

NATAL

CAPE COLONY

CAPE TOWN

Ujiji
Lake

Tabora

ZANZIBAR

Chitambe

Lake
Nyasa

MOZAMBIQUE

Zumbo

Kilimane

SOFALA

_____ missionary Journey
- - - - - Zambezi Expedition
~~~~~~~ Last Journey

## "*I too have shed light*"

Livingstone was in Bambarré, deep in the heart of today's largely ungovernable Democratic Republic of Congo (DRC), cast away among the villagers of Manyuema, on the west side of Lake Tanganyika, waiting. Weak and emaciated, he was too weak to move on alone. And where was he to go? It was October 10, 1870. He was now dependent on the Arab traders, who took a liking to him, for travel. He was less than three years from his deathbed in another hut, in Chief Chitambo's Zambian village.

With the slave trade raging around him, rampant and unabated, he reflected on people who had done noble battle in the abolition cause. He named rivers and lakes after them in his mind, Lord Palmerston, James Meeks. Then he thought of his early instructor in chemistry and lifelong friend, James Young. For him, he named the western branch of the Lualaba River:

> He has shed pure light in many lowly cottages and in rich palaces. *I too have shed light* of another kind, and am fain to believe that I have performed a small part in the grand

revolution which our Maker has been for ages carrying on... (LJ, 66).

What a striking statement! He had so many reasons for despondency. The darkness around him seemed never more intense. Yet he spoke words about shedding light, words that in themselves seem incandescent, "I too have shed light of a different kind." This reads like a man's bold response of faith to all the regrets and disappointments of life.

Indeed, as we look back at Livingstone now, with the twentieth century rolled out between us, enjoying the bright light of the Christian faith that he brought to this part of the world, all of his shortcomings are forgiven, so great was the light he cast. Such was the length and breadth of that light that his words from Bambarré ring like a prophecy, rising up from his most meagre hut: "I too have shed light."

Of course, he had no way of knowing the fullness of light that would come from his sacrifice. His prophetic word is cast like bread upon the waters of time, saying,

> Dark may be the day, stone cold the human heart,
> But let your one light shine, for this in time will spread
> and fill the earth with the glory of God.

## 1. He Put Africans in Their Best Light

Not only was Livingstone a polemicist, attacking the system that degraded Africans. He was also their apologist. He brought to light "African genius," as Basil Davidson calls it, as he pulled his African friends into the orbit of his Christian charity.

> Like Moffatt, his father-in-law, Livingstone emanated respect for the African...he recognized that Christianity appeared to Africans as subversive, aiming at "reducing them and their much-loved domestic institutions," and

he saw that this lay at the heart of their resistance to conversion. His open-minded tolerance astonished other missionaries, as when he asserted that polygamy could not be called adultery and that...tribal initiation rites were not black magic but a ceremony ensuring tribal unity.[1]

For Livingstone, unlearned Africans "showed more intelligence than is to be met with in our own uneducated peasantry." Although he wrote objectively of the degradation and sinfulness of Africans, his positive statement were more numerous.

With a general opinion they are wiser than their white neighbours. They go direct to the point, and in so doing show a more philosophic spirit than the Germans...They have few theories, but many ideas...They are not by any means unreasonable. I think unreasonableness is more a hereditary disease in Europe than in this land (ZT, 67).

Indeed, Livingstone encounters enough signs of exceptional people, past and present, that he bemoans the lack of an African literature to preserve their stories.

Men of remarkable ability have risen up among the Africans from time to time, as amongst other portions of the human family. Some have attracted the admiration of large districts by their wisdom. Others, apparently by the powers of ventriloquism, or by particular dexterity...have been the wonder of their generation; but...the wisdom of the wise has not been handed down (ZT, 253).

He saw the great potential of "native agency" in Christianizing the continent, a prophetic insight to be sure. He spent his first decade in Africa on the lookout for mission stations from which to send out native leaders:

> The more I see of the country, its large extent of surface, with its population scattered and each tribe separated by a formidable distance from almost every other, I feel the more convinced that it will be impossible...for the church to supply them all with Europeans. Native Christians can make known the way of life (LT, 78).

"The chief and the native pastor"—Livingstone grasped early on that here were the keys to establishing the faith in southern Africa.

The generosity of the African village was something that Livingstone grew to admire and to rely on, despite the bad blood that slave-trafficking was producing. Liberality was clearly a virtue among the tribes and had a significance among the people that was close to ritual. In his journals, punctilious manners are the prevailing impression of unspoiled African society.

> I must express admiration for the great liberality of these people to mine. They go into their villages and rarely return without some corn or maize...The real politeness with which presents of food are given through nearly all the tribes makes it easy to accept the gifts. It is as much the law from time immemorial for the chief to feed all strangers as it is among the Arabs. It is one of the arguments for polygamy, they imply. A man with one wife only could not feed strangers (LAJ, II, 386).

Courage was a quality that the intrepid doctor admired most, "not knowing what fear was" himself. When he finds it in Africa, he takes note:

> Both men and women submit to an operation without wincing, or any of that shouting which caused young students to faint in the operating theatres before the introduction of chloroform. The women pride themselves on their ability to bear pain. A mother will address her little

girl, from whose foot a thorn is to be extracted with, "Now Ma, you are a woman; a woman does not cry." A man scorns to shed tears (MT, 131).

The "nobility" of his men in the swirling rapids of the Mburuma mountains, where at least one life was saved, draws his attention:

After three hours' sail, on the morning of the 29th, the river was narrowed again by the mountains of Mburuma, into one channel, and another rapid dimly appeared. It was formed by two currents guided by rocks to the centre. In going down it, the men sent by Sekeletu behaved very nobly. The canoes entered without previous survey, and the huge hobbling waves of mid-current began at once to fill them. With great presence of mind, and without a moment's hesitation, two men lightened each by jumping overboard; they then ordered a Bakota man to do the same, as "the white men must be saved." "I cannot swim," said the Bakota, "Jump out, then, and hold onto the canoe," which he instantly did. Swimming alongside, they guided the swamping canoes down the swift current to the foot of the rapid, and then ran them ashore to bale them out. A boat could have passed down safely, but our canoes were not a foot above the water at the gunwales. Thanks to the bravery of these poor fellows, nothing was lost, although everything was well soaked (ZT, 326).

As for diligence and productivity, these are sometimes found wanting. But that is not to say they are entirely absent:

There is often a surprising contrast between neighbouring villages. One is well off and thriving, having good huts, plenty of food, and native cloth; and its people are frank, trusting, generous, and eager to sell provisions; while in the next the inhabitants may be ill-housed, disobliging, suspicious, ill fed, and scantily clad, and with nothing for sale, though the land around is as fertile as that or their wealthier neighbours (ZT, 366).

Among the Bakota, he writes:

The owners of huts lent to strangers have a great deal of toil in consequence; they have to clean them after the visitors have withdrawn; then, in addition to this, to clean themselves, all soiled by the dust left by the lodgers; their bodies and clothes have to be cleansed afterwards—they add food too in allocates of acquaintanceship, and then we have to remember the labour of preparing that food. My remaining here enables me to observe that both men and women are in almost constant employment. The men at making mats, or weaving, or spinning; no one could witness their assiduity in their little affairs and conclude that they were a lazy people. The only idle time I observe here is in the mornings about seven o'clock, when all come and sit to catch the first rays of the sun as he comes over our clump of trees, but even that time is often taken as an opportunity for stringing beads (LJ, 8 July, 1867).

Of course, Livingstone's main interest was in religious sensibilities, and these he finds far from backward:

The primitive African faith seems to be that there is one Almighty Maker of heaven and earth; that he has given the various plants of earth to man to be employed as mediators between him and the spirit world, where all who have here been born and died continue to live; that sin consists in offences against their fellow-men, either here or among the departed, and that death is often a punishment of guilt, such as witchcraft. Their idea of moral evil differs in no respect from ours, but they consider themselves amenable only to inferior beings, not to the Supreme. Evil speaking, lying, hatred, disobedience to parents, neglect of them—are said by the intelligent to have been all known to be sin, as well as theft, murder, or adultery, before they knew aught of Europeans of their teaching. The only new addition to their moral code is, that it is wrong to have more wives than one. This, until the arrival of Europeans, never entered into their minds even as a doubt (ZT, 521).

Through it all, there is little doubt about the affection that David Livingstone held for the people groups of Africa. As one biographer puts it, "The reason for the devotion of Chuma and Susi and the other longest-serving followers, had clearly been Livingstone's gentleness with them and with all Africans. Far from being flogged or chained to stop them deserting—as regularly happened on other explorer's expeditions—they had always been treated with courtesy and affection."

In Livingstone's words,

It ought never to be forgotten that influence among the [Africans] can only be acquired by patient continuance in well-doing, and that good manners are as necessary among [them] as among [people anywhere] (WGB, 104).

## 2. He Introduced the Light of Peace Where There Was no Word for It

Peacemaking was so much needed in Livingstone's war-torn Africa, the devastation and ruin of conflict so great. Working his way up the Shire on the Zambezi expedition, "in one region which was once studded with villages, we walked a whole week without meeting anyone." A European colony, he was sure, would be invaluable for "constraining the tribes to live in peace...Thousands of industrious natives would gladly settle around it and engage in that peaceful pursuit of agriculture and trade...undistracted by wars...and might listen to the purifying and ennobling truths of the gospel of Jesus Christ."

Livingstone scolded African chiefs who fuelled the slave trade by selling their neighbours. He reasons with Kakiku along the shores of Lake Nyasa:

> We mention our relationship to our Father, the guilt of selling any of his children, the consequences: it begets war, for as they don't sell their own, they steal from other villagers, who retaliate. Arabs and Waiyau, invited into the country by their selling, foster feuds, wars and depopulation ensues. We mention the Bible—future state—prayer; advise union, that they would unite as one family to expel enemies who came first as slave traders, and ended by leaving the country a wilderness (LJ, 126).

When he confronted the most antagonistic tribes with poisoned arrows on the way to Quilimane, 1856, the last resort for Livingstone was taking up arms in self-defence, even when it seemed he might be killed. "I will not cross furtively by night," he concluded. It would "appear as flight, and should such a man as I flee? Nay, verily, I shall make observations for latitude and longitude tonight, though they may be the last. I feel quite calm now, thank God."

Livingstone supported the "right to bear arms" before his time. While he was always sensitive on the question of guns and gunpowder, he could not bring himself to believe that it was unlawful to sell these articles. For him, having a gun could well "prevent the effusion of blood...and were the interior tribes well armed there would be fewer slave hunts." For him, a "real English musket" could be a reliable defender of liberty! Thus he was prepared to use arms in the righteous and good cause of ending slave running, "and if a few more guns would speed the process, then let the guns be available." He continued to pin his optimistic hopes on peaceful trading to "supplant by lawful goods the trade in slaves." But should that fail, he added, then force might become "inevitable" (LN, 78).

Everywhere Livingstone and his men went, they proclaimed that they were friends of peace. When they had to resort to guns against the Ajawa in 1861, Livingstone and his Zambezi expedition member Bishop McKenzie tried first to visit the chief, and "they fired in self-defence. It was the first time that Livingstone had ever been so attacked by natives, often though they had threatened him. It was the first time he had had to repel an attack with violence." The Ajawa were driven off without loss on either side.

In a letter to the Quakers, who had been active in the abolition cause in the West Indies, Livingstone rejects the pacifism ideal for Africa.

> I love peace as much as any mortal man. In fact, I go quite beyond you, for I love it so much that I would fight for it...Your principles to be good must abide the test of stretching...I am widely known as a man of peace...but I can never cease to wonder why the Friends who sincerely believe in the power of peace principles don't test them by going forth...as missionaries of the Cross. I for one would heartily welcome them from the belief that their conduct would have good influence, though it would never secure their safety.[2]

## 3. He Spread the Much-Needed Light of Civilization

We cannot follow Livingstone on his forays through nineteenth-century Africa without sharing with him a passion for civilization. There was very little of the "noble savage" concept in him, although he did very much admire the "African genius" here and there. For him, wherever found, uncultivated humanity was degraded and vile and had not changed since the days of Noah. "Commerce and Christianity" was Livingstone's solution.

His vision for civilization went back to 1840, while studying in London. He had attended a meeting sponsored by the Society for the Extinction of the Slave Trade and for the civilization of Africa. There he was inspired by Thomas Fowell Buxton, Wilberforce's successor, as he expounded his dream of Africans abandoning their participation in the slave trade for goods like wax and ivory. Commerce and Christianity together could achieve this miracle, it was said, not Christianity alone. This had been Buxton's theme, and for Livingstone it was the right approach. The world was marching on under divine control until the knowledge of the Lord would fill all the earth. This meant, among other things, civilization. There is a touch of the colonial spirit in his working out of the vision:

> Our dreams must come true even though they are no more than dreams. The world is rolling on to the golden age. The inmates of our workhouses have more comforts than rich chieftains in Africa have...persons in very moderate circumstance put on finer clothes than lords did at the time of Queen Elizabeth. Intelligence is communicated instantaneously, and travelers are conveyed on the ocean and onto the land (WGB, 135).

But this was not something he envisioned without application. He put his philosophy of Christian civilization into practice by becoming a "rainmaker" among the Bakwena—by irrigation!

> The doctor and the rainmaker among these people are one and the same person. As I did not like to be behind my professional brethren, I declared I could make rain too, not however by enchantments like them, but by leading out their river for irrigation. We have only one spade and yet by means of sticks sharpened to a point we have performed all the digging of a pretty long canal...This is I believe the first

instance in which Bechuanas have been got to work without wages (WGB, 46).

Once Lake Nyasa was discovered, Livingstone advocated a steamer to work its way along the shores, suppressing the slave trade and encouraging commerce. And his deep commitment to such advances becomes evident in his correspondence:

> If government furnishes the means, all right; if not I shall spend my book money on it. People who are born rich some-times become miserable from a fear of becoming poor, but I have the advantage you see, in not being afraid to die poor. If I live, I must succeed in what I have undertaken; death alone will put a stop to my effort...Our dreams must come true even though they are no more than dreams; the world is rolling on to the golden age (WGB, 119).

Northcott comments: "As a prophecy of what Africa would eventually see on the Zambezi in water over in the Kariba Gorge and the Kebra Basa dams, it is a shrewd thrust into the future, and the fact that he could record such prophecy in the heat of a wagon at over eighty degrees is a sign of his capacity for detachment."[3] The theme of expanding the influence of civilization continued to grow on him:

> I have found access from a good harbour on the east...and discovered a pathway into the magnificent highland lake region which promises so fairly for our commerce in cotton, and for our policy in suppressing the trade in slaves...I earnestly hope that God will crown our efforts by securing our free passage through those parts...and by enabling us to introduce civilization in a manner which will extend the honour and influence of the English name...Instead of trying to carry civilization to the interior...I am attempting to establish the system of the African proceeding on com-mercial speculation to the coast. There they can learn in a

short time to appreciate the power of Europeans and the inference naturally flows: if those who have so much power and wisdom believe and value the truths of religion how much more we? (WGB, 225.)

Civilization. Without it, said Livingstone, "it will ever be found that uncultivated man is a compound of treachery, cunning, debauchery, gluttony, and idleness."

## 4. He Shone the "lamp unto my feet"

Through it all, Livingstone brought the light of the Word of God, carrying the well-worn Bible which he read through four times while anchored at Bambarré in a hut. He taught from it regularly on Sundays, considering a Lord's Day ill spent when he had to travel or do otherwise. He explained its great truths simply and envisioned the coming days, when its truths would be translated into every "tribal tongue and taught by native evangelists and succeeding generations of missionaries." He continued using the Bible in his interaction with various tribes, translating sections into Sichuan by 1843. Occasionally he thought he could witness the effect of the scriptures on his hearers:

> It is a fact that men never cry...but when the Spirit of God works on their minds they cry most piteously. Sometimes in church they endeavour to screen themselves from the eyes of the preacher by hiding under the forms...as a remedy against their convictions. And when they find that won't do, they rush out of the church and run with all their might, crying as if the hand of death were behind them. One would think, when they got away, there they would remain; but now, they're in their places at the very next meeting...That such hardened beings should be moved at all is wonderful indeed (WGB, 42).

Whatever the effect, he continued speaking the Word of God:

> A large audience listened attentively to my address this morning, but it is impossible to indulge any hopes of such feeble efforts. God is merciful and will deal with them in justice and kindness. This constitutes a ground of hope...A permanent station among them might affect something in time, but a considerable time is necessary. Surely some will pray to our merciful father in their extremity, who never would have thought of him but for our visit (MT, 5 Aug., 1855).

For Livingstone, it was only the power of the Word of God that would effect change:

> I am thankful that I was permitted to sow the good seed among them and I believe that seed is not dead. It is the living word of the Living God. There are few souls which can withstand its force, and no hatred however deep can quench its power. I have strong faith in that vitality which God's word possesses and now record my conviction that the seed will yet grow among [them] though I may not see it (LAJ, 11, 303).

Today such words sound very prophetic, given the great harvest of the Christian faith which was to follow:

> We had good and very attentive audiences yesterday, and I expatiated with great freedom on the love of Christ in dying, from his parting address in John 16. It cannot be these precious truths will fall to the ground. But it is perplexing to observe no effects. They assent to the truth, but "we don't know" or "You speak truly" is their response. In trying to convey knowledge I use the magic lantern, which is everywhere extremely popular. Though they listen with apparent delight to what is said, a question on the following night

reveals almost entire ignorance of the previous lesson. O! that the Holy Spirit would enlighten them. To His soul-renewing influence my longing heart is directed. It is His Word and cannot die (LAJ, 315).

One might have expected a better response from the Makololo, Livingstone's favourite tribe, and the one with which he spent most time:

Sunday evening went over to the people, giving a general summary of the Christian faith and the life of Christ…I asked them to speak about it afterward. They replied that these things were above them—they could not answer me. I went on to speak of the resurrection…All were listening eagerly to the statement about this, especially when they heard that they too must raise and be judged…I spoke of blood shed by them; the conversation continued until they said it was time for me to cross, for the river was dangerous at night (WGB, 233).

Again with the Makololo, he shared the Word along the banks of the Chobe River, surely one of the most idyllic places on earth to hear the good news!

Preached twice to about sixty people. Very attentive. It is only divine power which can enlighten dark minds as these…The people seem to receive ideas on divine subject slowly. They listen, but never suppose that the truths must become embodied in actual life. They will wait until the chief becomes a Christian, and if he believes, then they refuse to follow…Procrastination seems as powerful an instrument of deception here as elsewhere (WGB, 118).

He continued with his Sunday services along the Chobe and found, over a two-year period, very similar hard soil for the good seed. Clearly this man's description of a "good and very attentive audience" did not mean "hearing with understanding"!

A good and very attentive audience. We introduce entirely new motives, and were these not perfectly adapted for the human mind and heart by their Divine Author, we should have no success...A good and attentive audience, but immediately after the service I went to see a sick man, and when I returned toward the *kotla*, I found the chief had retired into a hut to drink beer; and, as the custom is, about forty men were standing singing to him, or, in other words, begging beer by that means....So little effect produced by an earnest discourse conferring the future judgment, but time must be given to allow the truth to sink into the dark mind and produce its effect (MT, June 19, 1852).

Imagine the first-ever services of Christian worship along the beautiful Chobe River, where today elephants frolic and drink and the exotic flavour of Africa rises up from the waters as they widen and flow into the Zambezi! The missionary explorer described some of those gatherings among the Makololo:

When I stand up, all the women and children draw near, and having ordered silence, I explain the plan of salvation, the goodness of God in sending His Son to die, the confirmation of His mission by miracles, the last judgment or future state, the evil of sin, God's commands respecting it...The address is listened to with great attention by most of the audience. A short prayer concludes the service, all kneeling down, and remaining so till told to rise (WGB, 119).

Then Livingstone breaks into another prophetic statement about the ultimate effect of the Word of God:

The earth shall be filled with the knowledge of the glory of the Lord—that is enough. We can afford to work in faith, for omnipotence is pledged to fulfill the promise. The great mountains become a plane before the Almighty arm. The poor Bushman, the most degraded of all Adam's family, shall see his glory, and the dwellers in the wilderness shall bow before Him. The obstacles to the coming of the kingdom are mighty but come it will for all that (MT, Sunday, 19 June, 1852).

After seven years on the continent, he wrote to his father:

For a long time I felt much depressed after preaching the unsearchable riches of Christ to apparently insensible hearts; but now I like to dwell on the love of the great Mediator, for it always warms my own heart, and I know that the gospel is the power of God—the great means which He employs for the regeneration of our ruined world (April 7, 1848).

## 5. There Was His Eye for "all creatures great and small"

Philip Birkinshaw, in his charming book on Livingstone, notes that "as well as 'delicate sensitivity' to natural things, he added 'scientific direction and refinement,' which reads at times like a "Christian pantheism." One of his early notebooks quotes the Coleridge poem, *The Rime of the Ancient Mariner*:

'He prayeth well who loveth well
Both man and bird and beast;
He prayeth best who loveth best
All things both great and small;
For the dear God who loveth us,
He made and loveth all.'

For a man like Livingstone, Africa provided a vast and unexplored natural world to appeal to his wide range of interests. Birkinshaw notes that,

...the variety of African wildlife far surpasses that of Europe and America. Even in southern Africa...there are nearly 400 different types of mammal, including 80 game animals; 550 different reptiles and amphibians; almost 1,000 kinds of birds; 18,000 plant species, including nearly 1,000 trees; and of insects, well, 800 kinds of butterfly alone. Putting Livingstone in the midst of such plenty was like putting a cat in a dairy...It is not merely to the details of the African scene that Livingstone responds, but to its totality, the ecosystem in all its harmony...and he often calls it Eden.[4]

When we consider Livingstone's reflections on the grandeur of Africa, his encounters with big game and other fauna, his sympathy for the animals, we might conclude with Birkinshaw that he would have been a conservationist today. Here is Livingstone the naturalist, beholding the natural abundance of Africa:

When we came to the top of the outer range of the hills, we had a glorious view. At a short distance below us we saw the Kafue, wending away over a forest-clad plain to the confluence, and on the other side of the Zambezi beyond that lay a long range of dark hills. A line of fleecy clouds appeared laying along the course of that river at their base. The plain below us, at the left of the Kafue, had more large game on it than anywhere else I had seen in Africa. Hundreds of buffaloes and zebras grazed on the open spaces, and there stood lordly elephants feeding majestically, nothing moving apparently but the proboscis. I wished that I had been able to make a photograph of a scene so seldom beheld and which is destined, as guns increase, to pass away from earth (MT, 570).

In 1853, Livingstone was near the Kaprivi Strip, where these days we often take teams for safaris and game viewing:

The open glade, surrounded by forest trees of various hues, had a little stream meandering in the centre. A herd of reddish-coloured antelopes (pallas) stood on the side near a large baobab, looking at us, and ready to run up the hill; while gnus, tsessebes, and zebras gazed in astonishment at the intruders. Some fed carelessly, and others put on the peculiar air of displeasure which these animals sometimes assume before they resolve on flight. A large white rhinoceros came along the bottom of the valley with is low sauntering gait, without noticing us; he looked as he meant to indulge in a mud bath. Several buffaloes, with their dark visages, stood under the trees on the side opposite to the pallah. It being Sunday, all was peace, and...we could not but reflect on that second stage of our existence which we hope will lead us into scenes of perfect beauty (MT, 172).

While on a trip with young chief Sekeletu in 1853, Livingstone shot an eland and described the beauty of the creature:

We shot a beautiful cow-eland, standing the shade of a fine tree. It was evident that she had lately had her calf killed by a lion, for there were five long deep scratches on both sides of her hindquarters, as if she had run to the rescue of her calf, and the lion, leaving it, had attacked herself but was unable to pull her down. When lying on the ground, the milk flowing from the large udder showed that she must have been seeking the shade, from the distress its non-removal in the natural manner caused. She was a beautiful creature, and Lebeøle, a Makololo gentleman who accompanied me, speaking in reference to its size and beauty said, "Jesus ought to have given us these instead of cattle." It was a new undescribed variety of this splendid antelope. It was marked with narrow white bands across the body, exactly like those of the koodoo, and had a black patch of more than a hand-breadth on the outer side of the forearm (MT, 230).

Of course it is dangerous to build human habitation in the middle of African game—and share the neighbourhood with hyenas!

The people here build their huts in gardens on high stages. This is necessary on account of danger from the spotted hyaena, which is said to be very fierce, and also as a protection against lions and elephants. The hyaena is a very cowardly animal, but frequently approaches persons lying asleep, and makes an ugly gash on the face. Mozinkwa had lost his upper lip in this way, and I have heard of men being killed by them; children too are sometimes carried off; for though he is so cowardly that the human voice will make him run away at once, yet, when his teeth are in the flesh, he holds on, and shows amazing power of jaw. Leg bones of oxen...are by this animal crunched up with the greatest ease (LJ, 600).

Livingstone was interested in the question we often ask: why don't people hunt crocodiles and eat them? Are they not delicious? We've sampled crocodile at a various buffets and enjoyed it very much. They taste good and they are such a danger, lurking in the rivers. Why not hunt them? The answer we usually get is, "Because they eat people."

Crocodiles in the Rovumma have a sorry time of it. Never before were reptiles so persecuted and snubbed. They are hunted with spears, and spring traps are set for them. If one of them enters an inviting pool after fish, he soon finds a fence thrown round it, and a spring trap set in the only path out of the enclosure. Their flesh is eaten and relished. The banks, on which the female lays her eggs by night, are carefully searched by day, and all the eggs dug out and devoured... Our men were constantly on the lookout for crocodiles' nests. One was found containing thirty-five newly laid eggs, and they declared that the crocodile would lay as many more the second night in another place. The eggs were a foot deep in the sand on the top of a bank ten feet high...The yolk of the egg is nearly the same as the real white. In taste they resemble hen's eggs with perhaps a touch of custard, and would be as highly relished by whites as by blacks if not for their unsavoury origin in men-eaters (LJ, Sept. 1862).

Of course Livingstone could not do justice to African wildlife without some thought for snakes, some of which are

> ...harmless, and even edible. Of the latter sort is the large python. The largest specimen of this are about fifteen or twenty feet in length; they are perfectly harmless, and live on small animals; occasionally the steinbuck and pallah fall victims and are sucked into its comparatively small mouth in boa-constrictor fashion. One we shot was 11 feet 10 inches long, and as thick as a man's leg. When shot through the spine, it was capable of lifting itself up about five feet high, and opened its mouth in a threatening manner, but the poor thing was more inclined to crawl away. The flesh is much relished by the Bakalahari and Bushmen: they carry away each his portion, like logs of wood, over their shoulders (MT, 143).

And so the doctor's descriptions go on, describing the soko gorillas, who live in communities of about ten, zebras, buffalo, elephants. His instincts are on the side of conservation, and he is uncomfortable with big game hunters and their trophies:

> On these great flats all round we saw in the white sultry glare herds of zebras, gnus, and occasionally buffaloes, standing for days, looking wistfully towards the wells for a share of the tasty water. It is mere wanton cruelty to take advantage of the necessities of these poor animals, and shoot them down one after another, without intending to make the smallest use of either the flesh, skins, or horns.
>
> I could not order my men to do what I would not do myself; but though I tried to justify myself on the plea of necessity, I could not adopt this mode of hunting. If your object is to secure the best specimens for a museum, it may be allowable, but if, as has been practised by some who come into the country and fire away indiscriminately, great numbers of animals are wounded and allowed to perish miserably or are killed on the spot and left to be preyed on by

vultures and hyaenas, and all for the sole purpose making a "bag," then I take it to be evident that such sportsmen are pretty far gone in the hunting form of insanity (MT, 161).

## 6. He Opened Our Eyes by His Discoveries

Biographer Tim Jeal sets the scene: "When Livingstone landed in Simon's Bay in March 1841, the geography of the African interior was still as much of a mystery to Europeans as the whereabouts of the sources of the Nile and Congo."[5] For the civilized world, Africa was a mysterious land mass dotted by fringe settlements along the coast. Exploration and discovery was inhibited by all kinds of factors: the lack of natural harbours, mountains and cataracts, wild beasts, sudden and very abundant deaths from malaria, incessant heat and humidity. The challenge, for Livingstone, was redesigning the coastline!

> I am informed by the people here that the Kabompo contains a very formidable waterfall and that the Bashukulompo river is too spoiled by cataracts. The sea after all is the great civilizer of nations. If Africa instead of simple littoral outline had been broken up by deep indentations of glorious old ocean, how different would been the fate of its inhabitants. Commercial enterprise never entered the interior of the continent except by foot travellers. I am sorry for it. My dreams of establishing a commerce by means of the rivers vanish as I become better acquainted with them. But who can contend with nature? (Jeal, 287).

Seasonal rains could turn trails into impassible swamps and tropical forests abounded. There was the tsetse fly that could take out a whole herd of oxen in a week. For these and other good reasons, the continent remained largely undiscovered and unexplored. Its reputation as "the white man's grave" was growing.

Anyway, there was no pressing reason to explore Africa. To all appearances, the Africans possessed neither wealth nor an easily exploitable land. As Jeal puts it, "All interest in Africa might have died away in the sixteenth century, but for the use of one African commodity: the African himself!" (Jeal, 29.) Thus, it was most propitious that Livingstone arrived when he did. Enter a man who is as much explorer as anything else. The clustering of missionaries around the stations of Kuruman, close to South Africa's capital today, Pretoria, was to him something like the abandonment of a high calling. After just two years, he had submitted proposals to change all this and was more than ready to leave the settlements behind. In fact, he soon struck off to the north across the Orange River and wrote:

> I like travelling very much indeed. There is so much freedom connected with our African manners. We pitch our tent and make our fire wherever we choose, walk, ride or shoot at abundance of all sorts of game as our inclination leads us (CN, 29).

He made three journeys between 1849 and 1851, of some 300 miles each, out of the mission station in Kolobeng. He traveled as far as Lake Ngami, in the Kalahari desert, a five-month journey through 300 miles of the Kalahari. His party, which included his young family, were no doubt the first Europeans to see the lake, and a welcome sight its abundant waters were! But what a journey! People questioned his sanity on this 1851 venture, taking his young family, all at times very much at risk of dying of thirst, into the heart of the Kalahari desert.

> Shobo gave us no hope of water in less than a month. Providentially, however, we came sooner than we expected to some supplies of rain water in a chain of pools. It is impossible to convey an idea of the dreary scene on which we entered after leaving this spot: the only

vegetation was a low scrub in deep sand; not a bird or insect enlivened the landscape...and, to make matters worse, our guide Shobo wandered on the second day. We coaxed him on at night, but he went to all points of the compass on the trail of elephants which had been here in the rainy season; and then would sit down in the path, and in his broken Sichuan say, "No water...all country only...Shobo sleeps...country only"...The oxen were terribly fatigued and thirsty; and on the morning of the fourth day, Shobo, after professing ignorance of everything, vanished altogether. We went on in the direction in which we last saw him, and about eleven o'clock began to see birds, then the trail of a rhinoceros. At this we unyoked the oxen, and they, apparently knowing the sign, rushed along to find the water in the river Mababe...to the west of us.

The supply of water in the wagons had been wasted by one of our servants, and by the afternoon only a small portion remained for the children. This was a bitterly anxious night; and next morning the less there was of water, the more thirsty the little rogues became. The idea of their perishing before our eyes was terrible. It would almost have been a relief to me to have been reproached with being the real cause of the catastrophe, but not one syllable of upbraiding was uttered by their mother (LT, 46).

It was the third of these initial journeys that turned out to be the crucial one, where Livingstone's life's calling unfolded before him like the great rolling waters of the Zambezi. He had reached the upper Zambezi at its confluence with the winding Chobe in the vicinity of today's Chobe Game Park and Victoria Falls. It was a region where no geographical society suspected such a large inland waterway to be. As he stood on the banks of the great river, enraptured by what his wondering eyes beheld at the very heart of the African continent, an expanse of beautiful flowing water, deep and wide, in the majestic Zambezi—we hear something like the ecstasy of the prophet Ezekiel:

> The waves lifted the canoes and made them roll beautifully...An immense region God has in his Providence opened up...If we can enter it and form a settlement, we shall be able in the course of a very few years to put a stop to the slave trade in that quarter.
>
> It opens up the prospect of a highway capable of being quickly traversed by boats to a large section of well-peopled territory...I hope to be permitted to work as long as I live beyond other men's line of things and plant the seed of the gospel where others have not planted. But every excursion for that purpose will involve separation from my family for periods of four or five months (WGB, 94).

From this moment on, transfixed by the great Zambezi in its majestic flow through the heart of the continent, the man became, in Northcott's words, "a free-lance for God." He was to discover terrain unseen by European eyes, traverse the vast continent before him, trekking through southern equatorial Africa, across the central region of modern Zambia, from Portuguese Angola on the west to Portuguese Mozambique on the east, truly investing his life to his dying day as the great explorer of the continent, called to reveal treasures yet unseen to the eyes of a wondering world.

Along with great rivers, Livingstone was to discover new tribes, "strong black people who can carry the gospel." From the Makololo tribe, he had learned that the cotton they wore came from Portuguese Angola through intermediate African traders, the Mambari. Sebituane, chief of the Makololo, the fleetest and fiercest warrior chief Livingstone would ever meet, assembled a party of men to travel with him where they had never been, northwest along the upper Zambezi, out to the south Atlantic Ocean at Loanda, Angola.

The Makololo whom we met on the Chobe were delighted to see us; and as their chief Sebituane was about twenty miles down the river, Mr. Oswell and I proceeded in canoes to his temporary residence. He was about forty five years of age; of a tall and wiry form, an olive or coffee-and-milk colour, and slightly bald; in manner cool and collected, and more frank in his answers than any other chief I ever met. He was the greatest warrior ever heard of beyond the colony, for, unlike Mosilikatse, Dinaan, and others, he always led his men into battle himself. When he saw the enemy, he felt the edge of his battle axe and said, "Aha! It is sharp, and whoever turns his back on the enemy will feel its edge." So fleet of foot was he that all his people knew there was no escape for the coward, and any such would be cut down without mercy. In some instances of skulking, he allowed the individual to return home; then calling him he would say, "Ah, you prefer dying at home to dying in the field, do you? You shall have your desire." This was the signal for immediate execution (LT, 106).

This great transcontinental journey would rank Livingstone among the greatest explorers in history, opening up the continent east to west and leading the way for others. Livingstone the explorer is said to have had two additional aims: to find a malaria-free site on the upper Zambezi that would serve as a trading centre and mission station; and to open a viable route to the east or west coast of the content along the Zambezi.

The 1,200-mile journey to Loanda put him and his band of Makololo through every life-threatening onslaught imaginable. Payments of "hongo" tribute were demanded by hostile tribes along the route, apparently used to dealing with slave traders. There was danger from flooded rivers, with their crocodiles and hippos, the scourge of malarial fever and other diseases. Racing rivers, heat, dizziness, and tremors—all proved David Livingstone to be one very hardy and resilient explorer.

> Never did I endure such drenchings, and all the streams being swollen we had to ford many, the water flowing on the rustic bridges waist deep. Others we crossed by sticking to the oxen the best we could, and a few we made a regular swim of...Lying in a little gipsy tent with everything damp or wet, was sore against the grain.[6]

For all that, Livingstone cannot resist including the beauty of modern Angola as he makes his way toward the coast.

> The climate is so good they are either planting or reaping the whole year round. All the different grains, roots, etc, may be seen at one time in every stage of growth. Indeed, the country generally is fertile in the extreme, and very beautiful. It is flat but lies in ridges or waves, the edge of each wave covered in the dense dark forest, and the trough a pleasant valley containing a stream in its centre.

Seven months after leaving the Barostse valley, Livingstone arrived in Loanda on the coast of the southern Atlantic! Livingstone found one lone Englishman and fell into "an English bed" provided by Mr. Gabriel, close to death. He was nursed back to health and offered a ship back to England, where his fame had reached its peak. But this man was an explorer, heart and soul; plus he felt obliged to take his Makololo followers back to their homes; plus he was still looking for a trade route, linking the east and the west of the continent. And so Livingstone retraced his steps, in a decision that seems most heroic, declining safe passage back to England from Loanda. It took a year, but by late 1855 he was back at the centre of the continent, in the Makololo centre of Linyanti on the Chobe River. Along the way, he had discovered for European eyes the great Mosiatunya, "the smoke that thunders," one of our seven wonders of the world, which he named "Victoria Falls."

But this trek was only half over. In the space of a few weeks he was off again, this time to the east, with another large Makololo party, aiming for Portuguese Mozambique, to see what possibilities the Zambezi offered to the east as a navigable trade route. On finishing that journey he would complete the first authenticated west-east crossing of central sub-Saharan Africa. When he finally boarded a vessel for Britain, in 1855, two years of national acclaim awaited.

When Livingstone returned to Africa in 1858, it was as the head of the government-sponsored "Zambezi Expedition." Sailing up the mouth of the Zambezi from the Indian Ocean, it soon became clear that for David Livingstone, impediments were what God used to open up new territories! When he encountered the unexpected and impassable Kebrabasa rapids, some 100 miles up the Zambezi, he abruptly opted for a plan B. He turned his expedition to the north and sailed up the Shire River instead, into present day Malawi. Here was more uncharted territory—and some not so pleasant discoveries!

He reached Lake Nyasa as one of its first European discoverers. Alas, a second discovery awaited: the Arab Swahili slave trade had reached the Upper Shire. Livingstone was walking on the very slave route that linked Katanga in the interior, to the coastal town of Kilwa. How could his vision for European settlements be realized when the most suitable highland regions were being plundered for slaves by Arabs from Zanzibar and Kilwa?

Livingstone described his discovery of the beautiful lake Shirwa, surrounded by mountains, and continued to explore the Shire region, leading him to the discovery of Lake Nyasa to the north. Opening up beautiful, long Lake Nyasa to missions was to be a key entry for future mission stations and Christian expansion.

In the highland regions of the Shire Valley, they were to find an increase of energy, from the drier climate and the most viable for commercial and mission stations. This alone was the great achievement of the Zambezi expedition. Indeed, Livingstone had a grand and growing vision for the future of these lands:

> Water carriage existed all the way from England, with the exception of the Murchison Cataracts, along which a road of forty miles might easily be made. A small steamer on the lake could do more good in suppressing the slave trade than a half dozen men of war in the ocean. If the Zambezi could be opened to comers, the bright vision of the last ten years would be realized, and the Shire Valley and banks of the Nyasa would transform the region into the garden of the Lord (ZT, 93).

In the years to follow, it would become evident that his view was correct. This was 1859. Northcott notes, "He had the prophetic vision of what twenty or thirty good Christian Scottish families with their minister and elders might do on the fertile lands now stained by the tracks of slave trading."[7]

A third penetration of Africa awaited the great explorer, from 1866 to 1873, his final trip to Africa, this time to "discover the source of the Nile." How elated he was to be back on African soil! As Blaikie writes,

> In spite of all that he had suffered in Africa, and though he was without the company of a single European, he had, in setting out, something of the exhilarating feeling of a young traveler starting on his first trip to Switzerland, deepened by the sense of nobility which there is in every endeavour to do good to others: "The mere animal pleasure of traveling in a wild unexplored country is very great...The sweat of one's brow is no longer a curse when one works for God; it proves a tonic to the system and is actually a blessing" (WGB, 145).

There was also a mystical appeal about this search for the headwaters of the Nile, the great river having a sacred character in Christian lore. Moreover, for Livingstone, the discovery of its headwaters would give him an additional platform from which to combat the slave trade:

> I would not consent to go simply as a geographer...There must be practical consequences...The Nile sources are valuable only as a mans of enabling me to open my mouth with power among men. It is this power which I hope to apply to remedy an enormous evil (WGB, 275).

That discovery would elude him. But other discoveries along the way would prove most significant. As Blaikie puts it,

> Whatever might be his aims, it was ordained that in the wanderings of his last years he should bring within the sympathies of the Christian world many a poor tribe otherwise unknown; that he should witness sights surpassing all he had ever seen before of the inhumanity and horrors of the slave traffic—sights that harrowed this inmost soul (WGB, 135).

But this trek started out with some very hard going. By the time he and the remains of his bedraggled, recalcitrant team reached region of Lake Nyasa, they must have thought of abandoning the quest. This whole thing looked like a tactical error, and the temptation to turn back must have been overwhelming. The Rovumma, like most all African rivers, proved full of cataracts. The land was in the grip of famine and slave trading. All that Livingstone had learned from his arduous venture was that the slave trade was, if anything, expanding in the region.

Still, he visited villages and regions as the first European. And what lay ahead were his important additions to the field of geographical knowledge, with detailed surveys of lakes Mweru and Bangweulu, where he would end his days. Were such lakes the sources of the river Nile, as he anticipated? No indeed, he was closer to the headwaters of the great Congo River. But the discoveries of his third journey changed the world of geographical knowledge—and the course of history.

## 7. He Exposed Africa's Open Sore

If all of Livingstone's other achievements were forgotten, this one would immortalize him forever and warrant his place among the world's greats. While engaged in exploration, Livingstone opened to the eyes of the world the great atrocity that was the three-hundred-year slave trade in Central Africa. Today we would call it something like cultural genocide. Livingstone called it "murdersome." Abolition! For Livingstone, this was something worth dying for:

> No one can estimate the amount of God-pleasing good that will be done, if by divine favour this awful slave trade, into the midst of which I have come, be abolished. This will be something to have lived for! (Letter to Agnes, Aug. 15, 1872.)

Into this region of horrors, David Livingstone came with his admiration for the African members of the human family. He came with respect for tribal cultures and traditions. He came with charity, with his presence, the presence of a Christian in the midst of a world.

Of course this trade had its origins as early as the sixteenth century: while a few intrepid Portuguese were struggling up the Zambezi by 1500, their fellow countrymen were settling in Brazil, while the Spanish moved into the Caribbean, Mexico, and Peru. These were days of discovery, and the "new world" being colonized by the Europeans needed people. How were settlers to provide labour for the development of mines, sugar plantations, and cotton fields? It was at this juncture that interest in Africa picked up. The news that thousands of strong hardy black people were known to be living lives of apparent idleness on the other side of the Atlantic was transfixing to the mercantile mentality of the new world.

The trans-Atlantic slave trade was the result. With most European countries soon joining in and the European settlement of North America providing a vast new market for slaves, the trade flourished for more than three centuries before Wilberforce and the abolitionists began their thirty-year campaign to bring it to an end. Finally, in 1833, the British parliament passed their most belated legislation, banning slavery at home and setting a timetable for implementation of the ban throughout the British Empire. This was after the slave trade had prevailed over Africa for a full 300 years, tearing from the heart of the "Black Mother," according to historian Basil Davidson, some fifty million of its people. Davidson's graphic description gives the background to the world Livingstone was entering. The historian raises an interesting question when he speaks of European-African relations from 1450 to 1850: why did Europe prosper and Africa go backwards? For him it calls for a

> ...fresh look at the overseas slave trade, the steady year-by-year export of African labour to the West Indies and the Americas that marked the greatest and most fateful forced migration in the history of man...Through long years the "Black Mother" of Africa would populate the Americas with millions of her sons and daughters.
>
> There was misery, unending misery. There was so much death in the Americas that whole slave populations had to be renewed every few years...In 1829 an Englishman named Walsh took passage from Brazil on the North Star...Somewhere in the South Atlantic, he chased and stopped a slaver. Walsh described, "The cargo of 505 men and women—the crew had

thrown fifty-five overboard during seventeen days at sea. The slaves were all enclosed under grated hatchways between the decks. The space was so low that they sat between each other's legs and stowed so close together that [there was] no possibility of lying down, or at all changing their position by day or night. As they belonged to different individuals, they were all branded like sheep...impressed under the breasts or upon their arms...burnt with a red hot iron." Walsh was shocked but informed that this was "one of the best slavers on the sea."

Month after month, for three hundred years before Walsh took passage, such ships sailed the Atlantic.[8]

How many were the victims of the slave trade? Davidson raises the question, looking for round numbers, scouring scanty records.

But the Portuguese carried at least one million to Brazil between 1680 and 1780...British colonies received more than two million during the same period. In 1744, a typical year, 104 slaving ships cleared from Liverpool, Bristol, and London: the *Lottery* took 305 to Jamaica, for a profit of thirty six pounds per head; the *Enterprise* took 392 to Cuba...Liverpool slavers made a profit of 2,360,000 pounds between 1783 and 1793 on 303,000 slaves.

Davidson does the math and concludes that 15 million slaves landed alive and calls it a "very conservative figure...But many died in the process...in Africa...in the 'middle passage'...others were transported to Europe and Asia. Thus, so far as the African slave trade is concerned, it appears reasonable to suggest that in some way or another before and after embarkation, it cost Africa at least fifty million souls" (BM, 88).

The historian calls this a multiplied loss to Africa. First and foremost was the depopulation; second, there was the "steady and decisive damage" of economic loss. "Slavery suffocated economic growth and gave the maritime nations of Europe a long lead in economic development," as Africa sent away "the very men and women who would otherwise produce wealth at home. In exporting slaves, African states exported their own capital without any possible return."

Such was the world of unbridled rapine that David Livingstone entered in 1841. While he could not stop it, he could express the horror that was due. His written portrayals of "the trade from hell" raised the consciousness of his countrymen and contributed greatly to abolition. But meanwhile, he was exposed to a world of unending atrocity at every turn.

His exposure to slavery began early among the Boers of South Africa in the forties. It was broadened on his transcontinental trek to Loanda, where he wrote:

> The great bane of the Portuguese settlements was slavery. Slavery prevented a good example, it hindered justice, it kept down improvement. If a settler took a fancy to a good-looking girl, he had only to buy her and make her his concubine. Instead of correcting the polygamous habits of the chief and others, the Portuguese adopted like habits themselves...The whole system of slavery gendered a blight with nothing to counteract; to make Africa a prosperous land, liberty must be proclaimed to the captive, and the slave system, with all its accursed surrounding, brought conclusively to an end (WGB, 172).

His proposed cure to slave traffic was legitimate trade. The idea of English cottons as the current coinage of Africa grew on him, even through the exchange currency was only in ivory and beeswax. In his early travels, he was prospecting for Christian merchants as well as Christian missions. Together, he claimed, "they could drive out slavery in ten years." From Bashinge, on March 20, 1855, he wrote:

This slave agent...has two chainful of women going to be sold for the ivory...The Portuguese cannot send them abroad on account of our ships of war on the coast, yet will sell them to the best advantage. These women...were caught lately in a skirmish the Portuguese had with their tribe; and they will be sold for about three tusks each. Each has an iron ring around the wrist that is attached to the chain, which she carries in the hand to prevent it jerking and hurting the wrist.

Livingstone's thoughts turn to human depravity:

It is only the goodness of God in appointing our lot in different circumstance that we are not similar degraded, for we had the same evil nature, which is so degraded in them as to allow of men treating them as beasts.

This scourge would follow Livingstone wherever he went. In modern Malawi, he was met on March 5, 1859 by "a cargo of slaves (twenty men and forty women) in irons to sell at St. Cruz for exportation at Bourbon." In *The Zambezi and Its Tributaries*, he told of slave sticks and the rows of men, women, and children. Vaulter Golding carries the famous account of Livingstone setting free a long line of slaves near Lake Nyasa:

A few weeks later, in June 1861, the new steamer, called the *Pioneer*, reached the mouth of the Zambezi. At the same time, there came a party of missionaries under the brave Bishop Mackenzie, who had been sent out by the Universities of Oxford and Cambridge to settle in the Shiré valley...

He had halted his party in a village for rest and food, when suddenly a long file of eighty-four slaves came round the hillside towards them. The captives, mostly women and children, were roped together with thongs of raw hide, but some of the men had their necks fixed in a "goree," or forked slave-stick. The back of the neck was thrust into the fork, and the two prongs were joined by a bar of iron under the chin, while a slaver walked behind, holding the shaft of the stick, ready to wring the poor slave's neck at the first sign of escape. Worn out with pain, misery, and fatigue, the hapless slaves limped and staggered beneath their loads. The slavers, decked out with red caps and gaudy finery, marched jauntily along, blowing tin horns and shouting as though they had just won a noble victory.

Dragging him by the arm, and driving him with the terror of a spear-point, the Makololo brought the chief of the slave gang to Livingstone, who at once recognised him as a servant of the Portuguese chief officer at Teté.

The inhuman wretch said he had bought the slaves, but his prisoners told a different tale. They had been captured in war by the slavers, who had burnt their village, murdered their tribesmen, and marched them off in bonds towards Teté…Livingstone and his friends quickly set themselves to the work of cutting the thongs and sawing the slave-sticks off the captives, and while they were thus busy, the chief of the slavers escaped.[9]

The effect of this wholesale merchandising of humans, with the attendant wars and kidnappings, was predictable. Villages were depopulated, land that had been recently cultivated and was very productive was now razed and abandoned.

All the countries near to the Portuguese have been greatly depopulated. We are now ascending this river without vegetables, and living on salt beef and pork. The slave trade has done its work, for formerly all kind of provision could be procured at every point and at the cheapest rate. We cannot get anything for either love or money, in a country the fertility of which is truly astonishing (LJ, 65).

Throughout the region of Lake Nyasa and modern Malawi, it was the same story. When they took the four-oar assembled boat up in the lake for the first time, leaving the *Pioneer* on the Shire, they discovered that the placid beauty of Lake Nayasa/Malawi was only a veneer for terrible atrocities on every side. As Blaikie put it,

> The slave trade was going on at a dismal rate...Livingstone was informed that 19,000 slaves from this Nyasa region alone passed annually through the custom house in Zanzibar. This was besides those landed at Portuguese slave ports. In addition to those captured, thousand were killed or died of their wounds or of famine, or perished in other ways, so that no more than one fifth of the victims actually became slaves (WGB, 172).

### *"This monster iniquity"*

Livingstone's vision was for a small armed steamer on the Lake Nyasa, moving up and down the long shorelines for trade in produce. Surely, he said, it would stop "nearly the whole" of this wholesale robbery and murder. As a result of the appalling realities he witnessed, the cause of abolition became more urgent in his mind. Could it be that his discoveries had only stimulated the activity of the slave traders? Were the Portuguese local authorities actually promoting slave trading, despite their promises to the contrary and despite its inevitable desolation across the countryside?

> Wherever we took a walk, human skeletons were seen in every direction...A whole group had been thrown down a slope behind a village, where the fugitives often cross the river from the east...The sight of this desert, but eighteen months ago a well-peopled valley, now literally strewn with human bones, forced the conviction upon us that the destruction of human life in the middle passage, however great, constitutes but a small portion of the waste and made us feel that unless the slave trade—that monster iniquity which has so long brooded over Africa—is put down, lawful commerce cannot be established (ZT, ch.12).

Wars continued to spin out of slavery at every stage. The further Livingstone pursued his quest, the more apparent it became that this systemic evil was not abating. Moving up the Rovumma in 1866, he writes:

> The horror of the slave trade presented themselves in all their hideous aspects. Women were found dead, tied to trees...The slave trade utterly demoralized the people...The Arabs bought whoever war brought to them, and the great tracts of forest in the country favoured kidnapping...Marks of destruction and desolation again shock the eye (LJ, 56).

As for the European governments, it seemed there was much posturing: "Though the Portuguese government had given public orders that Livingstone was to be aided in every way...the Portuguese who were engaged in the slave trade were far too devoted to it to encourage an enterprise to extirpate it" (WGB, 345).

The worst blow for Livingstone must have been the realization that the effect of his opening up the Zambezi had been to afford the Portuguese traders new networks for conducting their "unhallowed traffic." The more he travelled, the more he realized that the slave trade was following in his footsteps. When he landed much farther north, in Manyuema, in modern-day DRC, he wrote:

> Many of the Manyuema women are very pretty; their hands, feet, limbs and form are perfect. The men are handsome...The way in which these...Zanzibar Mohammedans murder the men and seize the women and children makes me sick at heart. It is not slave trade. It is murdering free people to make slaves. It is perfectly indescribable. Kirk has been working hard to get this murdersome system put a stop to. Heaven prosper his noble efforts (LJ, 67).

Then came what some have called "Livingstone's My Lai," the Nyangwe massacre on the Lualaba. Some 400 Africans were at the market when the unthinkable happened:

A large party of Arab traders had arrived with one Dugumbé, trading in the markets, and intending to remain six or seven years. As he and his men were dealing in the village market, they were haggling about prices when shots broke out, for they had carried their guns into the marketplace. As the marketeers threw down their wares and fled in confusion, three of Dugumbé's men opened fire on the mass of people, while volleys discharged...by the creek on the panic-stricken women who dashed at the canoes which were jammed in the creek. As they scrambled for the canoes, shot after shot continued to be fired. Some of the long line of heads disappeared quietly; whilst other poor creatures threw their arm high as if appealing to the great Father above, and sank. One canoe took in as many as it could hold, and all paddled with their hands and arms. Three canoes got out in haste, picked up sinking friends, till all went down together and disappeared. One man in a long canoe, which could have held forty or fifty, had obviously lost his head; he had been out in the stream before the massacre began and now paddled up the river nowhere, and never looked to the drowning. By and by, all the heads disappeared; some had turned downstream towards the bank and escaped.

After the terrible affair in the water, the party of Tagamojo, who was the chief perpetrator, continued to fire on the people. I counted seventeen villages burning this morning. I asked the question of Dugumbé and others, "Now for what is all this murder?" All blamed Manillas as its cause, and in one sense he was the cause; but the wish to make an impression in the country as to the importance and greatness of the newcomers was the most potent motive. It made me sick at heart. No one will ever know the exact loss on this bright sultry summer morning. It gave me the impression of being in Hell (LJ, 1870).

It was that descriptive account, in 1871, which cemented the British resolve to abolish the slave trade.

## 8. "The light of his presence" (the Livingstone Touch)

No doubt this is a testimony to Livingstone's genuine conversion as a Scottish youth. There seems no doubt that he was "salt and light" in the world, that he brought the presence of a Christian worldview, that he conveyed something like Christlikeness to Africa. This was a genuine conversion, to be sure, young Livingstone's experience after a period of spiritual angst in his youth. The turning point seemed to be the assurance of James Matheson's book, that there was no conflict between Christianity and science. Once assured of that, the path was laid for David Livingstone, the scientist and naturalist. He could make a full commitment of his life to Christ. His conversion was followed closely by a sense of call. He was raised in a climate of missionary expansionism, and great missionary societies were sending his countrymen to the ends of the earth. He felt such a calling early and trained to make himself most effective. He was greatly influenced by Robert Moffatt of Bechuanaland, who encouraged his young hearer to catch a vision of the villages of Africa. What youthful idealism exuded from young David Livingstone as he arrived in Cape Town, 1841: "I leave the opium wars aside...I smell the smoke of a thousand villages." With such a divine call, and with his background of training in medicine, theology, and the natural sciences, how could the man not shed light?

Of course, the brightness that came from Livingstone's sheer presence was in contrast with the surrounding night. It was a

Christ-like light "shining in the darkness." As a newly arrived missionary, he could have remained among the southern Bakwena people and simply added the light of his candle to the already bright glow around the Moffatts of Kuruman. But this was not all his vision. Livingstone's light was a great light because it was mostly solitary, among people who sat in absolute spiritual darkness. He came with acceptance of the African as a human being, image bearer of the Creator. He came with respect for tribal cultures and traditions, even when he was surprised by ways of life that seemed passing strange. He came with charity, with his presence—the presence of a great Christian in the midst of a world of paganism, like the presence of the Lord upon the shores of Gadara.

Perhaps presence matters most. As Paul writes about "sincere love," it "weeps with those who weep...rejoices with those who rejoice...minds not high things...associates with people of low estate" (see Romans 12:14-16). This is the life of all the Mother Teresas of Christianity, among the wretched of the earth, doing something beautiful for God. It seems that somewhere early on, an unwavering conviction was born in David Livingstone that he should give Africa his *presence*. And his presence, ultimately, made all the difference. It was his presence that enabled him to respond to the social turmoil that he encountered. No doubt this was the only way he could really make a difference—as is no doubt true in any age, where truly impactful, Christlike ministries are carried out in all the far-flung regions of the globe as God's beautiful people carry Christ's presence and do his humble work, lifting the downtrodden, healing the sick, mending the broken. Christ is present as we incarnate his presence.

And what a presence Livingstone had! From his initial landing in Cape Town, northward through Kolobeng and Kuruman, along the fringe of the Kalahari, learning languages as he went, till he reached the Makololo people at the Zambezi. Not only did he walk across Africa on its foot paths, he sailed its rivers and lakes. To the end, when we find him meandering around Zambia's Lake Bangwelulu and crossing beautiful Tanganyika, Livingstone was committed to Africa body and soul.

Indeed, to a continent from which generations of Europeans had uprooted millions of people, destroying so many lives in the process, David Livingstone resolved to give one life back. It could never compensate for the incalculable toll of the slave trade, of course. Livingstone alone could never give "reparations." But it was fitting that one life should be given back to Africa in its entirety. "Only one life to offer, Jesus my Lord and King." This seems to have been Livingstone's song. He literally poured out his life on African soil, giving back to the continent the best that he had.

His last birthday underlines the totality of his dedication:

19th March, 1872—Birthday. My Jesus, my king, my life, my all; I again dedicate my whole self to Thee. Accept me, and grant, Gracious Father, that ere this year is gone I may finish my task. In Jesus' name I ask it. Amen, so let it be (LJ).

"I too have shed light?" Goodness, David Livingstone, you surely have! And it is not just the light of *your* personal presence in Africa, as great as that was. There is also the expanding light brought by those who would follow in your footsteps.

Indeed, there is the very bright light of my Zambian students, representing the Livingstone legacy, a radiant young church within a Christian nation.

# Part II

*Fast Forward to Modern Zambia*

oday's Zambia is shaped like a butterfly, spreading its wings in the heart of the African continent. But something must be wrong with the design of these nation states. How could *a butterfly* emerge from such an unpromising chrysalis? And today to spread bright wings in the sunlight? How is this possible? Does it not seem like light years from Livingstone's deathbed in Chitambo's village to today's Zambia, the "Christian Nation"? How can it be only a century, three or four generations, from those dark days past? The transformation of Zambia has been so sudden and full—it almost takes your breath away.

Ruth and I teach and work with a beautiful college community in the heart of Zambia, a 100-member student body that teems with young life and faculty colleagues who have emerged as top-flight African scholars and theologians, a dynamic *koinonia* community of faith. Of course there is some pushing and shoving in the Titanic, our venerable men's dormitory. And a young lady might get frozen out for a day or two. But we are so far removed from Livingstone's Zambia, where cruelty and fear ruled the day; it is like another world. This is the most peaceful and joyful community of faith you would find anywhere.

Hold for a moment the question of how this is possible; how in just over a century, such a radical, miraculous transformation could unfold, from cultures of bloodshed and hate into their loving and healing descendants, penetrating a society so deeply that an entire nation is known as Christian—entrenched in its constitution, no less! Hold that question of "How?" What we are saying here is that first and foremost, we must acknowledge that only God could span such a gulf, as the old hymn says:

Oh, the love that drew salvation's plan!
Oh, the grace that brought it down to man!
Oh, the mighty gulf that God did span at Calvary.

Never were those inspired words more true than in the birth of Zambia! Why not begin by simply admiring this unfolding, this bright sunrise, this radical transformation, this new birth of entire people groups, this conversion of an entire region. The Christian nation! Zambia! Shaped like a butterfly, spreading its wings in the heart of Africa!

But what kind of Christian nation is this? Can this be actually true Christianity? Oh, we could talk about those distinctives that have always marked the African: that they are probably louder and more rhythmic than the rest of the world; that they have a deeper spirituality that seems untouched by the entrenched secularism of much of the modern world; that they carry their Bibles—or Bible-app devices—to church on Sundays; and that they have national prayer days, regular overnights for prayer, and extended seasons of prayer and fasting. There is their appetite for learning and advancement, especially in matters of faith, which pushes them, usually at great sacrifice, into all kinds of academic upgrades. Their toughness in the face of the most daunting odds is really something else. Houses can be collapsing in torrential rains, but you will find many a Zambian at a worship event until the storm passes by. Even charity, that primary Christian virtue, is not lacking. How can this even *be*, you wonder, given where Zambia has come from? The charity is certainly not worn on coat sleeves; sometimes the culture seems callous and uncaring in the extreme. But as I watch ministries of compassion unfold, even around our campus where students minister to neighbourhood shantytowns, among the poorest of the poor, I know that Christian love is alive and well in the Christian nation.

In fact, I look around and conclude that the vital signs of genuine Christianity are very much in place in the Christian nation. Take the love, joy, peace, and longsuffering of the fruit of the Spirit. Here is a society that manifests those, in a corporate sense, quite a lot. In fact, over our twenty-plus years in Zambia, I have come to believe that despite its many complex challenges, the nation is under some kind of divine blessing. As I walk around on a sparkling African morning, everything soft and green after an overnight rain, the bright sunshine reminds me of the favour of God.

I wonder if any land has ever had a more "heart and soul" response to the gospel of Christ than this one. One nation, comprised of many tribes, all with their own language, now with their Bibles and burgeoning churches—this butterfly nation is spreading its wings!

## President Frederick J. Chiluba's
## Declaration, Vow, and Prayer

On December 29, 1991, seven weeks after being sworn into office, President Frederick J. Chiluba moved to the podium and offered a prayer to God on behalf of Zambia:

Dear God, as a nation we now come to your throne of grace, and we humble ourselves and admit our guilt. We repent from all our wicked ways of idolatry, witchcraft, the occult, immorality, injustice and corruption, and all other sins that have violated your righteous laws. We turn away from all this and renounce it all in Jesus' name. We ask for forgiveness and cleansing through the blood of Jesus. Therefore we thank you that you would heal our land. We pray that you would send healing, restoration, revival, blessing, and prosperity to Zambia. Amen.

It was a great moment. As popular as Zambia's first republican president, Kenneth Kaunda, had been, the perception was that he had drifted into eastern religions as part of his "humanism" philosophy and filled the statehouse with idolatry. When he repealed Article 4 of the 1972 constitution, which had guaranteed a one-party state for Zambia, it opened the door for Chiluba, who had experienced conversion in 1981 in prison, to assume the chairmanship of the MMD, the Movement for Multiparty Democracy. A short while later, he became the second president of the Republic of Zambia.

The president followed his prayer with his famous "Speech by the Pillar," in which he told the people that Zambia was changing because of the grace of God. Now was the time to enter into a covenant with God, in the spirit of King Josiah, who "stood by the pillar and made a covenant" (2 Kings 23:3). Thus the president of Zambia entered the Christian nation covenant:

> I declare today that I submit myself as president beneath the Lordship of Jesus Christ. I, likewise, submit the government and the entire nation of Zambia to the Lordship of Jesus Christ. I further declare that Zambia is a Christian nation that would seek to be governed by the righteous principles of the word of God. Righteousness and justice must prevail in all levels of authority, and then we shall see the righteousness of God exalting Zambia. My fellow Zambians, let this message reach all civil servants in all government departments. The time of corruption and bribery is over. For too long, these wicked practices have been destroying and tearing down the nation.

Then, in keeping with the spirit of David Livingstone, in some ways Zambia's "spiritual father," the president referred to the *spreading of light* in the nation: "My fellow Zambians, a new dawn has come to Zambia. May God bless and help us all to live according to his righteous laws."

What a statement it was, no doubt one that had never been made in such terms since the days of King Josiah! And Livingstone? Surely, never in his most rapturous dreams would he have imagined that such a thing could happen in the land of his death, within a little more than a hundred years. Sad that we don't live to see the full results of our labours. Mercy, if Livingstone were still alive to behold what his beloved Zambia has become, he might say, like Simeon, "Lord now let thy servant depart in peace!" But alas, like many great pioneers, he had to be satisfied with seeing the land of promise from afar. Another generation would inherit the blessings for which he had laboured—and endured more than his share of affliction.

Of course, such a declaration created ripples of concern. Some church leaders felt left out by the president's speech. The three Christian "Mother Bodies" were careful in accepting the declaration and concluded that "a nation could not be Christian by declaration, but by deeds"—and pulled out the "separation of church and state" rubric so that the church could always exercise a "prophetic role."

> The Christian church in Zambia would continue to collaborate and offer constructive criticism to the state where necessary...Christian principles should continue to have a positive impact on the development of the nation.

Still, the church leaders endorsed the president's declaration of Zambia as a Christian nation, as long as the rights of those practising other religions were respected. The Zambia Episcopal Conference issued a pastoral letter, reiterating that a nation is not Christian by declaration but by deeds:

> Zambia can be a "Christian nation" only if Zambian Christians follow Jesus in a life of love and respect for one another, a life of dedication, honesty and hard work. In particular, we must follow the example of self-sacrifice, even unto death on the cross...which enabled Jesus to preach the Good News to the poor, proclaim liberty to captives, and lift up the oppressed...It would be in deeds of justice and concern for the poor that we would know the Christian character of our nation.

And so the nation debated the implications, seeking to flesh out what such a declaration should mean. Five years later, the government included the declaration in the preamble to the constitution. Thus the preamble was made to read as follows:

> WE THE PEOPLE OF ZAMBIA by our representatives assembled in our Parliament, having solemnly resolved to maintain Zambia as a Sovereign Democratic Republic... declare the Republic a Christian nation while upholding the right of every person to enjoy that person's freedom of conscience or religion (The Constitution of the Republic of Zambia, Act 18 of 1996).

Again the church demurred. The leaders of the three Mother Bodies did not agree that the preamble to the constitution of the nation should state that Zambia is a Christian nation. Rather, they preferred the position that "Christianity or any other religion could be safely secured without any form of declaration...Zambia should not adopt a state religion or give Christianity a privileged constitutional recognition."

Such debates have been ongoing in the years to follow. But there is no sign that the entrenchment of Christianity in Zambia's constitution will be revoked any time soon. And many Zambians in our circles feel very much okay about that! They are the ones to whom the future belongs.

"For me, the declaration means Lordship," says Sunday Siwale, one of our third year students, preparing for service in the armed forces as a chaplain. "We have given the Lord Jesus Christ a place of Lordship in the country...and I'm sure he is not going to refuse the invitation!" We speak of the great verse in Ephesians 1:22, "He is made head over all things in the interests of the church."

"Can this be the case in Zambia?" I want to know.

"Of course," says Sunday. "He rules all things so that the church can grow and prosper."

"For me, the declaration means privilege," says Clara Daka, a member of our graduating class. "Privilege to worship God at any time, no fear, no interference...not like China...This is a great blessing. The declaration has brought more favour." Clara picks up the significance of a president making a vow and a declaration, as something official and governmental. Still, the declaration was "prophecy...and when you prophesy something it releases prospects for good...things will happen as you have prophesied....This is why we have unity and peace."

"For me," says Joshua Daka, one of our recent graduates and founder of Fountain of Joy Church in Chimwemwe, "it is important because it made the country more friendly to the gospel. Before the declaration, you would hear people saying that Christianity is 'foreign' and we need to get back to traditional beliefs. Now you never hear that and you can squeeze in a prayer at almost any function. The country is very amenable to Christian values."

Who is going to argue with the voice of the youth? Such reflections on the implications are all for the good, young Zambians wrestling with what their declaration means for them, its strengths, its weaknesses. I sense that the youth of Zambia seem to be enjoying the process of forging their own futures in their Christian nation.

Personally, I'm happy to leave that debate to my students, at least for the present. Theirs is the future, theirs is the nation; to them belongs the fleshing out of the implications of their declaration. From my side, I am more interested in *celebrating* the moment! What country, at least in the last 500 years or so, has formally declared itself Christian? What kind of modern novelty is this? A *Christian nation?* Is there any chance that, say, Canada might follow suit? Is this a theocracy, a Geneva revisited? Surely nobody is going to be locked up for being non-Christian? And what about pluralism, democracy's most sacred cow? Such questions will assuredly arise. But I like to just pause and admire this butterfly creation as a first step. Why not examine it in its best light? Why not let the butterfly spread its wings?!

In these pages, I wish to look at this wonder more closely on its own, without blurring the lines with larger debates about pluralism, religious tolerance, and respect for all faiths and so on. What if we looked at the full dimensions of this Christian nation to see in the best light its full length and breadth? And what about its depth and its height? Paul calls the church to "know what is the length and breadth and depth and height" of its faith (see Ephesians 3:18). Why don't we try for the same with His people, in a Christian nation?

We could apply the idea of *length* to the length to which men like Livingstone went to bring the good news to Zambia. Surely they went to extreme, sacrificial lengths! Or we might speak of the length to which this Christian nation is called to go in spreading its light beyond its borders!

But what about the *breadth?* Who could doubt that the Christian faith has a very broad span in Zambia in 2018? Prayer is *everywhere* in Zambia! Preaching the good news is *everywhere* in Zambia! The power dynamics of divine intervention are called down *everywhere* in Zambia!

Then we could think about *depth.* Is this Christian nation phenomenon merely "thousands of miles wide and only an inch deep"? Are everyday, grassroots lifestyles being affected? Is there any *theological* depth to the Christian nation or is this just some kind of "strange fire," as has been argued elsewhere? Is the nation's faith filtering down to where people live? Is there something like "trickle-down Christianity" going on as a result of what the constitution says?

We shall also consider *height:* does the Christian faith continue to have influence in *high places,* now that Chiluba and his successors are off the scene? What about Christian influence in the official policies and practices of Zambia? These are the questions before us.

# Is There Any Depth to This
## Zambian Christianity?

**W**hen I think about our students, I often marvel over their depth of commitment. These young people leave jobs, in a world where jobs are very scarce indeed, to check in to a theological college for four years, largely on faith. How I admire their profound commitment to the Lord and his high calling. They seem deep in prayer. They are deep in Christian ministry, responding to God's call with that totality that our Lord calls for. "If any one would come after me, let him deny himself, take up his cross and follow" (Matthew 16:24). That's Zambia. That's the students we work with.

I like the depth of theological grasp among these young people when they are given a chance at an education. Amazingly, and quite suddenly, the internet is now available nationwide in Zambia, even deep within the Gwembe Valley. And virtually all of our students get online with their smart-phones and devices. So the opportunities to open up to the world of scholarship and go deeper in the Christian faith have never been greater.

I sense real theological depth in my colleagues, Chanda, Mumba, Phiri, Kipimo, Chalwe, and Ntuntu. Research and doctoral programs have become available to them on the continent in all kinds of new packages. Dissertations are published that show a perception of theological issues that only people like them could bring to the table, combining cultural sensitivity and critical thinking. When they teach, they find, as I do, the seriousness with which our students take the issues of the faith and the background information they bring to class. All of this speaks to *depth*. And these very able young theologians are up to the challenge.

Such developments lead me to think that the tired line about the African church having no depth is a ruse—and a shallow one at that. To me it seems a failure to understand what is happening in the African religious world. Obviously African theology takes a different tack here and there from traditional reformation theology. I doubt that there is significant disagreement on fundamentals. But the emphasis is going to vary here and there. Nor is African preaching likely to line up with Haddon Robinson's principles of sound exposition. Africans love allegory, despite its limitations and excesses, and love to come at truth that way. And they like to get maximum mileage out of a phrase. Maybe it's right to say, as William Dyrness does, that theology in Africa has to do with a different kind of depth, something like "depth of mystery":

> African theologians have helped us see the importance of the intuitive and celebrative dimensions of faith and its depth of mystery. They have helped us see that what cannot be verbalized may still be danced or sung. And most of all, they have shown us the meaning of life lived in the presence of God and of each other. An old African proverb states, "One is human only because of others, with others, and for others." If we listen, we might learn from Africa that the least each of us owes to the other is to be completely present, just as God is present to his creation.[1]

# The African Church and
# "Bullet" Bob Hayes

Sometimes an Olympic athlete decides to change fields. As if life hasn't been demanding enough, he now wants to be a professional football player. In America! Even with gold medals hanging around his neck and a few world records to his credit! Maybe it's not about money. Maybe these guys just know deep down they can be impact players at another level. Or maybe they just sit down and figure it out: "I'm already the fastest human on the planet. All I need to do is learn how to catch an American football and hold onto it. How hard can that be? I can *do* this!"

Such an athlete was the great "Bullet" Bob Hayes, who revolutionized the National Football League's view of elite game-breaking speed. As the 1964 Olympic Gold Medalist in 100-metre and 4x100-metre relay, Hayes was identified as the world's fastest man. He ran an amazing 8.6 second relay split in a come-from-behind victory for the US at the Tokyo games. Switching to football, Hayes was drafted by the Dallas Cowboys, a team geared most toward running the ball. But Hayes made such an impact that he made the "long bomb" a staple in Tom Landry's offense, causing other teams to start looking for their own high-speed game-breaker and staying up nights designing defenses against the long aerial pass.

Hayes won a Super Bowl ring with the Cowboys in 1971 and finished his great football career with 371 receptions, 7,414 yards, and an eye-popping 20 yard-per-catch average. Bob Hayes guessed right! He could do this.

What a great impact Bob Hayes had on the world of American football! He was so fast and such a great athlete that it changed the whole game. Teams had to figure out how to defend against him. His presence called for major adjustments, from the more traditional ground-game football to the high-octane passing game. And of course, other teams started scouring the world of track and field for more Bob Hayeses—which they eventually found. Willie Gault, James Jett, Michael Bates—Hayes paved the way for a steady stream of great Olympians to liven up the American game, players who could break the land speed record and still catch the ball. And if they had a little height so the quarterback could hit them with a pass so high a defender couldn't reach it, so much the better! Bob Hayes was the blazing speedster that changed American football for good. The game-breaking wide receiver was now the player teams began to build their offenses around.

I think of African theology that way. These theologians have come late into the theological world. Not so long ago, they were so far removed from John Calvin, it was like they were living on another planet, never mind in another era. They were running in the track of African traditional religions—some good concepts of God, some not so good. But now they have joined Luther, Calvin, and Charles Hodge on those systematic tracks that have sustained the Christian church for centuries. Do we mind if they go outside the lines occasionally? Or, for that matter, broaden the running lanes, bringing their speed and grace into their new context? What if they bring their fresh perspective into the game called theology? Might it not be a timely adjustment?

There is *ubuntu*, for example, where the African worldview stresses community more than other cultures. "I am because we are." This runs counter to enough western stress on individuality that some lanes might have to be broadened. When a member of the community dies, the African says, "We are grieving" or "We have been killed." Why should not such an emphasis be most welcome in the world of reformation theology—especially when that venerable churchman-poet John Donne gave us his Meditation XVII 400 years ago?

No man is an island,
entire of itself;
every man is a piece of the continent,
a part of the main.
If a clod be washed away by the sea,
Europe is the less,
as well as if a promontory were.
as well as if a manor of thy friend's
or of thine own were.
Any man's death diminishes me,
because I am involved in mankind;
and therefore never send to know for whom the bell tolls;
it tolls for thee.

There is a different approach to the horizontal/vertical discussion as well. Western Christianity puts the vertical first: be reconciled to God, then secondly to your neighbour. African theology, on the other hand, focuses more on the horizontal: our relationships within community determine our relationship with God. Reconciliation starts with people being reconciled. Rather than a dualistic horizontal/vertical worldview, Africans view the universe holistically and believe that all creatures in Creation are linked. The idea is that when we reconcile the horizontal relationships, the vertical dimension follows.

Africa also brings a different approach to matters of conscience and sin. In western thinking, a good conscience requires justice, or obedience to norms. A bad conscience is the result of guilt, or breaking the norms. A guilty conscience is best resolved through reparation and retribution. Give back what you stole. In Africa, on the other hand, a good conscience comes from honour and acceptance in the community, through compliance with its ideals. A bad conscience results from one's failure to comply with the responsibilities of community, in which case the offender experiences shame from exclusion. A shamed conscience is healed through reconciliation and re-inclusion into society. In a communal culture, a transgression is never directly addressed because it may undermine a person's honour. The insult may be worse than the transgression. Thus the community addresses the wrong indirectly, though gossip, stories, proverbs.

The differences between the African perspective and the western on such matters are substantial, but they don't call for a rewriting of Louis Berkhof. Whereas western Christians conceptualize the source of evil as the devil or evil power, African religions incline toward finding the source of evil in the human world, or in a second phase, in disruptive ambitions and jealousies. When it comes to eschatology, Africans have been said not to have one—but that is surely an overstatement! According to John Mbiti, that timeless spokesman for African culture, the African has "little awareness or interest in the future." In his oft-quoted description of the African concept of time, the African "future" extends six months down the road—two years at the most. Events beyond that are not "actual time." "At the most we can say this short future is only an extension of the present." Thus concepts like the premillennial rapture of the church are a stretch for the African worldview, too otherworldly and abstract. Africans "cannot conceive that the end of the world is an ultra-historical myth unrelated to individual men and women in community."[2]

Hence the timely call to read African theologians with a view to broadening some lanes and, more importantly, to enhancing the field of Christian theology! As Edmond Sanganyado writes, "African culture may influence the Christian faith inconspicuously." Here are his some five reasons you should read African theologians.[3]

# 1. Christianity is not a white man's religion

There's an unspoken belief that western theologians are better than Latin American, Asian, or African theologians. They are extensively published and well-read across the world. Hence, western theologians are considered chief custodians of the Christian faith, thus reducing Christianity to a white man's religion. The Ethiopian eunuch was the first non-Jewish Christian. History suggests that the sons of Simon of Cyrene might have contributed to the spread of Christianity into Alexandria, Egypt. Through this community came several of the prominent church fathers: Augustine, Origen, and Athanasius. Above all, the canonicity of New Testament was first approved in Africa at the Synod of Hippo. When you read your New Testament, you need to remember that God used Africans as custodians of his word. African theologians helped in studying, practicing, and teaching God's word.

# 2. Western theologians may not teach you cultural navigation

Christians in Africa are Christians who are African. However, our Africanness is often reduced as demonic in western Christian thought. For example, many churches in Africa do not play maracas, drums, horns, or thumb pianos because these instruments are played at traditional ceremonies.

African theologians understand better the cultural dynamics through personal experience. Can a Western theologian answer a question on whether *lobola* is biblical? What about on women returning to their birth families after they give birth to their first child? Or on attending a funeral of an unbeliever?

## 3. African theologians went through what you're going through

African Christians have questions about AIDS, institutional corruption, tribalism, miracles, and infectious diseases. They're looking for practical answers not theoretical. Such questions are best answered by people who have experienced these things.

On several occasions, Paul reminded believers across Asia that the suffering he went through was for him to be able to minister to them better. Many African theologians know the pain of losing a loved one to AIDS, ebola, or cholera. For example, Emmanuel Katongole lost relatives in the Rwandan genocide.

## 4. African Christians are affected by African traditional worldviews

A worldview is a lens that you use to view the world. It creates a framework that you use to understand the world around you. Worldviews are a product of past experiences, background, and media. African worldviews are unique in that they dissolve the dividing line between the spiritual and the physical realm.

Until recently, when I sinned before God, I asked for forgiveness and prayed against evil spirits. If I lied, I would pray against the spirit of lying. In African traditional worldviews, evil spirits are responsible for sin, while the sinner is a mere victim. I learned I was wrong from an African theologian, Yusuf Turaki.

## 5. African Christians can understand the Bible too

Recently, the *Africa Study Bible* was launched. In 2010, the *Africa Bible Commentary* was published with commentaries written by seventy African theologians. Importantly, in the last two decades, several seminaries and Christian universities have been opened across Africa. Hence, Africans are making great contributions to evangelical scholarship.[2]

In short, it is good for us to interact with African leaders and learn to appreciate their unique perspective on the faith. They are very much abreast of theological issues, past and present, and they bring freshness to theological debate. My colleague, Victor Chanda, wrote as comprehensive a review of Word Faith Theology and its gnostic excesses as you would read anywhere, a biblically balanced and theologically informed treatise.[4]

When I interact with Victor and his theologian friends, I have to laugh out loud at the "theologically shallow" line or the idea that the African church is dealing in "strange fire." I ask, "Is there something so dynamic about the western church that anyone would deny the need for something like fresh fire?"

But what about the local church level? I ask my colleagues if they have concerns about the *depth* of faith among Zambian Christians, those who fill the pews of the churches week by week. Of course, they say, many people are theologically illiterate. But this hardly means that there are no programs of discipleship in place, no means to go "deeper" into the truths of the faith. They assure me that such programs are there in most churches and that anyone who wants to go deeper in the faith and even rise to the echelons of teaching a small group can find a way to do so very readily.

One indicator of this appetite among the laity is our Distance Learning program, designed for school teachers and business people who can only afford to come to college for intensive periods. In a given year, we will have as many as sixty of these people ready to sacrifice their leave days and come to TACU to upgrade their theological knowledge.

Of course you will find churches in Zambia, as elsewhere, that hardly bother to preach anything intelligible in a month—let alone "systematically intelligible"! Add to that the dearth of teaching during the week. The result is a local church that is emptying in every respect. These things are ever with us. But is the proportion of undiscipled Christians higher in Zambia than in other parts of the world? The short answer would be, I find that very unlikely.

I suppose you could use the fruit of the Spirit as a depth gauge, and call in the familiar nine to determine the depth of the faith in the Christian nation. The question would be, are those characteristics of the church of Christ strongly evident in the Zambian church?

When I think of love, I look no further than what is happening outside our campus gates. Barnabas Ambassadors of Hope! A soccer and discipleship ministry that calls forth bands of our students every week to share the love of Christ with shantytown youth. The big step here is that the entire ministry is "beyond the walls," surrounded by some of the most needy shantytowns anywhere in the world. These kids are so disadvantaged that the very idea of a formal league—with uniforms and soccer shoes and actual soccer balls and a youth centre, coaches and referees—this is like something fallen from the sky!

Speak of joy and need we say more? The effervescence of the Zambian church, sometimes in very austere circumstances, is, I think, its most salient feature. There is something incredible about the song and the dance when all indicators are adverse. It is an act of faith and of joy in Christ. This is special. In fact, a church like Zambia's helps us to define the true nature of joy: it is not in circumstances, but in the Lord. And *that* this church knows right well. Pierre Pradervand links this to the African nature:

The incredible vitality of African people...I believe there are simply no other people in the world who are as bursting with life as the Africans...African villagers are capable of dancing an entire night non stop. Such vitality is one of the most powerful qualities of black Africa. That after four centuries of the holocaust of slavery and centuries of cultural indoctrination...they have maintained this...ebullient stamina and still exude this potent sense of joy bursting at the seams is one of history's [miracles] and the most meaningful contribution to the people of the world...This exuberant sense of being totally alive is cousin to one of the most omnipresent qualities of Africa...joy. It is just everywhere.[5]

Peace is an interesting commodity, because Zambia is practically the only land of sustained peace on the whole African continent! Peace seems to be one of God's special gifts to the Zambian people. I hear occasional gripes about "our peace," that it only means non-confrontation. But I sense a "Shalom of God" upon the land, despite manifold hardships, which are quite heavy. Another way of looking at the peace that hangs over Zambia is that this is the "peace of God that passes understanding." There are plenty of grounds for anxiety and tension in Zambia, that is for sure. But somehow I think the peace of God rests upon the land in mysterious and undefined ways. And one thing you learn in Zambia is that even if people may sound like they are ready to kill each other, deep down, "He's my brother." Very much like family life! This is a most remarkable quality of the Zambian church. And in the nation, for some seventy-plus tribes to live in peace? Zambia's internal peace must be one of the great miracles of the modern world—especially when you compare this atmosphere to that which prevails in her neighbouring countries.

Again, "long-suffering" probably defines the Zambian community of faith more than most any church on the planet. The

Zambian people are infinitely patient when life brings toil and travail. As Pierre Pradervand says,

> Africa can teach us about time; not time tied to the pursuit of objects and money but to an openness and spontaneity—the time of just being and having relationships, rather than doing or achieving. Above all, it is the time of the present moment, of living in the now, rather than a constant projection into the future...the main sickness of industrialized society. Africa has unique sense of *kairos* (the unique moment of golden opportunity). If it is true that it needs to master *chronos* (the tick tock that keeps us rushing from one appointment to another)...we need African *kairos* more...Patience...the great quality of Africa, enables it to weather the onslaughts of history...Haste, Africa teaches us, may be the best way of not getting there...the haste of the race produces the stress that kills joy. Development in Africa is not so much a precise goal as a certain way of travelling.[6]

Pradervand here reminds one of the African proverb: "To go fast, go alone; to go far, go together." And so on with the fruit of the Spirit. If these are evidence of spiritual depth, the vital signs in Zambia seem very strong.

However, there is another dimension, to the "depth" question. When people say the faith of the Christian nation is "a thousand miles wide and only an inch deep," they are not talking just about theological depth nor the fruit of the Spirit. They are talking about lifestyle and ethics. They are saying that the Christian faith has not sunk down deep enough into the culture to transform behaviour.

This is a concern—so much so that we reserve comment on it until a closing chapter, The Butterfly Is Endangered. It is not just the church that is sounding the alarm over this lack of moral penetration. In fact, what I read is that the church, if anything, is complicit; that if the culture is slipping into a kind of free fall morally and ethically, the pulpits are not grasping the serious-ness of the moment, opting for the superficial, majoring on the quick fix, silent on holiness "without which no one will see the Lord." The question is, how can you have a Christian nation with a church that never touches holiness or raises a call for repentance?

We reserve discussion of this apparent shortfall to the closing chapters. For now let us simply register the concern: that the dec-laration of Zambia as a Christian nation is not always reflected in the grassroots, everyday lives of its citizens. In that case, the fur-ther question would be, how can you have a Christian nation that is not Christian in *deed*? This is a concern. So says the president himself!

# Chapter 6

## *How* **Broad** *Is the Faith of the Christian Nation?*

Looking at the faith of the Christian nation in its full dimensions brings us to a second question. How broad is this faith? Is it localized in certain areas, or does it cover the country, from city to village, from border to border? That is the question before us. The governing word for this chapter is *everywhere*! Whether it is prayer, preaching, or power dynamics— the faith of Zambia turns up *everywhere*.

## a. Prayer Is Everywhere in Zambia

We live close enough to Copperbelt University that I can go up to the campus for a morning constitutional on an energized morning, just up the hill along a winding Unity Way, past a funeral home, whose ancient sign itself needs to be buried as it hangs from a rusty iron post. This is old Northern Rhodesia property. My pace is slow enough to be called a "ralk"—half run, half walk.

Then along the hydro line, a nice, straight, red-dirt road that runs across the Copperbelt from Ndola to Chingola. Copperbelt

Energy does little to maintain it, so this hard-packed trail is only good for *ralkers,* like me, or bikes—or of course the interminable pedestrians. The median age in Zambia is seventeen. Youth are all over the paths and streets at all hours. So I like to get up to CBU and *ralk* among the young, kind of a vestige of a former era myself. At my age I prefer the six o'clock neighbourhood. I duck under the entry bar and greet the guards who are starting to shuffle around: *"Mwashabukeni Mukwai!" "Eya Mukwai!"*

But what's this? Just through the gates, three women are holding hands in a small circle along my perimeter road, which winds through the campus along the lines of an original plan, when Canada helped build a technical school here back in the sixties. I like the high ground of this campus. The air usually is clear, and the breeze sometimes carries the freshness of the Kafue River, which flows from here 300 miles to its confluence with the Zambezi. I'm treading softly as I make my way by. These women are coming to the throne of grace early to start the day. To my left a student is down on his knees at a park bench. I pass a smattering of different people standing, facing a tree or a wall in prayer. Some are bent over on benches. Prayer partners are seated on a concrete ledge, hands joined, feet dangling over concrete walls.

It's prayer time at CBU! Young men are striding along my road, calling down divine blessing. Here we have some authority declared, some binding and loosing. Whatever that means to the church worldwide, there seems to be no doubt about what it means here! As I round the Maintenance Centre, I cast an eye to make sure the noisy Ridgeback is chained. He always is, but he sounds so fierce, I like to double check. He's quiet today as if also under the spell of prayer. But these CBU prayers are generating some volume of their own! English, Bemba, the language of heaven—this campus is alive with warfare prayer to start the day—while I *ralk* my way along.

"What's happening?" I cross paths with a lady wrapped in a shawl. Small groups are lifting up a song. A student club has gathered in a cluster for prayer under an awning. From within the classroom block, I am hearing loud prayers from the charismatic contingent. "I thought the Day of Prayer was two weeks ago!"

"Oh, at this time we are praying for the nation every day," she says. What? My mind flies to the University of Manitoba, where I also have had many a morning *ralk* around a campus—a campus that is stone silent. Why did I never hear the student body of the U of M filling the moody Manitoba morning with campus prayers? How is it that Zambia's second largest government university is alive with prayer for the nation—at daybreak? Drought conditions have been bad, I am aware. Water levels are down, and power shortages are hampering life at every level. So the president has championed a national call to prayer. Turns out these CBU students have taken it up—and extended it!

The sun rises over the old campus, getting facelifts here and there. Things are green and lush, and the soft light through the mist is lovely. I am thinking, "The blessing of the Lord makes rich." I feel like my constitutional has been doubly blessed, along the lines of the text that says, "May your whole body and spirit be preserved." That is my blessing on this day of prayer. How wonderful, a national holiday enjoining prayer upon a nation with an annual reminder! Even better to see it spill over, as in Zambia, to successive weeks of prayer!

This National Prayer Day became a government holiday a few years ago. People gather on October 18th at campuses and stadiums for prayer all across the nation. At times, the Prayer Day may devolve into speech making and song and dance—always the preferred mode in Zambia. If song and dance can be interpreted as prayer, "so much the beta!" And we know that song and dance are a large part of psalmodic prayer in any case. Mercy, if prayer lacked physicality and energy, where would we be? Africa helps us to rediscover the physicality of the spiritual exercises. And I don't mean the *ralk!*

I laugh when I read one of my cherished old commentaries, that by Adam Clarke, that most prolific Methodist of the nineteenth century. "Praise him with the dance!" shouts Psalm 150. "This cannot mean anything but the ancient 'zither,'" says Clarke, who had doubts about music even being allowed in the church.[1] Try that out on modern Zambia, and the laughter would be loud and long! What? Prayer has many components! So prayer days can evolve into celebration, everyone of course enamoured with electronics. But the National Prayer Day also involves many more times of serious corporate intercession and fasting. And as I am discovering, this can even spill over into days of concerted prayer.

What gave the prayer days special urgency last year was the state of the Kariba Dam. It was rumoured that the government had mistakenly lowered the water level of the dam that supplies power for the whole country, in order to service the dam wall, which was built by the Italians in the seventies and is said to be moving an inch a year. Unfortunately it's hard to recover a gazillion gallons of water once it's been allowed to flow downstream into the Zambezi and out to sea, so the rumour mill said. It also said that the government decided to lowball bidding on the turbines and bought units that need more power to function and are less efficient than the original British units. Then the drought. Whatever the cause, we had a chronic shortage of power and water and the nation was suffering a lot.

So the prayers of 2016 were for copious rains that the reservoirs would be filled up; that the supply of power to the nation would be sufficient to supply all the mines, always a priority; and that "load shedding," that policy of prioritizing the power supply to where it was most needed, might end. Life was becoming extra hard for everyone. At our campus, we had to buy inverters and get a start on solar energy. The load shedding was so constant that it was nearly impossible to keep the college running. "God will visit us!" was the cry of the faithful. "Full dams! Surplus power! Even to sell to our neighbours!"

All of that is now one year behind us, and there has not been one day of load shedding around these parts! They tell me that the prayers of God's people brought on "the mother of all rainy seasons." We notice that increased hydro rates must also be part of the solution. But that national crisis, which low water levels had generated, was averted. Zambia needs diversification, which everyone talks about, and more sage decisions at the top government levels, but we're thankful for small victories!

Prayer power! My goodness, the reservoirs rose so high, the rivers were spilling their banks. Houses and retaining walls were collapsing under the torrential rains. It was a magnificent response from the heavens! Or we might call it the "heavenly realms"!

### *"Why Do You Sound Surprised?"*

When I received my doctor's report about ferritin level readings that had soared over the 700 level in a short time, I turned to our friend, Pastor Robert Kasema, for prayer. I had been donating blood earlier in the year, but now the iron levels were still too high for a body's good. My sister said she would welcome some of my iron! This was all about a peculiar chromosome that I alone inherited from both parents.

"I really need to have a ferritin reading of about 150," I said to Robert. "When it gets too high, it's very hard on the liver and other organs—and can do permanent damage. In fact, I need to be close to regular iron levels in order to remain in Zambia."

It turned out that our friend was leading his church in twenty-one days of prayer and fasting to start a new year.

"And also remember our friend Brian," I said. Brian had been diagnosed with prostate cancer back in Canada. "He's a strong supporter of the college, who we can't afford to lose. We want God to spare him and lengthen his days."

Well, Kasema's group are sustained prayer warriors! Over those weeks, a number of great things happened. One was that God touched Brian in a very powerful way and he got a good five-year extension on his days! During that time, he was able to help us build our Discipleship Youth Centre, outside the campus gates—which we subsequently named "Brian's Place."

As for my iron level, it dropped to the normal 150 range and has never shot back up since! "Can you believe it?" I reported to Kasema. "It dropped down to a very low range and never budged! This is wonderful!"

"But why do you sound surprised?" asked Kasema. "That is exactly what we were praying for!"

Oh those prayers of Zambia! Like laughter, they "do good like a medicine."

### Parklands

We enjoy a kind of prayer covering around our house in Parklands, the leafy central area of Kitwe. Some mornings I wake up to music, *"Tubalembe BaYahwe...."* It is the voice of women, the workers and cleaners at our neighbourhood properties, raising songs of praise to begin the day, as they take their straw brooms around the walkways.

One morning, I was walking over by "Nice Gardens," our neighbourhood garden centre, and heard a lone male voice from deep within the property, down by the creek. He had picked up a song and was raising a raspy tenor to start the day, a full, gravelly voice with soaring cadences, and quite uninhibited. What other neighbourhoods offer such a melodic start to the day?

126

We have churches nearby. The Lighthouse likes to bless some mornings with songs of worship as the saints meet for Rise and Shine prayers. This church also has regular "overnights." During such times we hear the sounds of worship and intercession covering our neighbourhood like a cloud. Of course, yes, we have neighbourhood bars as well! And they can raise a most unholy din with their woofers at all hours. But this prayer covering over Parklands! I miss it when I'm away.

There are ladies behind our property who like to partner in concerted prayer from time to time, clapping fervently in spiritual warfare, taking authority against all the programs of the evil one. I like to think we are included in that fervent intercession and that some enemies are being put to flight!

What a prayer covering we have in this Christian nation of ours! Of course, Ruth and I enjoy valued prayer support on the other side of the world. And how grateful we are for such things, given malaria and the one peril that Livingstone did not face: the growing insanity of the roads, as Japan casts off all its vehicles after five years and lands them all in Zambia. These Corollas and Spacios are bought cheap and put on the road as taxis—with some very inexperienced drivers behind the wheel. Our downtown is like a go-cart race around midday! And where are the police? It is rumoured that they *own* the taxis! Given the great challenges that daily life in Africa offers, with its constant financial crises and issues related to poverty, and cholera scares, the need for wisdom as to how and best to respond to needs—how conscious we are of the need for prayer!

As we benefit from the churches of our neighbourhood, the concerted morning prayers, and hear the ladies behind the property and join the sweet songs of the women around our block, I raise another raspy morning voice and try to bless the neighbourhood with my own rendition of "Bless the Lord who Reigns in

Beauty" or *"Shakalabee...."* How wonderful to live in an environment of worship. Blessed Christian nation! I walk the streets and bring my grandkids, my ABCDELN list (April, Betty, Charlie, Dottie, Emma, Lucy, and Nathan) under the covering of prayer myself. Somehow I know the great promise holds: "No one shall pluck them out of the Father's hand" (see John 10:29).

And I claim that great promise of Hebrews for Zambia: "Land that drinks the rain often falling on it and brings forth a harvest is blessed by the Lord" (see Hebrews 6:7).

### At Shoprite?

It was in the midst of the jams and jellies at Shoprite's grocery store that I picked up some familiar tunes on the intercom. *"Lesa Mwana, Lesa Tata...Twaminya Twamisumbula...."* "I know that song!" I said. "Blessed Father, Son and Holy Spirit!" We sing it in college chapels. Such a welcome background sound! "Lord, I give you my life...." The background music of Zambia amid the clatter of grocery carts!

Of course, this is soft background music and hardly noticeable in the din of the shoppers. But how nice to hear such music in a public place! Worship is everywhere in Zambia: *"Lesa tata, lesa mwana...."* Compare that worship of the Holy Trinity with the background sounds many people shop to, where on a good day you might be assailed by the original soundtrack of "The Runaways"—this is a rare blessing.

### Prayers of Intercession Are Like an Embrace

There is nothing like being upheld in Zambian prayers when you really need it. I remember my first bout of malaria and seriously thinking I might be passing from this earth. Not only was there dizziness, which is my first indicator, but there was this absolute malaise in every limb. I was new in the country and found it all, the chills, the delirium, the cramps, the Livingstonian fever, the near paralysis—all the symptoms were extremely worrying.

One of our veteran Zambian ministry friends happened by and gave us a parting prayer after tea.

*"We rebuke malaria!"* he shouted. Exactly the words I needed to hear. "You must *leave this body now!"* I felt a power greater than quinine!

Then there was a dream in which our two sons were in some kind of danger. A high speed accident, deep water—it seemed to me that a life had been lost.

I shared my worries in a circle of prayer during Spiritual Emphasis Days. "Here I am in Zambia, my family on the other side of the globe—what can I do to help? In my dream I thought somebody died!"

*"There will be no death!"* said one of our prayer partners as we formed a circle of prayer. *"There will be no death!"* Authority to the fore again. As he prayed, he drove back all the forces of hell and destruction, and I began to sense that the enemy was in full retreat.

There would be no death.

### Under Attack!

One of our students had been given a dream about the campus and shared it with me.

"Principal, the campus is under attack. In my vision I saw forces of evil climbing over the walls and infiltrating the place!" And why not? If the enemy was going to launch an offensive, why not direct it towards a training centre for spiritual leaders who would minister across Zambia for years to come?

We shared this among the student intercessors as they met during the week. We mentioned it at a larger prayer gathering. And God definitely "raised up a standard" against an enemy who wanted to come in like a flood. We had a season of spiritual awakening. And whatever attacks the enemy was planning went into full retreat. As some of our chapel speakers like to put it, "We deprogram the programs of the enemy!"

### The Upper Room

Our campus Upper Room used to be the viewing platform for horse racing! This was back in the colonial era. Our former racetrack is now becoming more habitable for humans. We had a couple of agronomists look the land over a few years back, and they declared the pH level so low it was practically "acidic...No future for agriculture on such soil." So we imported lime, and gradually the campus has filled up with plants and gardens, sweet potatoes and groundnuts.

Our nephew, Rob Hall, was helping with the construction of the Upper Room. He was using a grinder to cut a large piece of steel when the blade shattered. A flying projectile hit him square in the chest and killed him. Our Robbie bled to death right there in our Upper Room. He sealed the floors with his blood on one terrible day.

But today it is lovely to see the Upper Room, sealed as it is with such sacrifice, as a place where the campus gathers for prayer. We call on some of our student leaders to help us as we set aside a special week for prayer. They gather mornings at six in a large circle around the walls where Rob shed his blood, windows open to the north, south, east, and west. Someone leads in a song of praise, then a prayer follows. Then the whole Upper Room turns into a hallowed place, a true house of prayer. This is so beautiful, cascading down from the third storey heights, a prayer covering settling down upon an entire campus, over a hundred acres under the canopy of prayer, our "pillar of cloud and of fire."

Of course there is volume in these early mornings as the students gather. We invite pastors and leaders from nearby to join us for this week of corporate prayer to start off the new year. When the week is over, the Upper Room remains a go-to prayer centre throughout the year, sealed in blood. It's nice to step up for an hour during a busy day and join the spirit of prayer that rises from all over the Christian nation.

With its windows open toward all four points of the compass, our Upper Room instills a vision and becomes a vantage point where God might speak as to Abraham: "Lift up your eyes, look to the north and south, east and west...All the land you see I will give you" (see Genesis 13:14). So the Upper Room has become a place of vision. Some of our young friends have seen their ministries crystallize as they walk around the Upper Room.

"Why not out of Zambia?" an inner voice said to one of our visiting friends in the Upper Room. "Why not centre your ministry at the centre of Africa?" From the Upper Room, more than one ministry has been birthed and expanded around the world.

Hence a new name for our sacred space: "The Robert Hall Ministry Formation Centre."

Ministry Formation Centre! Now, on many a day, you will find future pastors and leaders walking the circumference of our Upper Room and talking to God about the future of their ministries. Indeed, some have come back years later and said, "God showed me the shape of my ministry right here! Now I am just checking things off as they happen!"

### National House of Prayer?

So it seems fitting somehow that we now have in this nation a "National House of Prayer." It is under construction in the capital city, Lusaka. This has met some resistance, as though there are better things to spend money on when the needs are so great

131

and "people can pray anywhere." But why not have a beautiful house of prayer in a Christian nation? It gives recognition to a national dependence on God. It says, "We are a nation of prayer, and we want this reminder and resource at the centre of our nation."

President Edgar Lungu was present when the foundation was laid early in 2016, and the *Times of Zambia* reported the event:

> President Edgar Lungu says he is proud to be part of the resolve to build the National House of Prayer because he is emulating King David and his son Solomon who built God a house of prayer.
>
> The Head of State said his personal desire to align Zambia to God was not born of his own human desire but was inspired by the Holy Spirit.
>
> "Considering what God's purpose is for the nation, Zambia, you will all agree with me that the construction of the National House of Prayer to honour our God is the right thing to do," Mr. Lungu said. Reading from 1 Chronicles 22:19, President Lungu said King David encouraged his son Solomon and all the leaders of his time to arise and build God's temple. "Our generation can, therefore, not be ashamed to emulate King David and his son Solomon to build God a house of prayer. I am proud to be part of this collective resolve to do so."
>
> He said it was his understanding that God's intention had always been that Zambia should become a mighty Christian nation that would be a beacon of light and a missionary country.
>
> Mr. Lungu said he knew without doubt that God had always been interested in the well-being of this nation and that he had a purpose and plan to prosper Zambia.
>
> The Head of State said there was need to understand that Zambia was a beacon of light from which the gospel of the Lord Jesus Christ, would shine across the continent of Africa and beyond.

"Considering the social and economic challenges that our country has been going through, invoking the presence of God into the nation's psyche is not just important, but a matter of duty for every Christian. This should be natural, given that we are a nation dedicated to God—a Christian Nation," he said.

Mr. Lungu said it was imperative for Zambians to realize that the nation was set to be the bread basket of Africa because agriculturally, the country had the potential to feed the whole of sub-Saharan Africa.

He said Dr. David Livingstone's last prayer reminded leaders to pray: "Lord from the land upon which my knees rest, raise a mighty Christian Nation, a nation that will become a beacon of light and hope to the continent, a nation that will take the gospel to the ends of the earth."

Mr. Lungu said Zambia was also a nation of refuge and, as a country despite a few challenges, citizens had never suffered the kind of civil unrest seen elsewhere and remained one of the most peaceful and friendly in the world. "On behalf of the entire nation, I wish to thank all participating churches, businesses, parastatal bodies, cooperating partners, and indeed all well-wishers in advance for your generous financial and material support towards the National House of Prayer."

Only in Zambia, one might say! But why should a call to prayer not be universal, in a world as troubled as ours?

## b. Preaching Is Everywhere in Zambia

### On the Bus?

I jumped on the 5:30 bus to get down early to Lusaka before noon. EuroAfrica! If you catch the 5:30 out of Kitwe, it puts you in the big city mid-morning, no fuss no muss.

Somewhere around Kapiriri Mposhi, about two hours out, where the great North Road will branch off to Luapula province and Lake Bangweulu, early travellers were waking up. Some were buying groundnuts or fruit from the ladies who came up to the windows with baskets on their heads. Some vendors got on board and walked the aisles with snacks. Then as we were pulling out, a nice little weathered man jumped on board with a well-worn Bible. *"Mwashabukashani,"* he said. "How are we this morning?" *"Nami Posha Mwishina ya kwa Yesu Kristu, Amen."* "I greet you all in Jesus' name."

And is it not a great day for travel? He greeted the driver and the front rows. Next thing we knew, he was reading a text and launching a homily! This was some strong Bemba preaching that would last until the next town, about a half hour down the road! As we neared Kabwe, he said, "Let us pray." Every head bowed. Then he talked to God on our behalf, for safety of passage for the travellers—something very much needed on these Zambian roads! He invoked God's blessing upon the home and the family of every weary traveller, this fine little man out of nowhere.

"In Jesus mighty name, Amen," he said. So ended the prayer. And all the people, all my fellow-travellers from front row to back, hurtling our way down the road to Zambia's capital on the morning express—all the people said, "Amen."

Welcome to Zambia!

### Preaching Points!

It used to be that our graduates could leave us with pretty good prospects of assuming an established church. This is no longer the case. Nowadays our grads have to tough it out from scratch in one of Zambia's well-churched cities or shantytowns to get something started. And what great perseverance they show, planting a new church on faith—and not much else!

So they start their own preaching points. Joachim finds a vacant building in Chimwemwe, which must be the most over-churched community in the world. He and Miriam transform this derelict structure into a house of God with very nice wall hangings. And every Sunday, dressed to the absolute max, the "praise and worship" team steps up to inspire the good people of Chimwemwe with the latest sounds of Zambian gospel.

"But this community is so over-churched," I say. Are you sure this is the place to start your church?" This is a pair of outstanding students, and we really would like them to do well.

"This is the place, Doc," says Joachim. "I felt it when I walked around for a few Sundays…so many people on the streets. Everyone here says they are 'Christian,' but no one is found in church. We plan to change that!"

So they turned this derelict makeshift building into a sanctuary! And they started running church. Before long, they had seventy worshippers joining them. But their vision is large. You get the feeling that these people are preaching to the masses. This is great. And loud! I always make sure I am out of line of the speakers, electronics being the fascination of the Zambian church as we speak. But if all else fails, I make sure I carry the camera. If decibel levels reach overdrive range, I step out and film the event from a safe distance!

"You can't plant a church without a keyboard," says one of our Lusaka graduates. This is because a Yamaha keyboard cranked to the max is more or less like advertising, as it pounds out its basic three chords on a Sunday morning, in Zambia's answer to the chimes that float over the towns of Northampton, calling the saints to the hour of worship. In some compact Lusaka communities, it is even protested as "noise pollution." So these small churches begin, little pockets of light all over Zambia. They begin, they grow, and before long, they surprisingly multiply.

Just down the road, very good student Yonah Mbewe is starting his own church from scratch. In Kamatipa, you have the Methodists with our graduate Madalitso Mulenga. You have Simon Nyirenda and his fine little church built with his own bare hands. Down the way is Maybin Malama. Newton Nkhosa. Mufika Bukasa, who plants a church with his family wherever he touches down, has a church nearby in a classroom. You cannot find a single school classroom in Chimwemwe that is not housing a church on Sundays. Nor is there a vacant building. Churches are like mushrooms—with more vitality of course!

### Unreached Territory?

But what about those unreached remote regions of Zambia? We challenge our graduates along such lines. "Don't just flock to the cities. Think rural! Many areas of Zambia need a church!"

"No, God is calling me to the city," they may say. "I know very needy areas," they say. And so in Zambia's major centres churches continue to be established, elbow to elbow. Yet it's not as though these city churches are stuck in just one location. Soon they are planting branch churches in their outlying communities, staffing them with their own people. That way some of our graduates, very capable guys, get to take up someone's small cell or branch church and try to turn it into something self-supporting and self-governing.

I ask David Chibale, our one-time missions director, about planting churches in unreached areas of the nation. Do any such areas exist? What is the most effective strategy? Chibale's heart beats for church planting and missions. We talk about his town of Chambeshi and the various "branch-churches" he has raised up on the fringes of town.

"Why? Will these people not find their way to the mother church?"

"One or two members, maybe. In fact they are the ones who usually want to start the branch in their neighbourhood. And they become the leaders! So there are two benefits here. One, a new church is planted and two, new leaders are being raised up!" Every so often, all the branch churches join the mother for a Big Sunday.

The same thing goes on with Bishop Chachi Chongo and Catherine up in another mining town of Kalilushi—only their branch churches are a little farther-flung, among small villages whose people would very seldom find their way to the mother church. Catherine takes a special interest in seeing these little churches flourish under their own elders, providing leadership training at the mother church midweek and visiting the small communities regularly. All of the poverty related problems of Zambia are evident in these small church plants, from child marriages to an inadequate supply of goods and services. But these small cells meet and worship and raise the great songs of praise that fill the Christian nation every Sunday. I enjoy their very attentive listening and excitement when I come by as a guest speaker. But these little churches hardly need the likes of me! They hear solid preaching every Sunday, from an elder who may be a small-scale farmer or a school teacher. In fact, these little branch churches may get more solid Bible, Sunday to Sunday, than some of their high-end, Lusaka counterparts!

"But isn't leadership a concern?" I ask. "Isn't this country riddled with fly-by-night false prophets who take advantage of untrained leaders?"

"Not at all," says Gabriel Mumba, who oversees a branch church himself. "We supply and train the elders and make sure the preaching is sound." Many of these churches make use of the material provided by CLTI, our Christian Leadership Training ministry, which is committed to raising up pastors and leaders right where they live.

"It's the New Testament pattern," says director John Morris Elliott. "Where did you ever find a Bible college or seminary in the New Testament?" Zambia has caught on to this concept, for sure. The country is awash in training centres for Christian leadership, running courses in two-week intensives or in night classes in major centres, all the way from Chipata to Nakonde, training people in the fundamentals of the faith.

Newly planted branch churches, highly motivated leaders trained on site—how do you beat a pattern like this? This butterfly nation has a New Testament thing happening! It's no wonder that it just keeps proliferating preaching points.

### Verbiage and Garbage

Sometimes a young church can be swept away by imported gospels wrapped in prosperity theology. This trash has a great appeal to people who struggle to keep food on the table every day.

"It's tough preaching straight gospel in Lusaka," says Jones Chiyana, one of our graduates who has built a great city church from scratch. "There is so much bad seed being planted from all over Africa, and it's growing like crazy because people have a huge appetite for anything that can give the 'quick fix.'" Charlatans sell "anointed brooms" to sweep out evil spirits and "holy water," taking the church back to the days of Chaucer's Pardoner with his relics. Shortcuts, quick fixes—"Prophesy over me, man of God! I have brought my offering! Sprinkle my head with holy water!" But faithful Chiyana and a host of his colleagues just do their job. Preaching the solid gospel. Bringing people to Christ. Proclaiming all those vital truths he learned in Systematic Theology 303. And this former banker continues to expand his thriving church, created *ex nihilo* in our capital city.

Our graduate Zacharia Banda says, "My people have so many Christian channels in their houses; no matter how poor they are, they might hear ten sermons on a Sunday before they get to church! I have a lot of competition!" TV is such a big commodity in the Christian nation. Zach's fine, growing church is in down-trodden Mucomfya, a marketplace suburb of Luanshya. If this place has satellite cable in every home, you can be sure that most every home in Zambia has the same. No wonder the parish minister is under stress! The whole country is inundated with religious verbiage—and more than its share of garbage.

Of course this is very much a mixed blessing. The problem is, according to my colleague Chanda, "Africa has received Word Faith Theology with both hands." The "Man of God" is somehow linked to the diviner of old African traditional religions. Fetishes have deep roots in the African psyche. It doesn't take much for new Christians to slip back into old traditions.

### Zambia's Most Needed Text

But I look at these young apologists, Chanda, Banda, Ntuntu, Chiyana, and company, and I just know there is a correction for every abuse. Of course, it's a bit disconcerting when you hear a pretty prominent pastoral leader going on about how people need to "leave a token behind" when they come for prayer. And some fly-by-night making money off of Acts 4:35 where the believers took their possessions and "laid them down at the apostles' feet." If St. Luke only knew how much abuse that verse would cause!

May God bless every Zambian apologist, I say, young, old, graduate or non-graduate. Good for them. The scriptures are there. They still provide "doctrine, reproof, correction, and instruction in righteousness." Plus, they provide a key text for today's Zambia! "If a man purify himself from these"—that is, the conveyors of false doctrine—"he will be a vessel for honour, sanctified, useful to the Master, prepared for the Master's use!" (see 2 Timothy 2:21).

In short, in a country like this, preaching is everywhere—good, bad, and indifferent! The good news is that there is hardly anywhere in Zambia where you do not stand a pretty good chance of hearing the gospel proclaimed.

### Remy Could Have Been an Imam!

Where would Remy Mwense be if not for a little branch church in Kashikishi? Remy is our very gifted fourth-year worship leader, getting ready to graduate and return to his home province of Luapula. But if it hadn't been for that cell group, he might be an Imam! "My father left my mother when I was in secondary school," says Remy.

> I had to drop out of school due to financial challenges. Since I was just doing nothing, my uncle advised me to follow my father to his new home in Northern Province. It turned out he had remarried and I was not exactly welcome. I stayed with him for seven months, then he left, leaving me with my stepmother. I had no choice but to remain in that northern town with a woman I barely knew...no money, no family. A short time later, my father died, and my stepmother went back to her original home in Congo. So I was left alone in that northern village.
>
> I had no friends. There was no Christian church in the village. We just had a mosque for Muslims, and witchcraft ruled. I decided Islam was my best choice, knowing I wanted to serve God somehow. I got so committed to the mosque that in a short time I knew a lot of things, more than even the people I found there...so much so that I became the second leader to the Imam. While there, I was against Christianity and discouraged Christians from following Jesus. I thought I was working for God, but that inner peace was not with me.
>
> Gradually I began to sense I was missing something, and out of nowhere began to lose interest in Islam. It started

coming so strong that I started thinking, "The moment I get out of this village, I will stop being a Muslim." As things were, I was leading the people at the mosque as usual. The Imam was a businessman and used to travel a lot. So often I remained in charge of the mosque, leading people into prayers, five times a day every day. Even though I had lost interest, I was afraid to denounce Islam due to the influence I had as a leader in the village. If I had come out against Islam, that would have been the end of the mosque there. And my life would have been in danger. So I continued going through the motions, even though my emotions were already detached.

In 2008, I made up my mind that no matter what, I must get out of this place, go back and find my mother and family. In May, I made my move to Kashikishi in Luapula province and was able to be reunited with my mother and family. One happy day that was!

I arrived home on a Tuesday night. On Wednesday, my mother took me to a small cell meeting that had started up near our place. This was before I even knew what church it belonged to. I found out my mother had connected with this cell group and joined the Pentecostal Assemblies of God. On Sunday we went to the mother church, and that was the day I gave my life to Jesus Christ.

I started feeling so strong upon my heart that God had called me into ministry, but how was I going to do it? My education had been cut short. Mum had been married to a difficult man with quarrels almost every day. Still to my surprise, he supported my secondary schooling until I finished in November 2012. And then he died.

To my great surprise, the small church I had joined agreed to sponsor me to go to Bible college and train for the ministry. It felt like a dream because the church at that time was small and very low in finances. They had never supported a college student, not even for one semester! But now they were accepting this big challenge!

They have never failed to support me for even one semester. And they are committed to underwriting my studies all the way through college.

### ZAFES: Zambia's Fellowship of Evangelical Students

I was back at CBU one evening to join a Christian student group for an evening at the invitation of Jeff Kuntamoya, one of our graduates. It was at the chapel, a multi-denominational building on the edge of the campus for use by a variety of churches and student life groups The main attraction of the chapel property is that it is a hot spot for WiFi. Thus it became something like an outdoor student lounge; the future leaders of Zambia sprawled about on the walkways, propped up against the walls, tapping away at their devices—no doubt expanding on their academic research!

Forty students or so showed up for our ZAFES meeting. People got reacquainted and then we went into something like campus church. Four of the young women led us in some praise songs, the leader raising a verse or two, the rest of us following up with a descant. Zambian music, tracing its way back to deep roots! *"Mwe lesa amweo...."* Get some clapping going, and *Chiweme, ba yawe* can go forever.

The student leader followed up with a brief exhortation, then shared various prayer needs. "Now let us pray for those not well," he said. He began to pray audibly, not as though directing the prayer, not as though to be heard above everyone else, but more as a signal for everyone to join him. And the whole room was filled with the sounds of prayer, everyone talking to God in a great swell of intercession. Later he said, "Now we shall pray for the issues at Student Union." And again, audible corporate prayer filled the room.

"We have seventy-three ZAFES groups across Zambia," Jeff

told me later. "All on different campuses." Seventy three? I didn't know there were that many campuses in Zambia!

"Are they politically active?" I'm asking the question that prevails on the university campuses of the world. "Do they take to the streets on occasion?"

"Well they do...but mostly if food allowances are late!" Jeff laughs. But he tells me that these students are active in Student Union life and share the concerns of all Zambian students for democratic process, for transparency and justice. Often, he tells me, this crowd can function as a calming influence on campus when things are tense. They meet for fellowship and prayer. They share their needs in small groups. They interact with their circles of friends about the challenges of university life in Zambia, the competition out there, the job prospects. This is a crowd of engineering students. Some are in law. Some in IT.

"And now we shall pray for next week's outreach to Petauke!" While they pray, I wonder what is happening. I thought next week was the break-time week! Were they taking their break week to do door-to-door evangelism in Petauke?

They were and they did. I was so impressed. I wondered what I could say to such a crowd; this most inspiring audience of students at Zambia's second-largest university. I resorted to the mustard seed parable, with that "smallest of all seeds" that becomes a very big tree. I reminded my young friends that they are living in such a tree in their Christian nation. They are the branches and fruit of the seed that David Livingstone planted over a century ago. And now they were planting more of the good seed of the good news.

They had every reason to rest assured, that every good word of witness they shared in Petauke would bring a harvest.

## c. Power Dynamics Are Everywhere in Zambia

Of course proliferating churches is one thing. Even the JWs do that with their gangrenous heresies. But you need to have centres of "power dynamics." As distinguished Pentecostal philosopher James K.A. Smith says, the primary hallmark of Pentecostals is their "radical openness to divine surprises."[2] That more or less defines the Zambian mindset. Not for Zambia the secularism that Charles Taylor describes so aptly in *A Secular Age.*[3] No desacralizing of the world here. The Holy Spirit has given gifts to the church, has he not? Let us claim them and run with them!

### *"These signs shall follow them that promote!"*

I scroll around Facebook to find out what some of our recent graduates are up to. I find many who are pastoring churches— and doing it with flair! They are raising the promotional standard much higher than when I and my class of Swordsmen started out more than five decades back. Theirs is not the somewhat pedantic pastoral role that has often defined the church since time immemorial. Theirs, rather, is a pastoral role with a power dynamics component.

Here is Field Ngalande, one of our finest recent graduates, tall, good-looking, great mid-fielder on the college soccer team, and very good student:

> And my year ends like this....Now the man of God hosting you on this one I call Him Spiritual Pilot. The reason is simple. He flies us higher with his preachings to the Glory of God! I wonder what kind of dynamics of his preaching he learnt this week and which Bible he reads!

> Meet your Host Pastor Field Ngalande as he hosts and flies

us higher into 2018! Believe me, in 2018 Your Name shall be Great!

Pretty upbeat start to a new year!

I think Field is renting a temporary hall in Mansa for his young church. But his big bright poster for New Year's Eve features a "Prophetic Service and Cross-Over Night." New Years does not just arrive unannounced in Mansa! The prophetic service will run from 9 to 12 in the morning, the cross-over service to follow at 2200 hours, lasting until 5 am!

This congregation may be struggling to make ends meet, but their pastoral leader, Field Ngalande is "Living Under Open Heavens! As Jesus said to Nathanael, 'Thou Shalt See Greater Things Than This...You Shall see Heaven Open.'"

What are you doing New Year's Eve?

Further along the Facebook trail, I find Pastor Stephen Nyirenda, who has raised up a church in the nation's capital, Lusaka. This is not just any church. This is "Perazim Christian Embassy," and they are ending the year with "Three Days of Prophetic Utterance" in the Burma Road Primary School. Guest speakers are Professor Jonathan Botha and Pastor Moses Sikazwe. Other highlights at Perazim are "A Night for the Move of the Holy Spirit" and in December, "A Night of Prophecy and Answers!"

Stephen takes to the Facebook forum to expand on the gift of prophecy to the church:

> The gift of prophecy has been lost in the Church even though we have prophets. The gift of prophecy has an implication of gushing forth from the inner man. You begin to speak by inspiration from the mouth. It falls under vocal gifts like tongues and interpretation. As with the mother of John the Baptist to Mary the mother of Jesus, immediately when the Spirit came upon her she began to well up and utter the

words of encouragement to Mary.

Many prophets of our times have specialized in words of knowledge, but few are flowing in the gift of prophecy. As a result, the church has Superstars. There is no wide impartation of the gift of prophecy.

The gift of prophecy comes with revival. The Bible says when you prophesy, if there is a non-believer in a place, the secrets of his heart are revealed. He will say, "God is in the place!" But what is happening now, after people have given words of knowledge with no presence of God, which is mind blowing, people go back to sin. They only praise the Superman man of God. But when the true gift of prophecy is manifesting, there is fear of God.

Years back in the UCZ youth fellowship at St. Margaret, there were brethren flowing in the gift of prophecy. When they uttered prophecy, we would hide under the chairs, the presence of God was so much. We would fear that our sins would be pointed out.

Child of God, it is time to desire spiritual gifts, "especially that you may prophesy." We need the gift of prophecy to confirm us in all areas of our lives. I mean spiritual confirmation. "I have established David my servant by my hand." Let us "stir up the gift in you which was confirmed by the counsel of elders through prophecy."

Right now as I write, I feel the unction welling up on the inside.

Good for Mark Zuckerberg and his Facebook providers for giving such a forum for Spirit-driven churches! I wonder if that was in the original FB business plan?

Following our service with Redson Banda, a deeply spiritual man, we found the pastor under a tree with a queue of people. Was this counselling?

"Yes, and he is speaking a word into people's lives," was the answer. And so prophetic words may be given in a directive prophecy: "I hear the Lord saying...."

Is this not an abuse of the New Testament gift?

"It is certainly being abused," says our pastoral friend, Musolo. "The country is full of fly-by-night 'prophets'...They promise people the moon and even lead some away from solid churches where they will hear the word of God. They promise a rich husband and a vehicle...It is very enticing for people who are poor, and they can get swept away. Oh these false prophets," he shakes his head. "They make their living out of robbing the people! You don't get out of the place without leaving a big offering behind!" But Musolo believes that this is all a fad and it is passing. He quotes the great text: "The word of God standeth sure...and the Lord knows those who are His" (see 2 Timothy 2:19).

Still, for all the excess, these young Zambian preachers have left us far behind, me and my Swordsmen class of many moons ago, back when the Beatles turned the world of music on its ear. Surely we Swordsmen could have used a lot more of this bold, assertive zeal of my Christian nation graduates! How can you not love that kind of passion for ministry, fresh out of college, starting a church from scratch in rented halls—preaching as though this small church were reaching the world—which through modern communication, it well may be! The start-up may be small, but the vision for divine intervention is huge!

And these former students of mine are not mountebanks or charlatans. Far from it. They can think critically. They have a grasp of the long history of the church and reformation theology. They can certainly preach and do reasonable exposition. They just are deeply persuaded that the divine encounter is what people need and seek. And they major on that.

I think this dynamic young Christian church of Zambia absolutely loves hyperbole! The more grandiose the claims and more radical the promises, the greater the chances of some power dynamics! Their cardinal text must be, "These signs shall follow them that believe."

Believe and promote!

It is time to pay a visit to Gilbert Bwalya. From his student days, Pastor Gilbert has always loved crusades and healing evangelists, so after graduation he turned his Luanshya church, booming as it is, into one extended healing crusade, housed in a large abandoned theatre. This church is an ongoing Benny Hinn crusade.

We visit on a Sunday. During praise and worship, prayer for the sick and prophetic words of knowledge are the main event as Pastor Gilbert moves among a long line of people, laying hands on the sick here, speaking into lives there. This is a forty-five minute event, because the queues are long. Some people fall down around the altar area, under the power of a divine touch. Pastor Gilbert focuses on the sick and the needy. He has interviewed these people beforehand. Later he will preach, raise an offering, and that's it.

But what amazing growth this church has had in ten years, starting from scratch, now numbering over a thousand. "This is a process," says Gilbert Bwalya. "First they must attend our interview clinic for a few weeks. This is where we interview, pray, and seek guidance about the real need. Often people come for prayer without knowing what their real need is. It takes prayer and conversation and discernment to reveal these things."

"We could never have a ministry in this area with preaching alone," says another friend who has planted his church close to an inner-city market area. "These people come in with very great needs. They need the word of God, yes. But mostly they need God to touch them. They need a divine encounter."

The whole event is beyond deafening to be sure. This church must want the entire market area to know they are open for business! And the preaching is not as biblical as my friend is capable of, that's for sure. A lot of allegory, very liberally applied! I feel badly because this man is one of the best Bible expositors around! But here, for today, the power encounter has become the main event.

"Make sure you don't miss tonight! God is going to do wonders!"

### Dealing with Demons

"I've just been dealing with a very stubborn demon," says Lewis Kalaba, in the after service of a missions conference. This is common. Demons manifest as the people of God worship. Leaders take the possessed person out to a ministry room and get that demon cast out in Jesus' name.

Sometimes there is a "charm" involved, attached around the waist of a young woman or carried somewhere else on a person. This must go, and some additional space for ministry is needed! Once the charm is off, out with the charm goes the demon. "In Jesus' name!"

I joined our friend Robert Kasema at a crusade in Mwinilunga, bringing together several churches to hear Kasema's power-packed ministry. Many people were brought to Christ as the gospel was preached, many delivered from various afflictions and oppressions. God was definitely touching people in powerful ways.

After the event, as we were driving back our long and winding road, Kasema said, "Discipleship is so important. Without discipleship, you could come back next year and do it all over again."

It was a reminder of the balance needed in the local church. Power dynamics are a key component to a rounded ministry, to be sure. And so is teaching. It's a matter of getting the house clean and then reinhabited!

# Is There Any **Length** *to This* **Zambian Christianity?**

**W**e have looked over this faith of Zambia in its depth and its breadth—trying to inspect the full dimensions of our Butterfly Christian Nation's faith. And we have put forward the obvious, to anyone who spends any time in Zambia: this church has some *depth* and has a very *broad* reach. No matter where you are or who you are, the church is there for you. You don't have to take Blaise Pascal's wager and "act as though God exists," to see if He does not meet you. In Zambia, it's like the whole country has taken that wager and has turned its corporate heart in the direction of the Almighty. *"Lesa musuma!"* God is powerful! If Pascal is right, that God "hides himself from those who test him and reveals himself to those who seek him," people must be finding God weekly in Zambia. The whole atmosphere is filled with God-seeking.

So much is this the case that we would wish great *length* to this Zambian Christianity, that it might have enduring influence and *go far*! That, as President Lungu affirmed, it might be "a beacon of light for generations to come." Wonderful words. But *how long a run* can a Butterfly Christian Nation have in the rough and tumble world of the twenty-first century? What can be its length? That is the question before us.

One thing in Zambia's favour for the long haul, as with Africa, is its youthfulness.

George Ayittey, in his much-read *Africa Unchained* compares Africa to the cheetah. He says, "Africa's youth is its great advantage. Africa comprises the youngest market in the world; more than half the population is under twenty-four. This is one area where Africa leads the world; in its youthfulness."[1]

While Europe will decline by sixty million souls by 2050—barring another huge influx of North African refugees!—Africa will add 900 million people, double its current population. Of course there will be issues of food supply. Seven of the ten most populous countries in the world will be in Africa! But along with those challenges, there are some definite advantages. With its growth rates, Africa is "growing younger every day." Who among my generation would not want such a blessing? It's like Africa has discovered the fountain of youth!

Zambia is at the centre of this youth explosion, and its "young cheetahs" are poised to carry the ball into the future. Thus Vijay Mahajan, in *Africa Rising*, says it is time to "run with the cheetah generation," that crowd that is faster than "the hippos," the over sixty-five crowd, "holding the reins of power, mired in the past."[2] (Uncomplimentary, I would say, to we hippos!)

But the hippos only comprise seven percent of the population in Africa. "They complain about colonialism and imperialism, while the fast moving cheetahs demand democracy, transparency and an end to corruption." Mahajan says, "the future of Africa is on the back of these cheetahs." They are the ones who will change the politics, drive economic growth, and redefine Africa's consumer market. As we find with our graduates, in their bustling church plants all across Zambia, "these guys are fast and well connected." Mahajan says, "One cheetah with a cellphone can transform an entire society."[3]

I hear a few hippos saying, "Scary thought."

This strikes me as very good news for countries like Zambia and for the "Christian nation" in particular. If one young cheetah with a cellphone can transform a whole society, Zambia must be poised to have a great, enduring impact.

When Ruth and I first came to Zambia in 1996, there was hardly a cellphone to be found. People with old established property had landlines, and for a year or two they were pretty efficient. Then all of a sudden, communication towers were going up all over the country and fibre optic cable was being laid along the highways. Then, from one year to the next, students showed up on our campus with cellphones complete with a Bible, concordances, Facebook, WhatsApp, FaceTime, and every other app known to man. Getting a student to bring a Bible to class was suddenly an old-fashioned request!

I figure all of this stuff must come pretty cheap because most of our students, like students everywhere, are so broke they can't top up their phones with "talk time." When they call and hang up before I have a chance to answer, I know this call has to be on my kwacha! But they all have cellphones as a matter of the most urgent necessity, broke or not. No cellphone, no Christian ministry. What are we thinking?! Life must go on! And they are all young cheetahs. So I'm betting on them being able to take the Christian nation a long way.

I like Mahajan's take on the Siemens commercial featuring a young Tanzanian who flies back to Dar Es Salaam after a time abroad and phones his family from the airport: "I have a surprise for you." The surprise is a new "leopard" hairstyle, his head shaved with spots like a leopard.

> But admirers with cellphone cameras take his photo in the city and then send the image across the country, even to his home village. While he is in transit, all the hair salons begin offering leopard hairstyles. By the time he arrives home by bus, everyone in this village is sporting the same hairstyle. When his family asks him about his surprise, he just shrugs.[4]

Mahajan concludes, "Through connection and speed, the young generation has gained a different view of the world. One cheetah...connected with a cellphone can transform the entire society, not only in superficial ways such as hairstyle but in more fundamental ways too."

When I read Mahajan and his incredible optimism for Africa's "rising," I can't help thinking about the promising future of the butterfly Christian nation of Zambia. I see continuance, endurance, and influence, built for the long haul. And something much more important! Imagine a band of young Zambian emissaries of the Good News, whose mission is extending the kingdom of God, carrying the missionary zeal of their forefathers, moving with their speed and connectivity across the continent. Why should the butterfly nation not take wings? Why should the Christian nation not have great, enduring length and lasting influence? My reading is that the prospects for "length" in the Christian nation are very good indeed.

Indeed, it may only be the youth that can carry the gospel to the north of the continent, and this for one simple reason. They speak the language. Or shall we say, the "lingo" of Africa. Mahajan speaks of the special language of youth, including the Kenyan dialect Sheng, a hybrid of Swahili and English used by the rappers. "Sheng cuts across difficult demographic segments. It is not the language of the rich teenagers or the poor. It is the language of youth." Such egalitarianism makes the young cheetah generation more "open" to contemporary presentation of the

Good News. "African youth have a complex and textured experience connected to global trends and local traditions. Old and new existences are side by side, like English and Swahili, coming together to create Sheng."[5]

English, Swahili, Sheng—Africa is filled with languages. Communicating the Good News, or any news for that matter, is a big challenge—bigger than that faced by David Livingstone's successors. According to Mahajan, there are 250 languages in Nigeria alone and 400 to 500 dialects, "so that a Nigerian might drive a half hour to work and have trouble understanding a conversation...This patchwork of languages means that pan-African brands and advertising have to move beyond words to emotion, music, images, and other non-verbal messages."

Indeed, there is one language that the youth of Africa *all* speak, and that is music. Music is the universal language of the cheetah generation. Music pulsates across Africa with the rising of the sun—or especially the moon! And it is probably the best way to build connections with youth markets. Mahajan relates how in Ghana, Nescafé started an annual contest similar to American Idol, designed to discover and nurture young African musical talent through west and central Africa: "By helping to make these young musicians known, the company has built its own brands. The group was offered a contract to record their music and given heavy promotion via television, radio, print, billboards, and live entertainment."

When it comes to advertising and promotion, Mahajan demonstrates how this universal cheetah language can be used to promote a product:

> An advertising campaign for Fanta in Nigeria showed a group of young people in an open-roofed, four-wheel-drive vehicle stuck on one of the ubiquitous traffic jams in Lagos. A girl and her father and mother are in another car. They

crank up the sound and open up bottles of Fanta. It now doesn't matter that they are stuck in traffic. It doesn't matter what life throws at you, there is always an opportunity to find music or humour in it.[6]

All of that to point out the great advantage that Zambia has to take Christian nation values across the continent. Its youthfulness and its music—both are bursting with life across the country. Zambia is so overrun with such fantastic and gifted musicians that you just know it is going to "run with the cheetahs" in its universal language.

Of course, music is a great medium for the Good News. Should it not have power to lead young listeners to faith? Has anyone been brought to faith through contemporary music? When we hippos are running for earplugs, we seriously doubt it!

But I ask Mike Love that question in a quick email. He runs YC, an annual youth convention weekend event in Edmonton, Alberta where for several years some 16,000 young Canadians gather to hear some of the best communicators to young people, whether they be preachers, teachers, or musicians. It's a great weekend to connect with other people from other churches to build unity and friendships. These gatherings feature the latest artists in contemporary Christian music: Switchfoot, Michael W. Smith, Chris Tomlin, Newsboys, you name it. More than 30,000 young Canadians have professed faith in Jesus over two decades of YC.

So here's our question for Mike: "Would you say that contemporary Christian music has power to bring young people to faith?"

"Yes of course," he says. "Whatever carries the gospel carries that power, whether it's music or anything else. Music draws young people in. It's been that way for generations. No matter where you go in the world, music is highly important to people, especially young people. They love to sing it, play it, and dance to it. Music is most effective when the tune gets in your head and the message gets in your heart. Like a car, music is a vehicle that can carry the gospel in a powerful way. It's just one of many delivery systems available to the church. We should embrace it."

This is good to hear, especially for those of us who had our doubts! The universal language of youth can carry the gospel! "Another beautiful thing about music is that it evolves with every generation in its style and its cultural relevance and therefore can be effective to reach youth at a very deep level. Then when a youth speaker gets up and invites them to Christ, their heart is wide open to respond. I pray that God will raise up many more musicians around the world."

I think Mike would be happy to see how Zambia is responding to that prayer. One of the young music cheetahs of Zambia is Kings Malembe Malembe. When he and his band go into his great "Favour" song, you just *know* that this is the vibrant declaration of Zambia, the nation under divine favour: "Favour on me, speed on my feet, increase in my hands...." How do you beat that song? And I mean "beat!" I'm sure Kings' "Favour" song is the roar of the cheetah!

This is all about the favour of God, celebrated in the butterfly Christian nation! "Pressed down, shaken together, running over with the favour of God." These guys love the song of Jabez—and I read somewhere that things worked out very well for him! "Bless me, bless me indeed, enlarge my territory." Zambia's cheetah musicians love nothing better than celebrating God's favour on their Christian nation. And why should they not carry it long, give it some length of influence and blessing? May it be so in Jesus' name.

Yes, the Christian nation has much to offer the world. Truly, its "product" is something much more saleable and urgently needed than any other commodity: the life-changing, ever-new, best news of the gospel! So if music can be used to engage young people in addressing health and social challenges, like the Population Services International's Youth AIDS project to help stop the spread of HIV/AIDS—why should music not be used to help stop the spread of sin? PSI's project was designed in 2001 to *go long* and to reach 600 million young people around the world. "To treat malaria, PSI uses social marketing to make prepackaged therapies widely available and affordable through commercial outlets." PSI, a model for Zambia's young cheetahs![1]

What a great moment it was when Stoppila Sunzu scored the winning goal and Zambia's Chipolopolos knocked off heavily favoured Ivory Coast to win the Africa Cup of Nations, 2014! All of Zambia took to the streets in a night-long celebration. And who can forget the Chipolopolo team's celebrations on the field, as the young footballers fell to their knees, taking their Christian values to the world as they gave thanks to God. "Futbol for God"—that is the motto of today's national team. Here is another great advantage that Zambia has in taking Christian nation values global, its great national soccer program. The universal language of sports is one that Zambia is already very involved in, another channel for carrying its values *long* and *wide*.

As I look at our young graduates, shooting for the moon in their new-look churches, promoted with their high-tech glitz and glamour and lot of now-generation networking, and I think of all the new languages and messages among the young—I'm pretty much convinced about the *length* to which this Christian nation can go. These young cheetahs are just getting up to speed! They will be building God's kingdom long after we hippos are grazing in other pastures!

# Questions of Height: Does Zambian Christianity Have Influence in High Places?

We have looked at the *depth* dimension of the Christian nation's faith, along with its *breadth* and its *length*. Now we ask the remaining question, what about its *height?* We are asking, "Does the faith of the Christian nation have *influence in high places?*"

It's unusual in a world like ours to have Christian influence in high places. Christianity is not like other religions, which impose their values on a state and make the state an arm of the church. These are far from the days of Innocent III and Gregory the Great at the apex of the power of the papacy. In such late medieval times, the church could impose its will upon the state and demand compliance. For them, the church was the sun in the world, while the kings were the moon, whose only illumination came from the sun. The power of kings was a reflective power, derived from the sun, which gave the world its illumination. No doubt the medievals got that part right!

Teaching church history, I always enjoy coming to this section. This church was so powerful that it made a king walk through the Alps to apologize to the Pope—who then would leave him standing out in the cold for a time. It forced another king to annul a divorce and take back his wife. The power of the one and only Catholic Church was such and the credulity of the masses so great that withholding the Mass was enough to bring the king, any king, to his knees. My impression is that these Zambian students would be happy to return to such times—as long as they are the ones wielding the papal power!

No, in Zambia we are a long way from such influence. Yet still, the church has some considerable clout.

## Unrest Among the Mine Workers

A few years back there was unrest among the miners. They gathered in Lusaka, all carrying sticks and spades and causing a lot of disorder, near riots in the streets. Timothy Kaimba was one of our students at the time and working for the Red Cross. He was called to drive ambulance during the unrest.

"Any casualties,?" I asked Timothy after the dust settled.

"No, there are no guns out there. Just some injuries here and there...wounds from sticks and stones."

"So how was it resolved?"

"The bishops came on the radio and told the people to go home."

Simple as that? What they had said, apparently, was, "Your grievances have been noted. They are being addressed through official means. You are just creating confusion. Just go home."

And then, everyone went home.

## Correcting, Rebuking, Instructing

Zambia has three "Mother Bodies," the representative groups of all Christians in the country. This is a very powerful lobby. Put the

Catholic Council of Bishops and the Evangelical Fellowship of Zambia together with the Council of Churches body, and you have some 75 percent of the nation represented. So when a president decides to run for a third term because "the people are demanding that I stay," the voice of the church is strong enough to rule that out.

And when a president begins to act too autocratically, the influence of the church is such that it can preempt dictatorial tendencies. Our current government opted to lock up the leader of the opposition over dubious offences and charge him with "treason." In many countries, it might have been terminal. But there is enough strength in the church of Zambia to dissuade a government from such heavy handedness. Venezuela could never happen here.

Opposition leaders might have their doubts about justice, and the *Independent Post* newspaper was stripped of its publication powers. Yet a detached observer might say that these voices of opposition were just unwise in their choice of language, first-naming the president and agitating to an extreme. There is a high level of emotion running through a culture like Zambia's. Inflammatory language can be truly inflammatory.

## The Mother Bodies Protest

In mid-2017, the Mother Bodies of Zambia had had enough and rose up in protest. The opposition leader had been arrested over what seemed like a small traffic offence and jailed. It was time to file a united protest. According to Vatican Radio:

> Alarmed by a rapidly deteriorating human rights and political climate in Zambia, the three church Mother Bodies issued a strongly worded public statement at a press conference, critical of Zambian President Edgar Lungu's leadership.

The Zambian Church leaders called for the immediate release of Zambia's main opposition political leader, Hakainde Hichilema (popularly known as HH) whom President Lungu has confined in a maximum security prison, even before trial for an alleged treason charge, is determined.[1]

The bishops went on to declare they were united and unrepentant: "Zambia eminently qualifies to be branded a dictatorship. The fact of the matter is that only leadership that does not have the will of the people on its side...uses state institutions to suppress that same will of the people."

Whether or not such statements from the church are actually *heeded* by a government, Zambia is privileged that it has such stature. In the modern world? To be able to correct and rebuke a head of state? How rare is this!

## The Mother Bodies Call for Peaceful Process at Election Time

Following some political violence at a 2013 byelection, the leaders of church Mother Bodies took to the airwaves, addressing a media briefing at Kapingila House:

We are repeatedly saddened at the rampant political violence that keeps on popping its ugly face especially in the recent byelections. As people who have a God-given mandate of exercising the prophetic mission in our nation and in our time, we cannot tolerate such abominable and immoral acts being committed right before our very eyes. Our nation today, faces...increasing levels of poverty among the majority of our people, a pervading cancer of rampant corruption, escalating youth unemployment, the growing gap between the rich and the poor, an education system that is falling apart, a poor health service delivery coupled with the unclear constitution-making process, the gagging or muzzling of people's freedoms, the arrests of the opposition party leaders and human rights violations. As Zambians, we all need to examine our conscience, seek the truth, and work towards bringing back hope to our people.[2]

The bishops had appealed for calm in the aftermath of the violence in the run up to the byelections in Livingstone:

> Our politics have sunk so low as we recently experienced loss of life during political campaigns. This development is unacceptable and must not be tolerated...We must create a new democratic dispensation. Our democracy came at high cost and we should all endeavour to protect it and help sustain this philosophy of governance. We should all seek to come together to safeguard and promote the culture of peaceful, genuine and democratic elections in this great nation which for many years now has been the pride and envy of this region and the continent of Africa.

Political process drew the bishops' ire. Were the byelections really necessary?

> More and more byelections being instigated or motivated by greed, individual interests, and a selfish propensity for political dominance by the ruling party and the desire for ministerial positions by the MPs that are lured into resignations from their political parties...What value are these byelections adding to our political environment? Why are our leaders so ready to waste such colossal sums of money in the campaigns whilst our hospitals still face a critical shortage of medical staff, equipment, and essential drugs? We question the integrity of those who are crossing the floor in parliament for the sake of receiving political favours or appointments.

While at the podium, the Mother Bodies called on the police to be impartial and just in their imposition of law and order; and they called upon the media to do their job with courage and reliance, but also with fairness and respect for everyone.

Then in a parting note, the bishops called on church leaders to raise the bar and do their jobs better:

> We hereby exhort you to continue performing the God-given mandate of providing a prophetic voice in our society. Do not abuse the pulpit for partisan politics and do not ever fall prey to political enticements and corruption. Do not be afraid to preach the truth in love and we urge you to continue to call the powers that be to do greater justice...Never tire at proclaiming the message of truth, justice, peace, love, unity, forgiveness, and reconciliation. May God bless this great nation. (Mar. 15, 2013)

## We Say No to Police Brutality

In April 2017, the police got carried away on the side of law and order and left a lot of people fearing police brutality. According to the Catholic News Service, the Mother Bodies strongly protested police brutality connected with partisan politics:

> Zambians are living in fear as police brutality increases and the southern African country approaches dictatorship, Zambia's Catholic bishops have said. The bishops "are deeply saddened" by police officers' "unprofessional and brutal conduct," arbitrary arrests, "horrific torture of suspects," and the "careless, inflammatory and divisive statements of our political leaders...." Anyone who criticizes the government for wrongdoing is sure to have the police unleashed on him or her.

"The country's judiciary has let the country down," claimed the Mother Bodies, by failing to stand up to "political manipulation and corruption...Our democratic credentials...have all but vanished in this nation that loudly claims to be God-fearing, peace-loving, and Christian."

As a result of brutalizing the people through the police, Zambians are reduced to fear so that the order of the day is corruption and misuse of public funds. There is fear and trembling among the people, shown in the way they are afraid to speak out against injustices. The bishops called for an immediate halt to intimidating statements by ruling party leaders and said, "the continuous tension" between the ruling party and opposition affects the lives of the public. Zambia "is now, all except in designation, a dictatorship and if it is not yet, then we are not far from it," they said. "We therefore demand" that the government "puts in place concrete measures to reverse this worrying and dangerous trend" (Catholic News Service, April, 2017).

At the same time, the bishops denounced "attacks on the Law Association of Zambia and the government's plans to undermine it," an independent body with a membership of more than 1,000 legal practitioners, which should "play its rightful role as one of the most effective checks and balances in a true democratic dispensation."

## Helping to End Child Marriages

On a more positive side, the Zambian church can often affect government policy.

Raising consciousness of social problems like domestic violence and child marriage is a vital mandate. Zambia has one of the highest child marriage rates in the world. So serious has the issue become that recent first lady, Dr. Christine Kaseba-Sata, and the current vice president, Inonge Wina, declared child marriage a national crisis and called for its criminalization in Zambia.

The problem is the discrepancy between Zambia's statutory law, which sets the age of marriage as eighteen for females and twenty-one for males, and traditional law, where marriage can take place at puberty. It is common for girls to be married or have sexual relations under the age of sixteen.

Of course, child marriage is associated with high levels of poverty. Poverty leads many parents to withdraw their daughters from school and offer them for marriage to older men (in most cases) in exchange for payment of *lobola* (a dowry for the bride). It is estimated that thirty-eight mothers die each month due to complications relating to pregnancy and childbirth in Zambia. These conditions are disproportionately pronounced among teen mothers. Thus, maternal mortality is still high and only declining at a very slow rate from 649 deaths/per 100,000 live births in 1997 to 483 (UNFPA 440) in 2010.

World Vision Zambia has been quite active in helping shape government policy in this area. It works closely with the provincial and district ministries and departments in order to curb rising cases of child marriages:

> As a result of such collaboration, World Vision Zambia, under the Child Protection and Advocacy Project, successfully managed to facilitate the withdrawal of 150 girl children from child marriages in the three project sites, Mweru, Luampa, and Mpika, during Feb. 2014.[3]

The government identified traditional leaders as one of the key drivers to the successful elimination of child marriages. World Vision Zambia strengthened collaboration with traditional leaders and found many champions in the fight against child marriage.

Maybe Zambians don't realize what a rare gem they have in this "Christian nation." This is something to be cherished and upheld in a world where

- many nations don't even tolerate Christianity, let alone give the faith an official endorsement;

- many nations attack Christians as being subversive and even look the other way on Christian martyrdom; or

- many nations are so secular that they relegate Christianity to the fish tank of all the world's half-baked religions and say, "Enjoy the swim."

Being officially a Christian nation surely brings divine favour and blessing. It implies Lordship. And Christianity has come to Zambia at such a great price. How wrong to take such a gift lightly! "Her gift is far above rubies."

I rather think that Zambians should wear the badge of their Christian nation declaration proudly and invite other nations to follow suit! As David Livingstone liked to remind us, "The knowledge of the Lord will fill the earth."

# Part III

*How Did This Wonder Emerge?*

It's really a miracle, there's not much doubt about that. I mean, how do you get a Christian nation, and a pretty solid one at that, out of 1890 origins? This is like the days of creation when "the Spirit of God hovered over the face of the deep." Theologians like to remind us that creation was not *ex nihilo*, out of nothing, but out of *chaos*. That was central Africa at the end of the nineteenth century.

Yet now to see the butterfly nation of Zambia lustrous with the light of the liberating gospel—this is the stuff of wonder. How do you bring order out of that kind of chaos? It must be the word of God, the Creator, still generating life! In the words of Hopkins' poem:

> Oh, morning, at the brown brink eastward, springs—
> Because the Holy Ghost over the bent
> World broods with warm breast and with ah! bright wings.

J.D. Greear comments on the Genesis text:

> I have to admit, I've often found that statement odd, "the earth was without form and void." It looks like God intentionally begins his creation by making a dark, empty mess— and only then, in "part 2," does the Word go to work with the famous "Let there be" lines.
>
> But this is actually significant. And I believe this was intentional. By starting with chaos and darkness, God teaches us two things about how he works:

1.  The Word brings order out of chaos.

    When God created everything, he did it by starting with a formless void and then shaping it with his Word. He did that to show that, in the same way, our lives are a formless void until God's Word comes in to bring life and peace, beauty and order.

2.  The opposite is true as well: when God's Word departs from our lives, they descend back into chaos.[1]

## *The Chaotic Scene of 1873:*
## *Befriending and Baptizing the Ngoni*

The biggest challenge for the early missionaries who followed David Livingstone in a great stream, many filtering in from the Livingstonia Centre in the east, was convincing the Ngoni to give up war. This was no easy task, the tribe being so deeply imbued with warfare from their earliest days. It seems the tyrant Chaka had left his ruthless personality deeply imprinted upon his people. This tribe was so dominant in 1873 on the east side of present Zambia that everything had to begin with them. They were not the only major tribe that had made present-day Zambia home. But flanked as they were along the mountainous high country that rose up from Lake Nyasa, the powerful Ngoni overran so many lesser tribes that they became the virtual gatekeepers of the east. If Livingstone's successors were going to bring the good news to present-day Zambia, they would have to deal with the Ngoni off the top. And it was not going to be easy:

> I have seen an army, ten thousand strong, issue forth in June and not return till September, laden with spoil in slaves,

cattle and ivory, and nearly every man painted with white clay, denoting that he had killed someone.[2]

So records a mission journal in 1883. How could such deeply ingrained DNA ever be changed?

This was the daunting task facing the intrepid band of missionaries that rallied to the cause of Christianizing Central Africa only two years after the doctor's death. Indeed, the response in Britain to Livingstone's death was so strong that many missionary societies felt an immediate surge of new life and interest. The Church Missionary Society, the London Missionary Society, and the Scottish Presbyterian Churches took up the vision of penetration from the east coast, which Livingstone had devoted his latter years to. Similarly, the Universities Mission to Central Africa focused on the east coast as a beachhead. And the Catholic White Fathers, birthed in Algiers a decade earlier, did the same. Within the space of seven years, *seven different missions* were established along the borders of modern Zambia; meanwhile, the Plymouth Brethren were making inroads from the west to become a major missionary force out of their strong local churches in London.

What an environment these intrepid pioneers were entering, marred by the endless slave trading and accompanying warfare and the demonic oppression that hung over Central Africa and the regions of modern Zambia. These stalwarts were the pioneers. The cost was great in those days that preceded malaria medication. But these were true "soldiers of the cross." They befriended the chiefs. They translated the scriptures. They brought literacy and schooling to tribes that had never had the opportunity to read. They modelled peace and reconciliation. They broke the bondage of the witchdoctor with their medical care. They taught moral purity. They introduced concepts of justice and righteousness in places where they were "foreign concepts" in every sense. They spoke of a better life. They valued people as image bearers of God, regardless of tribe or status. Respect, love, trust, patience—these qualities characterized the new arrivals as much as they had their forerunner. And within a decade, they began to see the first results for their labours. We do them scant justice in these pages. But fortunately they left us some records of their labour from which we draw much inspiration. Laws, Elmslie, Stewart, Fraser, Arnot, Coillard, Dupont, Fisher—such great, effective ministries in a world of spiritual darkness! Together, they turned Livingstone's lone candle into a very bright glow over Zambia.

The journals of the medical doctors William Elmslie and Robert Laws, both out of the Free Church of Scotland, give us a pretty good picture. It was Elmslie who moved into modern Zambia and worked among the Ngoni, so fierce at the time that every proximate tribe lived behind barricades because of them. We are indebted to his book, *Among the Wild Ngoni*, for insights into Elmslie's most challenging environment.

Elmslie was born in 1856 and attended the University of Aberdeen, graduating in 1884, the same year he was appointed to the Livingstonia mission. A doctor and a missionary, Elmslie was also a scholar. While among the Ngoni, he acquired a detailed knowledge of the Tumbuka language and was the first person to reduce it to writing. He produced the first Tumbuka grammar and translated into that language the gospel of Mark, St. John's epistles, and Paul's letters to the Corinthians and Colossians. In 1924, he returned to Scotland where he worked as a parish minister until his retirement in 1931. Five years later he died.

Throughout his season in Ngoniland, Elmslie patiently introduced Christian values into the ruling oligarchy of chief Mombera, which was unpredictable and prone to warfare. The stakes were high and called for perseverance and vision. To win here was to gain influence over a very large region of eastern

Zambia and impact all the surrounding tribes. The culmination of the struggle was the simple victory of Christianity over the legacy of Chaka.

Elmslie's writing traces the Ngoni migration to Zambia beginning with the birth of Chaka in Zululand early in the nineteenth century. It's amazing to think that David Livingstone and Chaka were born around the same time, the one an agent of healing and liberation, the other one of the most ruthless warriors the world has ever seen. By the time Chaka died, over one million Africans owed their deaths to him, largely because he had learned the European "art of war by regiments and companies." He "improved" on the skills of his instructors, not satisfied that conquered tribes should be so generously treated as to be assimilated as vassals: Chaka's idea was more along the lines of crush and dismember. Following an attack by Chaka and his hordes, tribes would be left incapable of rising up ever again against an invader. Elmslie writes a gripping description of Chaka's mercifully short season:

> His brief reign of seven or eight years was a period in which more blood was shed, and greater upheaval among native tribes induced, than in any other place in the world...War poisoned all enjoyment, cut off all that sustains life, turned thousands of square miles into a howling wilderness, shed rivers of blood, annihilated whole communities, turned the members of tribes into cannibals, and caused miseries and sufferings the full extent of which can never now be known (Elmslie, 15).

By the time Chaka died in 1828, he had led his Ngoni people on their migration far into central Africa, and every step was marked by blood. Reflecting on the nineteenth-century Ngoni migrations, Elmslie gives a poignant panegyric:

> What might not have happened had the dawn of this century witnessed the enthusiasm of the Christian church in the cause

of foreign missions which is a feature of its close! What achievements for Christ there might have been! Here we stand at the Zambezi and look back at the reigns of Chaka and Zwide and see the rise and fall of kingdoms; rivers of bloodshed; a million or more massacred, condemned to cannibalism or starvation; fathers slaying their children and children their fathers; and God's fair earth made worse than hell—all for want of the gospel...The church of Christ was at the time ignorant of her duty and was not impressed by the opportunity of extending her Lord's kingdom (Elmslie, 29).

"What might not have happened?" "All for want of the gospel!" Such laments raised up about the church! May we not have to hear them again in our time.

When the Ngoni first crossed the Zambezi into modern Zambia, they were in the country of the Senga, who were easy prey; this tribe submitted and were assimilated. They continued their journey north until they came into the region of the Tumbuka, who covered a wide area along the border between Malawi and Zambia. They lived in small villages, an industrious agricultural people. They also submitted readily to the Ngoni. Chaka's son, the ruthless Zongandaba, was paramount chief of the Ngoni by this time. By means of the witchcraft brought to him by his Tumbuka vassals, he applied treachery to his subject tribes and nearly massacred all the southern Tongas. Only a handful of this branch of the Tonga, who had left their original homeland to settle along the west of Lake Malawi, were spared by the end of the Ngoni wanderings.

But this warrior tribe had not finished its migration. They pressed northward in 1885, to the south of Lake Tanganyika, now northern Zambia, where Zongandaba died, to no one's regret. Here the Ngoni tribe, having come so far out of Zululand, broke up. Some continued north and settled in present-day Congo and Tanzania. Others went east and settled

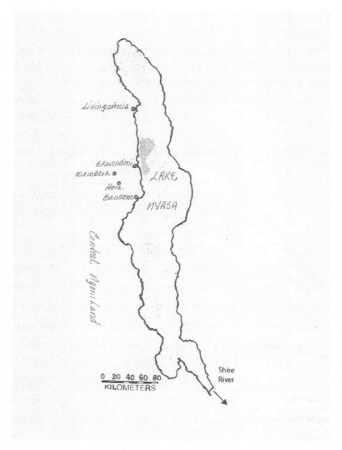

*Ngoniland, 1890.*

around the north end of Lake Nyasa, and others more south-
ward to the Henga in what had been Tumbuka country in the
east of modern Zambia. Here a large group of Ngoni settled
under Chief Mombera, close to the southwest shores of Lake
Nyasa, and became the focus of the early missionaries out of
Livingstonia. This dominating tribe now looked like the key to
the whole region.

178

Elmslie describes the physical features of Ngoniland, including much of what is now Zambia's Eastern Province, in terms that had made it attractive to his predecessor, Livingstone:

> About 4,000 feet above sea level. Leaving Lake Nyasa at 1,500 feet, we have to cross the broken mountain ranges, rising to as much as 7,000 feet, which form the eastern boundary of Ngoniland. Hundreds of square miles of open undulating country...treeless, patches of bush...ant hills all over, resembling stacks of hay. The villages situated near the streams.

Villages were only built to last three or four years, after which "white ants attack the wood and grass of the hut; the bugs and jiggers disturb the peace...It is time to seek a new home." Moving a village did not happen without ceremony. This was one of the major events, marking a division in the calendar, and became a highlight from which people could keep track of the months and years. Moving called for certain religious rites, the sacrifice of cattle as a sacrifice to the village ancestral spirit. Elmslie comments, "Though many religious rites of the people appear grotesque and unreal, yet a close examination proves the existence of their belief in a Prudence, a Judge, and an Almighty King."[3]

Establishing a new village meant building new huts, in circles around the cattlefold, the sun, moon, and horizon providing the template, the circular shape reflecting heat and rendering it comfortable in the cold nights, writes Elmslie, who lived in such villages for twenty years and preserved interesting descriptions of a typical day:

> On a typical day, everyone is up early. The women set off to the river with big earthen jars on the head. Brewing is solely a woman's occupation, and a great reputation for a woman can be gained by excellence in the craft! Planting and reaping produces much drunkenness because large pots of

strong beer are carried to the garden for workers. Quarrels ensue, and harvest seasons can be very degrading. When hundreds of baskets of maize are carried home, or the beer crop is cut stalk by stalk and gathered, beer drinking brings all the workers together. Inferior wives end up doing most of the work. There are many brawls, but an Ngoni must never strike a women or he will be known as a "bad man"—in which case he might as well go and hang himself!

Among the Ngoni, the main meal of nshima corn meal is in the evening. Following the meal, the youths and maidens go to cattlefold to the dance. The Ngoni have a great love for recreation...On a clear night it is nice to listen to their songs. Some observers might come away from such scenes with an impression of the glamour of native life, with its apparent peace and joy (Elmslie, 40).

Indeed, the a cappella sounds of singing in an African village still carry the same beautiful sense! But the missionary guest is aware that "such scenes do not cover the unhappiness, the slavish fear of evil spirits...the secret immorality, the lying, stealing, and murder which abound in every native community." When Donald Fraser joined Elmslie and began to move among the Tumbuka and Tonga slaves, as well as among the Ngoni themselves, he wrote about the "moral degeneracy" that prevailed all over Central Africa: there was the "great moral evil" of polygamy; all who bore arms were entitled to capture women as their wives, the chief being the worst offender, having many villages under his oversight, with a wife in each, the woman his way of claiming the village as his own.

In Ngoniland, any man could raise a case against a neighbour at any time, even though everyone had to bow to a neighbour to avoid offence. In such a setting, with charges and countercharges abounding, the *itshanusi* or witch doctor made a living off of the credulity of the people. If a sick person was deemed bewitched, friends and family would carry him about from place to place to "cheat the charmer." But if the man concluded that he was to die, he would lose his desire to fight for life and simply resign himself to the end. This was the case even among the youth.

Elmslie records that many members of the tribe died by drinking the *"muave cup."*

> When someone was accused of some offence, the itshanusi is called and a sentence of death pronounced for people accused of witchcraft. In such cases, the whole community turns out with jeers and waits for the accused wretch to vomit the poisons.

If the accused began to quiver and then collapse, the man would be accursed and condemned to death. The doctor noted that the mauve cup was prevalent during such dark days, especially among the Tonga and Tumbukas. Of course,

> ...the poison was linked to the supernatural, with its appeal to a power outside themselves. It was part of their religious system. The witch doctor was seen as an agent of ancestral spirits. While these people did not worship God, they had a strong belief in a Supreme Being, Chiuta, and they could approach him through ancestral spirits (Elmslie, 64-66).

This was something to build on. Over time, Elmslie and his colleagues recognized that the truths of Christianity had an open door to the Ngoni mind and to their subject tribes:

> These people live continually in an atmosphere of spiritual things. All the customs are connected with the world of spirits. In our preaching, we merely unfold God's character. They bow to his sovereignty. We have but to unfold truth to them.
>
> Regarding life and death, all natives have the story much like all the Bantu tribes. A dream is a conversation with a departed friend. Belief in spirits was constant. Certain hills

were worshiped among the Ngonis, and they retained a belief in Hades for disembodied spirits.[4]

Every year during the dry season, the Ngoni armies raided the quiet and industrious Chewa, or down to the lake they would come against the Tonga, or northward to the Nkonde or westward into "the land of fat sheep," going as far as Bangweulu in their savage attacks, near the site of Livingtone's death. According to Elmslie, "it is impossible to estimate" the loss of life in peaceful tribes or measure the anguish and distress, all because of the war and the power of the Ngoni. When Laws and Stewart passed through Ngoniland in 1878, they found such villages struggling for survival from Ngoni raids. Some people were practically driven into Lake Nyasa by fear of them. Protective stockades ran thirty yards into the lake. Scores of poor Tonga, Tumbuka, and Henga joined remnants of broken tribes in the hills. People fled into the dark forests in fear for their lives. Some whole villages settled along the cliffs, "living between earth and sky in small huts for fear of Ngoni." During one terrible period, many Tonga fled in terror to the lakeshore, while the Tumbuka were forced up Mount Hora, where they were starved into surrender by siege warfare. When finally allowed to come down to drink at the fountains, the Ngoni fell upon them, and many hundreds were massacred. Elmslie and the early missionaries were to survey the skeletons crowded around the foot of horrible Mount Hora.

The Ngoni dominated a sprawling area in which there were representatives of at least sixteen different tribes, mostly found among their slaves. In 1878, Dr. Laws and James Stewart founded a site for the new station on Mount Kaningina on the fringes of Ngoniland, between it and Lake Nyasa. Here the African missionary, William Koyi, fluent in the Ngoni language, settled for a time to observe. In time they got an introduction to

Mombera, the chief of the Ngoni, and Mtwaro, his brother and successor.

The Ngoni were suspicious of the mission locating itself among their Tonga vassals on the lakeshore. But Koyi was received in a friendly manner by Chief Mombera and there grew a relationship of mutual trust and respect, which was to be very key. Once trust was built, schools could also be built! In 1879, Dr. Laws from the Livingstonia Mission Centre came to meet Chief Mombera for a second time, and the two men strengthened their great and enduring friendship, Mombera expressing his affection for "the father of the white men." Like that of Robert Moffat and Umziligazi, chief of the Ndebeles, this friendship was to yield very positive results along the way. Elmslie comments on the power of these surprising friendships among men so different in many ways, yet drawn together by mutual respect:

> Mombera and Umziligazi, two bloodthirsty, despotic chiefs, far apart but of the same blood, visited by two missionaries of the cross, and forming a strong attachment to them and till death maintaining it, and speaking often of it! This attachment to Dr. Laws made Mombera hesitate to sanction war. Thousands of Tonga men and women owe their life to Mombera's affection for Dr. Laws...Indeed, happy must he be who was thus used of God in saving the lives of so many people, that they might hear and receive God's word (Elmslie, 94).

It seems the good Dr. Laws must have visited Mombera in the mornings! That's when his temper was best:

> Mombera had a dual character. He was at his best in the early part of the day, before he became intoxicated, and so by sunrise people with cases to be judged went to see him. Then his affability and generous behaviour were pleasant to see, but toward afternoon when the beer he continually

sipped began to act, his civility was at an end for the day and he was foul mouthed and quarrelsome. When he was sober, he delighted to play with his children, and manifested a very pleasing interest in them and their mothers, but when drunk, he drove them from his presence with obscene curses (Elmslie, 117).

When Dr. Laws made his early visits to Mombera's village, "we explained to him that the object was to be friends of all the people, to teach them about God and what he has done for us, to teach the children so they could read God's word for themselves." Mombera thanked these emissaries of the missionary community for their visit, but wondered why they should not come and live with him. "Can you milk fish that you remain at the lake?"

In fact, the mission was moving westward, ever closer to Ngoniland. With the founding of the Bandawe station along the western shores of Lake Nyasa, they were now settled within its borders. But peace among this tribe was by no means assured. Raiding continued by the "wild youth" all round Bandawe. And the unsettled conditions among the Tonga made mission enterprise very difficult. Tonga Chief Chikoko came seeking missionary intervention with the "wild beast" Ngoni: "They are like the snake: we are a frog." Would the missionaries supply guns and powder? Would Dr. Laws please intervene? All the villages of the Tonga had been destroyed for miles north.

At length, in 1882, a shaky peace between the Ngoni and surrounding tribes was secured. William Koyi went to meet Mombera and brokered an agreement, while much prayer was being raised by the missionaries to "take possession of Ngoniland for Christ." But long traditions of warfare resurfaced and were proving hard to break. By 1883, the Ngoni had broken the peace agreement and attacked a Tonga village, burning down the Bandawe mission school in the process.

War, bloodshed, famine, and death were again the order of the day, with untold misery among those spared... countless thousands over the region raided by the Ngoni (Elmslie, 98).

Still, there was a flicker of hope for progress among the missionaries. They resolved to stay in Ngoniland and work in Mombera's village until they were expelled, with faith that the gospel would win its way. Africa's missionary, William Koyi, "was doing such a noble work among the Ngoni, which no European could have accomplished," that he gradually broke down all their suspicions.

How do you get such warlike people to lay down their weapons for good? This could only happen through something like the "sincere love" of Romans 12—a quality that Elmslie and his team seemed to have had in abundance:

> Love must be sincere. Hate what is evil; cling to what is good. Be devoted to one another in brotherly love. Honor one another above yourselves. Never be lacking in zeal, but keep your spiritual fervor, serving the Lord. Be joyful in hope, patient in affliction, faithful in prayer. Share with God's people who are in need. Practice hospitality...Do not be proud, but be willing to associate with people of low position...If it is possible, as far as it depends on you, live at peace with everyone. Do not take revenge, my friends, but leave room for God's wrath (vv. 9-16).

Such love must be present and peaceful, among other things. And it was to prove triumphant in breaking that warrior spirit.

## No Word for Peace

Gradually, in fits and starts, Elmslie and his colleagues began to see an opening up of the Ngoni people to their ministry. They met with hundreds of head men and explained that Koyi wanted to settle,

185

teach the Word of God, and heal the sick. Such ideas were well received until Ng'onomo, a prominent Ngoni sub-chief, got to his feet and commenced a war dance. "We will not give up war!"

"This book says we must live at peace," said Koyi, holding his Bible. But as it turned out, there was no word in Ngoni for "peace"! And little wonder, with their tribal history. The closest they had was an imported term, "to visit one another." In time the translators would have to find an Ngoni word for that most precious commodity, peace.

The prominent headman, Ng'onomo, was adamant. "Let the Tongas bring back our wives and children"—or there would be no peace. But Koyi and Elmslie refused to attempt to settle old disputes. They simply continued to live among the Ngoni, knowing them to be the key to the region, and said, "We didn't write the book, we simply communicate it." Yet Koyi's speech, clear and pointed, reminded Mombera and his people that "the book" was stronger than medicine and gives peace. They were "stubborn," said Koyi, not to allow the team to build schools. "Let us go about the country." But this was five years of painfully slow progress. Gifts were exchanged. Long speeches made. When it was all said and done, in 1882, the missionaries were restricted to Mombera's own palace. And their colleagues from Livingstonia advised, "Proceed slow...grace, gumption, and go"—in due order!

Thus these early missionaries entered the time of "mission work in the dark days," unable to move around, besieged with the clamour for gifts all day. No doubt they had many occasions to be reminded of God's calling to Paul:

> *I am sending you to them to open their eyes and turn them from darkness to light, and from the power of Satan to God, so that they may receive forgiveness of sins and a place among those who are sanctified* (Acts 26:17).

At times it seemed they were under orders like Israel in Egypt: "Make bricks! The village headman wants them!" And "Why could they not pay the people to attend church?" Then the entire village would break out in dances that would last the whole night. In those days of very basic village structures and living in close proximity to the people, the missionaries had many a sleepless night, deciding it best to "allow them to dance till they are satisfied then calmly say, 'Good morning.'" As though to make their mission even more difficult, there were constant beer fests, "which we only endure for the Lord's sake." Guns were fired off on Sunday morning to disrupt mission plans for worship. People would gather for a Sunday dance, sing, and get drunk, so that the sacred day was filled with unhallowed sounds, to end in fights and bloodshed. It was a season of ribald songs and war dances. They were continually harassed because they would not give cloth and beads. And through it all, there was not one single convert.

Such a season was so much like David Livingstone's seasons of futility they must have wondered if they were repeating the same seed planting in vain. Was sharing the Good News in word and deed *never* going to show results? Where was the harvest? It was a season of patiently sowing the good seed, living out the words of James:

> Be patient, then, brothers, until the Lord's coming. See how the farmer waits for the land to yield its valuable crops and how patient he is for the autumn and spring rains. You too, be patient and stand firm (5:7-8).

During this driest season, they must have had many inducements to abandon Ngoniland and look for "more promising soil." It seemed that their presence was a matter of absolute indifference among the Ngoni. The building of schools was prohibited. They wondered if they were accomplishing anything. All they could do was speak of spiritual things with the builders and boys around a building project. They tried holding a service of worship on the Sabbath, with "open preaching of the Word." The service was tolerated, attended by a few women and some fully armed men. But even this proved futile, devolving into an uproarious event, with dogs fighting in the midst and shouts of "It's all lies, give us cloth!"

Of course there was no limit to the demands for medical work, and this was important in building relationships with the people, who came in crowds. Medical treatment was gradually overthrowing the authority of the native doctors as "common people were delivered from the bondage of their incantations." While response to preaching was nil, medical missions was conveying the message of God's love and care.

Finally, after seven years, the turning point came when Elmslie and Koyi started to hold small meetings for the Tumbuka slaves. Some of their youth came for more teaching. The missionaries were young themselves and attracted young people, who started to speak up on their behalf. Ngoni youth began to meet with them for prayer and to sing hymns. These youth were marked out for persecution as "bricks." But this was the "beginning of fruit."

By the end of 1885, after seven years among the Ngoni, young men were visiting Elmslie at night, saying they "wanted to pray to God." *Teach me to pray!* The request must have been music to the missionary ears! There would be persecution of these young men who wanted to learn how to pray. But at least they would not be executed, as was the case in Matebeleland! This was a triumphant moment, the ingathering of the first fruits. After seven years' hard labour!

## "But can you bring rain?"

The year 1886 was a landmark year, for "it marked the triumph of the gospel among the Ngoni." Interest had grown as more Ngoni youth came by night to be taught to read. Three sons of Kalengo, the witch doctor, were among the first: Chitezi, Mawalera, and Makara. These were very bright young men who made rapid progress in reading and writing. In the process, their minds were opened up to receive Jesus as Lord. Chief Mombera began to look on young Chitezi as "our man" and liked what he saw. He began to give the missionary enterprise more space. Elmslie recognized that "Mombera knew all" and often had reason to thank God for the presence of the chief on the throne.

These young converts were praying for their witch doctor father, their friends, their chief, the head men. Prayer became the vital centre of their new life. It was a powerful revelation when they saw God as Father, guiding and sustaining the world, inviting them to come to him in prayer. Their young minds were growing through the scriptures. A "new bond was formed, born of the Holy Spirit." After dark, these three Ngoni youth would gather to pray and Dr. Elmslie himself was receiving fresh inspiration by their devotion: "Mission is not about sacrifice. It has advantages to one's spiritual life. I have fresher interest in the word. Such simplicity of trust in these prayers!"

It was just at this time, with such a beautiful, growing response among the Ngoni youth, that the chief called for young warriors. He needed an additional residence—to add to the seven he already had! So he gathered a young army to go forth to conquer a village and "wash their spears in blood." It was a critical juncture for the growing young Christians. How could they be part of yet another bloody Ngoni foray? They banded together, prayed, and stood their ground. They refused to go to war. Like the three Hebrew children, these Ngoni youth defied the chief and said they would not enlist. And just as with the three Hebrews, God backed them up! Chief Mombera pulled back from his plan in a most uncharacteristic gesture, thought better of his housing needs, and another bloodbath was avoided.

The event speaks volumes for the profound power of the gospel. What respect and credibility these young new believers had already garnered in the tribe! For Chief Mombera himself to be dissuaded from war! It must have been a landmark day.

This season of first fruits was critical in other ways. Compounding the tension was the famine and drought that prevailed across the land. Planting seed in 1886 was a useless endeavour. What was the cause? Could the missionaries not help? Cattle were sacrificed to ancestral spirits, trying to propitiate the gods and bring on rain.

"Why do you not give rain?" Mombera looked to the missionaries and wanted to know. "What does the Book say?"

"We will pray for rain tomorrow," they said, summoning up their faith. "But it is important to come to God with the right spirit. You people don't even believe in our God."

By the next Sunday, a large crowd gathered to hear Elmslie preach on "Drought" from Isaiah 58:

> *Why have we fasted, they say, and you have not seen it? Why have we humbled ourselves, and you have not noticed?...Is this what you call a fast, a day acceptable to the Lord? Is not this the kind of fasting I have chosen: to loose the gains of injustice and untie the cords of the yoke to set the oppressed free and break every yoke?...If you do away with the yoke of oppression...then the Lord will...satisfy your needs in a sun-scorched land and will strengthen your frame. You will be like a well-watered garden, like a spring whose waters never fail (vv. 3-11).*

The people heard that God desires other things in place of animal sacrifices: learning his word and seeking him. He does not respond to "hands defiled with blood." It was an appeal to the war-like conscience. But none of the warriors responded in any way.

Then followed a war dance that lasted all through the evening—and until four in the morning. Meanwhile, on the other side of the village, the missionaries were praying for rain long into the night, "knowing we were under threat." As they were rising from their knees, they heard the sounds of a slight rain—the first in months! They found their way to bed feeling very hopeful.

The following day, another service was held to pray for rain. By two o'clock, prayers were fully answered and a heavy rain fell! January 18, 1886 was a landmark day. The most welcome rainfall came down upon the parched land! Elmslie records that this made a "profound impression and greatly advanced our work." Seed planting went into operation. Two councillors brought a sheep as thank offering.

From that day forward, common people started attending services boldly. Sabbath meetings were more firmly established and even included the presence of the witch doctor, *amaduna*. Interest in the Book was growing. The missionaries were granted extended areas for evangelism. Every village headman in the surrounding area was very ready to have their ministry. They found themselves preaching far and wide—in the middle of a very heavy rainy season!

Sadly, William Koyi died just as this expanded influence was really gaining ground. His last words, when he heard that more areas were opening up for schools and the gospel, were, "Lord, now let your servant depart in peace, for mine eyes have seen your salvation." Elmslie was left feeling "so lonely and helpless" without his African missionary friend. "How I loved him."

Restrictions for building schools had been removed. The two brother-chiefs, Mombera and Mtwaro, now reconciled, and the Ngoni kingdom was kept intact. They started a school and recruited two natives able to read to come and help teach. "You must not plant your garden only in one place," said the chief.

More schools! More reinforcements! Njuyu was still the centre, but "our influence was spreading across Ngoniland!"

## "He that finds a wife..."

Meanwhile, Elmslie left for a few months of furlough—and returned with a wife!

> The reception accorded us on our arrival was very warm, and an explanation was given of the scanty respect shown on some former occasions. The chief said, "Yesterday you were a boy; today you are a man and can speak." The Ngoni accorded the privileges of manhood, such as transacting business, to married men, and as long as I was unmarried, it was contrary to their habit to have to treat with unmarried persons whom they considered to be boys (Elmslie, 186).

## The Crossroads of 1887: "What if the Ngoni rise up?"

1887 was a bright new year in Ngoniland. "We had a little school of 22 scholars and a class of young men too old for school, but anxious to learn the Word of God!" After seven years of contact with the Ngoni, six years with nothing to show, now Dr. Elmslie and his team had free access to go to any village for teaching. The band of young men who had come by night to learn to read and pray stood by them and were becoming strong Christians, explaining to others the way of salvation through faith.

The witch doctor was seven miles away. When the drums began beating, he would come to ply his trade in the tribe. But Chitezi, his son, stood strong. Medical missions had won the day. The thatch-roofed school that they had been using was replaced with a brick building and soon attracted 400 children per day.

Unfortunately, just as the work was swelling, six Tonga carriers were murdered by the Ngoni under Nawambi, a very cruel warrior. This was so regrettable for many reasons, including the reigniting of the warrior spirit in the region. The old spirit of Chaka was back to life! Blockades sprung up and deprived the mission band of their communication link. Mombera intervened with Nawambi but vacillated so much that mission confidence in the chief was shaken. He did not take up the murders with any kind of interest.

It was a season of much anxiety. Dr. Laws revisited the area for the first time in four years, carrying a handsome present for Mombera. But there was little courtesy from the chief. And no sense of responsibility for the murder of the Tongas. Suddenly the missionaries were blamed for internal strife in the tribe. Mombera was being harassed and opposed by his brother, Mtwaro: "You keep all the missionaries to yourself! Dr. Laws must come back and visit with us!" And as always, the missionaries were called upon to make things right.

"Where are our Tonga wives and children? We gave up war, not to be poor. You people must enrich us! All members of your mission must leave Bandawe on the lake and come to our part of Ngoniland!"

It was a dilemma. Ngoniland could be held by agreeing to Ngoni demands, but that meant losing a vital link to Lake Nyasa's waterway of communication and "casting away the Tonga for attack." Meanwhile, Elmslie's wife fell sick and Laws was delayed—things reached a very low point. The connecting road to the lake was closed. They were left in terrible suspense, fearing that all their labours might all be ruined by war. It was truly a dark hour. When Laws wrote from Livingstonia, he said, "We should prepare at both places to be driven out!" Dr. Elmslie made provisions by burying his medicines at night, in carefully sealed and stoppered bottles. They were fearing the worst.

In mid-September, Dr. Laws and some missionaries gathered the Tonga people together and tried to settle the tensions. Giving up their women and children was not an option, in that "the Ngoni stole them in the first place!" There was no solution apart from the Ngoni withdrawing some of their demands. With the breakdown of trust and communication links, the missionaries had to make a decision. Would they abandon the post or stick it out? Fortunately they were guided by courage and conviction: "We must do our best to stick to both stations and trust the Heavenly Father." Letters from Dr. Laws at Bandawe on the lake to the inland Ngoniland missionaries reflected the tension of the times:

> The matter comes to this, we must do our best to stick to both stations if it is possible for you up there to do so with safety. If you must leave, then some other point than Bandawe must be the point aimed at on your return, for to come here would be simply to be fixed in a trap with the rest of us. Tonight I feel that here I have sought to do everything that prudence might suggest for the safety of lives and property. Now we are hemmed in, and we can only await to see what may be the next indications of God's providence, trusting our Heavenly Father to guide us to do what is right, just, and true, and altogether according to His holy will (Elmslie, 244).

Elmslie writes, "For a month longer, the suspense had to be endured...Each letter was closed, not knowing what might transpire before another could be sent...not knowing *what was to be done should the Ngoni rise up.*" Would a fragile peace hold, or would the drums of war be heard again?

It all came down to a very big and very crucial *ndaba*, called by Mombera, on October 27, 1887. The gathering convened at eight in the morning and lasted until four in the afternoon.

"All missionaries must come and live with me," said Mombera.

"But we need our Bandawe station on the lake," they said. "And we need our station in the hills to reach the Ngoni people up there!"

"There will be war."

"There must be no war around our mission stations."

"We will not submit!" It was Mtwaro's group, brother to the chief, who at first was not willing to give up war.

But surprisingly enough, it was around *them* that the resolution was found! Why not build another mission station in Mtwaro's very district! Mombera dragged his feet on the proposal, but his brother Mtwaro was delighted, and the high level gathering of headmen was nodding in agreement.

No one was more delighted than Dr. Elmslie and his band of missionaries after that momentous *ndaba*. If it had gone the other way, the missionaries would have been driven out, the land plunged back into warfare, the work of many years destroyed. A decade later, he looked back:

> With light hearts we went home and soon messengers were speeding through the forest, over hill and mountain torrent, bearing the glad news to our friends who had meanwhile been left in uncertainty at Bandawe. And hearty were our praises that night at worship...The Tonga who had been confined to the station...now freely and joyfully mixed with our Ngoni neighbours. Peace had been declared and at *no time since* has it been broken (Elmslie, 247).

Under the cover of night, the doctor went to his home and dug up the medicines he had buried. The dispensary shelves were full again. A new station was opened in Mtwaro country at Njuyu with schooling and church services. There was a great extension to preaching and teaching. Best news of all was that by

1889, there were several candidates for baptism in Chief Mtwaro's very village.

In January 1890, Elmslie recorded new additions to their staff and the baptism of converts. What delight he must have had in seeing their very first converts, Mawalera and Makara, sons of the witch doctor who had come by night to learn to pray and read, being baptized. Both would turn out to be widely respected Christian leaders. Five new schools were instituted in 1890. It was a great year for evangelism in Ngoniland. "A beginning had been made, and the long, weary years of waiting crowned with liberty to go about and 'heal the sick...and say unto them, the kingdom of God is come nigh unto you."...Our brick building...in a few months proved too small to accommodate the scholars..." (Elmslie, 252).

## "Can this be the Ngoni?"

By the end of 1890, Elmslie was celebrating as his team were baptizing Ngoni converts! Because the father of Mawalera Tembo and his brother Makara was a witch doctor, the brothers were very familiar with the ceremonies and had even been initiated into the practice in days gone by. But now, Mawalera "carries a peculiarly happy countenance, and his merry laugh makes him a favourite with all classes. From the first his profession of Christianity has been frank and powerful. Those who know him understand how, in private discussion and by personal testimony, always given humbly and with respect for his seniors, his influence has been wide and permanently good."

His brother moved to the new site as a teacher, "where he was most successful with the work, leading to the conversion of many."

He was the means of breaking the war-spirit in that district, and one of the first converts was the eldest son of the chief, who before was a notoriously passionate and cruel man, and ruled his slaves with an iron hand. His first act was to give his slaves their freedom...Nawambi, the ferocious war-dancer...became a new man...under Makara's influence, and a school has been carried on in his district, also by Makara (Elmslie, 286).

The "first fruits" were now bearing more fruit! Elmslie concluded:

Within a short space we had given up two European workers in Ngoniland and developed native agency...a real advance, proving both the permanence of the work among the natives, and the possibility of speedily evangelizing the country by means of native agents. Africa must be evangelized by the African, and although our native helpers are only moderately equipped, their work and influence serve to show that [with] more fully trained agents...we may hope for greater results than we now see (Elmslie, 287).

As for the Ngoni, "in former days the troublers of their mission stations," they were now in their new character "as peaceful worshippers of God." They were very ready to assist a far distant mission at Mwenzo with construction. This was like the transformation of the Corinthians, whom Paul categorizes among the worst of transgressors:

Do you not know that the wicked will not inherit the kingdom of God? Do not be deceived: neither the sexually immoral nor idolaters nor adulterers no male prostitutes nor homosexual offenders nor thieves nor the greedy nor drunkards nor slanderers nor swindlers will inherit the kingdom of God. **And that is what some of you were.** But you were washed, you were sanctified, you were justified in the name of the Lord Jesus Christ and by the Spirit of our God (1 Corinthians 6:11, emphasis added).

*"Such were some of you!"* (KJV). The exclamation reads like a great shout of triumph. The gospel has prevailed! Old inveterate sinful habits have been dislodged! Towering strongholds that seemed immovable have come crashing down! This was the Ngoni experience of 1890.

> Now the Mwenzo people...who knew the Ngoni only as cruel warriors, raiding their neighbours...saw them in their midst with the implements of peaceful labour in their hand, and the Word of God in their hearts, and on their tongues...They aided in the work...at the same time by life and word, proclaimed the reason of the change in their manner of life. The effect of this has been very great! (Elmslie, 288.)

By 1896, the region was part of British Central Africa and the Commissioner, Sir Harry Johnston, sought to administer it. Elmslie writes,

> The Ngoni remain to this day the only tribe not under the direct jurisdiction of the British government. They are, however, no less helpful than others in the great task of the redemption of Africa...Many hundreds go every year to the coffee plantations of the Shire Highlands, and to the trading corporations...where they prove steady and successful labourers, without whom...the commercial interest could not prosper...all through the preaching of the gospel of Christ (Elmslie, 295).

So deeply had the gospel taken hold in the tribe that when paramount chief Mombera was to be succeeded, a call was made to Mawalera Tembo to be present and "remain throughout the ceremony," as they did not wish to do anything wrong.

> It might be said that our teacher-evangelist was the most important individual there, as he was consulted on every point. He turned the occasion to good account by

conducting religious worship, and subsequently addressing the assembly on the foundation of good citizenship and good government, charging the chief to rule his people by the word of God, and *forever sheath the sword* of his fathers (Elmslie, 296).

Surely no one's joy on that festive occasion surpassed that of Dr. Walter Elmslie, about to depart on furlough: "One of the first acts of the new chief, Mperembe...was to request that schools be established in all his villages and he himself desired to become a pupil."

Missionary Donald Fraser, "the man who made friends," arrived in Ngoniland at this time and enjoyed the fruit of Elmslie's labours, baptizing twenty-nine at Ekwendeni and ten more at Hora, including "the young son of their chief," forty-four at Njuyu, and many more. On four successive Sundays in Ngoniland, eight adults were admitted into membership of the church while several hundreds professed their faith. The last of the doors in Ngoniland were opened to the work of the mission. The number of schools had been increased so that sometimes as many as 4,000 students were under instruction. Ten years earlier, the first schools with twenty-two scholars had been opened.

> They now leave school able to read the word of God for themselves, and possess a copy of it...The people who were wont to steal rather than work, now give a month's labour for a copy of the Bible...Men with the marks of old battles on their bodies may be seen earnestly labouring at what once was considered ignoble work, in order to own a copy of the precious word of God (Elmslie, 303).

When a large communion service was held among the Ngoni at Ekwendeni, May 1898, hospitality and fellowship prevailed— and a Tonga observer could not believe his eyes:

As I saw this I marvelled...small companies gathered by themselves for prayer and many melted to tears—as I saw these I greatly marvelled...Then...as I saw those who were to be baptized coming forward one by one, and receiving the rite until Mr. Fraser's arm grew tired...I saw men with scars of spears and clubs and bullets on them...I said in my heart, "Can these be the Ngoni submitting to God, the Ngoni who used to murder us, the Ngoni who killed the Henga, the Bisa, and other tribes?" And then at the Lord's Table, to see these people sitting there in the still quiet of God's presence, my heart was full of wonder at the great things God had done (Elmslie, 306).

A visitor from Britain was traveling with Fraser during these times and recalled a great baptismal gathering in 1898:

The first comers were from Mperembe's, the raiding chief who had only recently agreed to have schools...By Tuesday evening the footpaths were full. Whole families were coming, the mothers and daughters carrying cooking pots on their heads and bags of flour...Most of them were dressed in snowy white calico...We could see them coming along straggling Indian file, which changed into solid masses as they crossed the river...It was then that I realized the nature of the work that was being done among the Ngoni. The swinging pace could not be mistaken...It was the fighting men, the men in the prime of their strength that the gospel had laid hold of. A fitter looking set of men and women it would be hard to find anywhere. What a promise they are of the speedy coming of the kingdom of Christ in that land (Elmslie, 308).

By Saturday, over 3,000 people surrounded the 195 who were to be baptized. The visitor recorded:

Such a sight was never before seen among us, and rarely in the whole history of the spread of our faith. Oftener than once the head that was bowed before us, as they came forward to receive the rite, was scarred with an old wound; for several of these baptized had taken part in the very last raid of this section of their tribe. It was a wonderful ingathering that we were privileged to see...The day was of the Lord (Elmslie, 314).

## An African Pentecost

If there was ever a missionary one might like to have met, it was Donald Fraser of Livingstonia, "the man who made friends." Coming on the Ngoniland scene from the Keswick Convention just as Elmslie was enjoying these much-celebrated breakthroughs, he started out conducting baptisms at different stations in 1899. He remained on the scene until 1913. Fraser held "a preeminent place among African missionaries of this century." His biographers record that "throughout a great part of Nyasaland he was the chief founder of a new civilization and the spiritual father of a people. He was one of the most romantic and captivating of missionary pioneers. Beyond everything else he was a great Christian." A compact biography by his wife, Agnes, is said to portray the man "as his friends knew him, the many-sided, versatile, Greatheart, the prophet, the evangelist, the happy crusader for Christ."

One account finds Fraser with some Ngoni teachers, raking around the gravesite of the late Bishop Steele, who had died prematurely in Ngoniland in 1879:

Dr. Elmslie and Mr. Stuart had been telling their newly arrived colleague of the superstitious horror with which the Ngoni regard a grave; so taking a hoe, Fraser went forward and began to clean the ground himself. By and by the teachers approached, very silent. Presently they began to converse in whisper. Fraser continued his work, occasionally making a remark about Dr. Steele, who had won a great place in the heart of the people in the short time he had lived among them. At last a teacher approached, and inquired, "Do you want to do this alone?"

"No, if you like you may clean up too; Steele would be glad to know that the teachers love him still." In a few minutes as many as could were down on their knees silently removing the weeds, and cleaning down the encircling bricks. When they had finished he suggested that they should pray together, and beside the little mound they knelt, two of them asking God to teach them, too, to live and die for others. Then quietly, without noise or laughing, they finished their work and went away.[6]

Agnes Fraser wrote, "It was in this way, not by argument or scorn, but by silently encouraging them to overcome their fears, that he began the long campaign against superstition. He hated its hold, for he saw in all its stark reality the suffering and cruelty and terror to which it gave rise."

He was also very opposed to the oppression of women and they were among the "friends" that "Frasara" made in Africa: "He was keen that the degradation that so appalled him in Africa should be overcome, and a fight put up for the Christian ideal." His very considerate treatment of women was noted in a small incident by Mrs. Fraser:

The intuition of the best of the women made them appreciate his attitude towards them. When I asked one of them one day about a case of discipline in which I was interested, she replied, "She has confessed it all to us women; we will try to help her. But we are very grateful that Frasara says the men of the session need not hear all the story. He has chosen many good ways for us women."

When he was in South Africa, each Sunday the Christian women had to hear any news of him that had come, and they always prayed for his work. "He's back; he's back!" this woman elder came rushing to tell me when the distant sound of his bicycle had been heard. "Yes and Oh! Mama, my heart was welcoming long before my ears caught the sound of his coming." Well might they feel like that! Not only did he recognize their need and possibilities and plan for their proper place in the community but he took infinite trouble on their behalf (Fraser, 193).

## A Pentecostal Outpouring

It was in the same season that the Ngoni experienced a Pentecostal outpouring! Of course, 1910 was the time when the Asuza Street revival was in full sway in distant Los Angeles. It was the birth of the Pentecostal movement in America. But who knew that at the same time the people of Ngoniland would experience their own Pentecost! Indeed the great promise of a last days' outpouring of the Spirit upon "all flesh" was being fulfilled on the other side of the planet as another "Asuza Street" broke out among Zambia's Ngoni people!

Special meetings had been called by Mr. Fraser among the Ngoni in 1910, in the hopes of a divine visitation. He was the interpreter for the visiting speaker, Mr. Inwood of England's Keswick Convention. After two days with a large crowd gathered, Fraser was pretty discouraged. Nothing, it seemed, was being accomplished. "For a day or two, it seemed as if less, rather than more was being made."

By Friday he was all too aware that those who had come with a great thirst and expectancy were not getting what they longed for—and now only two days remained. And so he called his European guests to gather for prayer. Even yet, he said, their great expectations for a move of the Holy Spirit could be met.

Saturday morning, the place was jammed, African style, and

203

Fraser was filled with anxiety for a divine visitation. Mrs. Fraser describes what happened:

> At the end of the address on the Holy Spirit, those who wished to receive the Spirit were asked to stand. Perhaps there was some confusion in their minds as to what was asked of them. There was a pause, and only a few seemed to be standing. Then suddenly a wave appeared to pass over the packed congregation, a murmur of voices, then a rising volume of sound filled the place. Into one's mind instantly came the phrase, "a mighty rushing wind," and no sooner had the phenomenon been so described than it became clear what made that sound. It was 2,500 people, each praying individually, apparently quite unconscious of any other...It had all come suddenly and overwhelmingly upon people who had never before gone through any such kind of religious excitement, their training having been all along the lines of Scottish Presbyterianism. Each had now found a tongue with which to utter this revelation that had come to them. To their missionary moving among them, it seemed that for some it had come as a new sense of need and unworthiness; for others it was the voice of worship and praise.[7]

Thrilled by the gracious move of the Holy Sprit, a group stood outside waiting for Fraser.

> When he came, he caught Dr. Chisholm's shoulder and said, "Chisholm, you are a level-headed chap and a doctor. Tell me what you feel about this?"
>
> "I can only say, 'I believe in the Holy Ghost,'" was the reply.
>
> The wonder and thrill of it lasted through the remainder of the day and the Sunday that followed, and on into the weeks ahead as we travelled along the villages....
>
> The leaders of the church were filled with gladness...there had been confessions and reconciliations...

Again on the Sunday there was the same spontaneous outbreak of prayer. What struck us almost more than anything was to see our cook, not present the Sunday morning for the first time...standing praying with a face that would have served as a model for Stephen's, so transfigured did it seem. The church knew now what Pentecost meant...There was a great awe over the land, for the news of this thing that had happened had spread far and wide (Fraser, 199).

Of course, we know much more a century later. With 100 years of church growth, fuelled by the great Pentecostal outpouring of the Asuza Street revival, which has spanned the years—we can safely put this early Zambian Pentecost under the heading of the Apostle Peter in Acts 2, when he said, *"This is that!"*

No, this is what was spoken by the prophet Joel: "In the last days, God says, I will pour out my Spirit on all people. Your sons and daughters will prophesy, your young men will see visions, your old men will dream dreams. Even on my servants, both men and women, I will pour out my Spirit in those days, and they will prophesy" (Acts 2:16-18).

What the ancient prophet foresaw, and what Peter witnessed, was a very liberal outpouring of the Holy Spirit in the last days, an inclusive event upon all people everywhere. The good news for Zambia was that this 1910 visitation was just the beginning of a mighty outpouring of the Spirit that would lead directly to becoming the "Christian nation."

## Filling the Zambian Sky—
## the Faith Spreads Across Zambia

S uch a dramatic transformation among the Ngoni might well have been all that was needed to transform Zambia. But this was just one beam of the great light of the gospel that was starting to spread across the butterfly nation at the beginning of the twentieth century. This was the dawning of a new day. Livingstone's death had evoked a great missionary response. Only two years after his death, the Free Church of Scotland re-entered the Malawi highlands and founded the Livingstonia Mission Centre, which would generate a tidal wave of evangelism across the southern half of the continent.

Education proved to be the access route to these Zambian tribes. By 1894, a mere decade after Livingstone's death, Livingstonia had built 18 mission schools with over 1,000 pupils in Nyasaland. By 1906, they had 107 schools with over 11,000 pupils. Livingstonia's strong English curriculum, through its Overtoun Institute, soon began to produce strong African leaders. The centre also sent some of its best men to the Bemba, including John Afwenge Banda in 1904, the Chewa evangelist and father of

Dr. Hastings, first president of Malawi. Tonga evangelist David Kaunda, father of Zambia's first republican president Kenneth Kaunda, followed a year later, building up the Chinsali station and guiding rapid expansion.

Hugo Hinfelaar wrote of the Kaundas, David and his wife, Helen:

> Both husband and wife exerted a wholesome influence on the local people, and they accepted Christianity with enthusiasm...Helen Kaunda...was a forceful person with...the spiritual ideal to return to the innate religiosity of the people. This was expressed in the maxim: *Ukubwelela ku chishinte*, to go back to one's origins. She preached a lifelong commitment to monogamy as the moral basis of the clan—family. To stress this commitment, Christian families began to take the totem of their clan as surnames. The evangelists were called *Nkombe*...envoys, heralds, who had come to show the people the new *nshiba ya kwa Lesa*, the way to God. "We knew of course the High God, but we did not know so well the way of talking to Him here on earth," they said...The missionaries were perceived as being the "messengers from the East who brought new hope and vision."[1]

Thus, the seeds sown at Livingstonia's Overtoun Institution were blown all over East and Central Africa.

One of the great early developments was when the mission sent African missionary William Koyi to the Ngoni, speaking their own language. Before long, the newly evangelized Ngoni had produced fifty new hymns with their own flavour. Donald Fraser and others witnessed a corporate exodus from old tribal ways into the church. The Tumbuka-Henga community, which had been driven to near extinction by the Ngoni, was now truly "saved," in the fullest sense of the word.

Meanwhile, the gospel was moving northward into Zambia's Barotseland. By 1875, French missionary Francois Coillard, of the

Paris Evangelical Mission to Lesotho, was building a mission station among the Lozi. Schooling began for the children of Chief Lewanika. In 1894, Coillard opened a Bible school with four pupils. From the south, Baptist congregations in South Africa sent missionaries like D.D. Doke, a well-known expert in Bantu languages. Frederick Stanley Arnot (1858-1914), a true spiritual successor to David Livingstone and fellow Scot, arrived in Barotseland with the Plymouth Brethren. He proceeded to walk through Central Zambia, Angola, and Katanga for thirty years, advancing the gospel and planting mission stations everywhere he went. Methodist ethnologist and Bible translator E.W. Smith arrived in the region in 1902, building up mission stations that produced such African leaders as David Mibiana, the most powerful first-generation preacher of the Zambezi valley. David Funane and Johannes Mdima were also educated in mission schools and joined the ranks of Zambian Christian leaders early in the twentieth century.

But how was sprawling Bembaland to be reached? It was not until the remarkable Dr. James Chisholm, another missionary from Livingstonia, started his Presbyterian hospital there in 1900 that enduring and positive relations with the Bemba people were established. Chisholm was an example of permanence and longevity winning the day for missionary advance. He remained at Mwenzo among the Bemba from 1900 to 1935, starting from scratch. By the time he left, there were nearly 1,400 full church members and 28,000 annual outpatients at his hospital. Other people who "came to stay" built strong relationships with the people and had enduring impact: Malcolm Moffatt, with his station at Chitambo (1900-1930); the Roses of Kamobole (1903-1939); Walter Draper of Kawimbe (1902-1927), who earned the title "best loved man in Central Africa"; and Dr. Walter Fisher of Kalene Hill (1906-1935).

# Moto Moto

Some of these amazing pioneers achieved such favour that they even become temporary chiefs!

The same year that Mwenzo was opened, the White Fathers out of Algeria, known for their white flowing robes, won a foothold in Bembaland with the very outgoing Pér Joseph Dupont (1850-1930). Dupont was nicknamed Moto Moto ("fire fire") by the Bemba people for either his personality or his crack-shot skills with a rifle. He was a pioneer missionary in Zambia's Northern Province from 1885 to 1911. He persuaded the Bemba, who were feared as much by the European colonizers as by neighbouring tribes, to allow him to become the first missionary into their territory around Kasama. At the time the British South Africa Company (BSAC), chartered by Britain to administer Northeastern Rhodesia, was doing its best to assert control on the territory.

Dupont was born in Gesté, Maine et Loire, on July 23, 1850 to a peasant family. After a short stint of military service, he joined the White Fathers missionary society, now called the Society of the Missionaries of Africa. He was sent to the Karema Mission on the northern fringe of Zambia in 1892. Here, the paramount chief of the Bemba, the *Chitimukulu*, opposed any incursion by missionaries. But Dupont, not to be denied, befriended other Bemba chiefs as he moved around the country and found that some of the independently minded chiefs were otherwise minded. One of them, Makasa, gave Dupont a foothold in his area in 1895. Dupont tried to expand his influence into the Bemba heartland, and though he gained favour from many of the chiefs, was still opposed by the Chitimukulu.

A story goes that one day Chitimukulu VII (Sampa Kapalakasha) sent two warriors armed with bows and arrows to kill Dupont. They hid, waiting to ambush him where he used to shoot guinea fowl. Suddenly a bird burst from the bush and Dupont felled it with a single shot. This put them in such awe of his firepower that they stayed hidden and did nothing. Out of such incidents came his nick name, Moto Moto.

On another occasion, the record states that Dupont arrived to follow up on an appointment with Chief Makasa—only to be denied admission! "The chief refuses to see you," they reported.

"Ah, so Makasa refuses to see me?" he shouted. "Well, I don't refuse to see *him!*" And with that, he took his trusty rifle and fired several volleys into the air, announcing his arrival to all within earshot! Moto Moto—the indomitable French peasant priest—had arrived!

## Chief for a Season

Dupont's sending body noted his growing influence among the Bemba and appointed him "First Vicar Apostolic" over a huge stretch of Zambia. As such, he was called upon to oversee a delicate succession event among the Bemba after Chitimukulu VII died. When potential successor Chief Mwamba II fell ill, he sent for Dupont, who managed to nurse him back to health. When the chief died a short while later, his council was sufficiently impressed by Dupont that they asked him to succeed as chief! This was an unheard-of honour for a European, and Dupont humbly accepted for the short term, on the grounds that it would avoid bloodshed. Undoubtedly it was the only time in African history that a European was invited to succeed an African chief!

But this also provoked a crisis. For one thing, the coronation of a new chief required human sacrifice. And secondly, a Bemba civil war was brewing. It was only Dupont's great interpersonal skills, with his knowledge of Bemba culture and traditions, that spared the region a huge conflagration.

"But I cannot accept this position," said Dupont, "without also taking to myself all of Mwamba's wives." It is reported that he said this in jest! Meanwhile, he gathered support from the thirty-three subordinate Bemba chiefs to surrender the region to British control and let them pacify it. This bold move—a Frenchman pushing a territory into the British Empire—probably immortalized Dupont in Zambia's annals of history.

In 1899, this bold peasant priest founded the Chilubula Mission enclave, which still stands today near Kayambi in central Zambia. He held this office until 1911, when he resigned and left for Thibar in Tunisia where the White Fathers had a retirement home. There he died in 1930 and was buried. His impact on Zambia is still commemorated by the Catholic Church. His remains were reburied in 2000 at the church he had built at Chilubula. And today, a museum stands in his honour in northern Zambia: the Moto Moto Museum!

## Indigenous Churches on the Copperbelt!

After World War I, Zambia's Copperbelt, the world's second-largest copper deposit, became a growing population hub. With the expansion of the mines, workers from all over southern Africa flocked there for work. This Copperbelt province is like a constellation of seven towns, with Ndola, Luanshya, Kitwe, and Mufilira forming the corners of a rectangle. Trailing off from them to the northwest, you have Kalulushi, Chingola, and Chililabombwe.

As these mining towns grew, a surprising indigenous African church grew with them. This came as a discovery to the missionary community in 1925, when missionaries further afield passed through: "The phenomenal development of the work at Ndola is the outstanding feature of the year. The secret of its success lies largely in the fact that it is a spontaneous native movement."[2]

That year at Ndola, this autonomous African congregation had elected its own board of elders to organize the work of the church, attend to discipline matters, and recommend candidates for baptism. Sixty-four baptisms had taken place at one local church among the mine workers in 1925. "A considerable fund had been raised, out of which the congregation was supporting its own evangelist. A successful school had been opened and, in their spare time, the Christian miners evangelized not only in the compound but in the Lamba villages round about."

When South African Baptist A.J. Cross came to the Copperbelt in 1927, he again found that a self-supporting, self-governing native church had sprung up among the migrant labour force. But where could the African leadership have come from for such a strong, unexpected, and growing church? Cross discovered that these were Nyasaland believers, products of the schools that sprung up around Livingstonia under Dr. Laws and his team of educators in the first years of the century! They had carried their Christian faith on their migration west, to work in the Zambian copper mines. And an entirely indigenous, growing church was the result.

> Passing through a compound after dark on almost any night, you could find little groups of people gathered round the light of an underground worker's acetylene lamp, singing Christian hymns. At last someone struck the bright idea of building a church, and this they did with their own hands, calling it the Union Church of the Copperbelt (Taylor, 47).

At the Roan Antelope Mine, another indigenous congregation of mine workers spent many Sundays making sun-dried bricks and eventually built a church. This congregation supported their own full-time evangelist, another product of the Nyasaland schools that the missionary educators had established early in the century. These mine workers were fervent Christians, won their fellow miners to Christ, and had regular baptisms. At Mufilira, another active congregation was established among mine workers at the site where the Pentecostal movement made its first appearance. By 1930, Missionary Cross had become familiar with these indigenous churches and registered his amazement at their spontaneous strength:

> A self-supporting, self-governing native church has grown up and it is daily gaining strength and experience. A very vigorous evangelistic work is carried on by the church on its own initiative and responsibility, not only among the mining employees but also in the unevangelized villages...A body of elders ably governs the church; these elders arrange the church's evangelistic programme and the instruction of converts, besides the ordinary services of the church. In the pastoral work they are particularly successful...dealing with difficult cases of discipline or...restoration of erring members.

What impressed Rev. Cross the most was the unity of these indigenous churches, bringing together, as they did, people from many of Zambia's multitudinous tribes:

> ...widely varying tribes, speaking different languages, whose ancestors were once hereditary enemies, are making the grand experiment of working and worshipping in closest unity and cooperation. Not only are they drawn from varying tribes, but their spiritual history is associated with missions of various denominational connections; but they give objective proof of their oneness in Christ (Taylor, 47).

Nothing would have pleased the missionary pioneers more than to hear such a report!

Mission organizations were a bit slow, it seems, to recognize the centrality of the Copperbelt cities for church growth in

Zambia. In the thirties, Anglicans still preferred to do baptisms in the rural areas, rather than around the mines. Yet by 1940, virtually all of the children in Copperbelt schools had left permanent village life behind. Young people were becoming urbanized, and it would be the wise church bodies that opted to follow the trend. Meanwhile, African congregations were allowed to be "the church" on the Copperbelt, forging their own future as they built their own organizations. When various mission groups did come into the field, it was to join hands with a self-governing, self-supporting, self-propagating indigenous African church.

Despite the major slump of the 1930s, which hit the Copperbelt cities hard and reduced labour forces drastically, these mining cities were on a long-term track of growth. Thus, as the Pentecostal movement became established, focusing on the cities became a major and very timely strategy. Here were the centres that would attract the educated, entrepreneurial young Zambians who would be raising their families. While much remained to be done in the rural areas, it was time to prioritize the cities of Zambia and seek to establish strong churches. And it was in the cities that the first Pentecostal ministries began to take root. As early as 1933, Joel Chizakaze had planted the first Apostolic Faith Mission Assembly at the Kantanshi Mine in Mufilira.

The Pentecostal Assemblies of God Zambia grew out of the ministries of Canadian missionaries in the fifties. Jack Muggleton and Robert Skinner seem to have recognized that the future belonged to African leaders and established the Mwambashi Bible College between the Copperbelt towns of Kitwe and Chingola. The fledgling school produced some early leaders for the Pentecostal movement, such as Paul Malesu and Luke Sefuka, with the first recorded graduate in 1967.

According to Adrian Chalwe, the mission thrust was praying and preaching, with Glenn and Ruth Kauffeldt in particular working very hard, leading evangelism teams. Glenn Kauffeldt encouraged prayers for revival in Pentecostal churches in Zambia while Muggleton went on bicycle undertaking door-to-door evangelism. Another notable contribution made by Glenn Kauffeldt, as the first principal of the Bible college, was to insist on high academic standards.[3]

Canadian missionary Scott Hunter relates that when he came to Zambia in 1972, the Pentecostal movement was not advancing; so much so that the Canadian mother body was considering transferring their personnel to other fields. At a major *ndaba* in 1973, at which Hunter must have filled the role of Chief Mombera, the missionaries made a major strategic decision, which may well have set the course for the future of Pentecost in Zambia: "Close down the Mwambashi mission, phase out the Bible school we were operating there, put the missionaries in the cities to pastor the city churches, and go after the young people in the cities."[4]

Thus began a radical change in emphasis and direction. The Pentecostal Assemblies of Zambia became very much an urban presence and directed its evangelism toward the young. Vern Tisdalle assumed the pastorate of the Northmead church in Lusaka and began to change the personality of a largely ex-pat church to a more youthful, Zambian congregation. As Hunter tells it, "the Tisdalles went to UNZA (the University of Zambia) every Saturday for many months with hundreds of invitational handbills cranked out on a hand-powered Gestetner duplicator...Gradually the students began to respond."

Meanwhile, David Way came from Canada to pastor the new-look Eastlea church in the Copperbelt city of Mufulira. Here the emphasis was the same. Hunter records, "Ten years later...the general superintendent, the assistant superintendent, and the principal of the Bible college were all products of David Way's very fruitful ministry in that Mufulira church."

Youth ministry continued to be the focus as the Pentecostal movement gained momentum. At one youth camp, organized by the Northmead church, Hunter relates that "there were about twenty young people who came, and we were thrilled. That weekend seven of them were filled with the Holy Spirit. It is quite possible they were the first youth to have that experience in our churches in Zambia."

Many of these young people had come to the city to get a job and enjoy a better life than that which they had known in the village. The idea of going into Christian ministry was something new that began to burst in on their plans. Missionaries like Hunter had designs on them for ministry:

> We used to talk about getting them in the front door of the church, then getting them to the altar for salvation, then back to the altar to be filled with the Holy Spirit, then back a third time to wrestle with God's calling on their lives. As soon as they made the decision to surrender to that calling, we tried to get them out the back door for training for ministry! That was what these city churches were for; not to become an end in themselves, but to be the first major source of quality personnel who would open Zambia to the gospel.

And so the Pentecostal movement in Zambia expanded among the young. Missionary personnel continued to target youth through 1970s and even into the early 1980s under such missionary pastors as Vern Tisdalle, Ken McGowan, David Way, Elmer Komant, Gary Skinner, Winston Broomes, Bob Seaboyer, P.J. Mitchell, and Ray Callahan.

As young Zambians began to experience revival and respond to God's call upon their lives, the need for ministry training became acute. But was it time to get back to the rural campus at Mwambashi stream? Not at all. This movement was now so thoroughly urbanized that a city centre campus was opened in

Kitwe. Under the inspired leadership of West Indies missionary Winston Broomes and Canada's Brian Rutten, young Zambians were moving strongly into crusade evangelism and church planting. Fourteen very sharp young men comprised the first class on Kanyanta Street and it was evident that a new era in Zambia was unfolding. As former college principal Adrian Chalwe puts it, "The graduands of this period have put the PAOGZ on the Zambian map through their revivalistic preaching. Zambia's religious verve has been permanently transformed by the graduates of 1980. It is no wonder that they...called themselves 'the pioneers' of the PAOGZ."[5]

In some ways, this was the Ngoni miracle relived. Christian education among young candidates for Christian ministry—again this turned out to be the key. It would unlock the nation for gospel penetration. It would raise up a host of very able, world-class leaders. It would see the establishment and expansion of major city churches across Zambia.

## Oliver Mulenga

Our friend and colleague, Oliver Mulenga, was born in 1947 and grew up in Moto Moto Catholicism in Bemba country. He was raised in Luapula Province, by then largely Roman Catholic, and was on route to the priesthood. But by a stroke of divine fortune, he was spared those austerities and had the joy of marrying Petronella and producing his beautiful family of nine children—and, currently, about the same number of grandchildren!

It seems only fitting that today he leads an "Advocates for Life" ministry, which provides help and counsel for young women with unwanted pregnancies!

*"Is abortion a problem in Zambia?"*

"Yes. Officially it is illegal, except under certain circumstances. But it has become virtually 'on demand' in hospitals and clinics, and the government is doing nothing about it. It is safer than it used to be, but still not at all the right choice."

*Are you okay with encouraging women to keep their babies when they can't afford to take care of them? Is abortion in Zambia a desperate measure for people who are poor?"*

"Yes, I'm very much okay. I have plenty of women coming back to see me and thanking me for helping them keep their babies. The women are doing well and the babies are their delight. Why would anyone want to deprive themselves of this new life? We even help them find a skill!"

I say it is fitting. Oliver has found such joy in his own remarkable family of engineers, pastoral leaders, soccer players, enterprising daughters, lawyers, and entrepreneurs, his home always full of the sound of young voices—it seems only right that he should be encouraging others to enjoy such blessings!

"Back then," he says, harking back to the fifties, "Catholic missionaries came down from Chilubula and set up seminaries and schools around Kasama and my village of Mporokoso. I was the goalkeeper for a city team while attending the seminary where my grandfather had me to train for the priesthood after secondary school. My grandfather loved football and used to come to watch me play. And I was picked up by another team.

"One game was very tight and came down to a penalty shot between our team and the seminarians. It turned out that I stopped the shot! Well the seminarians wanted to reclaim me for their school, asking, 'What are you doing attending that heathen school?'

"'No, Father,' I said. 'I am an only child and I promised my mother a large family.' That seemed to satisfy him!"

While in that secondary school Oliver first heard the message of salvation from friends and teachers.

"I heard the voice of God on three occasions calling, 'Oliver.' And my school friends were telling me I had to be *born again*. 'Born again?' I said. 'I was baptized when I was two weeks old in 1947! What are you talking about!'

"But I started thinking about my Catholic faith, built so much in those days upon confession and mass. Their teaching was that you must be holy to enter heaven. And holiness comes through the Mass and Confession. But I was worried about the in-between times! I remember watching a man cutting branches high in a tree and thinking, 'What if he should fall from that height and die instantly? Would he be holy enough to go to heaven?'

"'Why don't we just pray, Oliver,' my friend said. 'You've got nothing to lose.'" Oliver's friends were pushing for a decision. Finally they were leading Oliver Mulenga to Christ. "We got beyond talking about it and started praying about it. And that's when I invited Jesus into my heart. Secondary school! It was a great day!"

After graduation, Oliver was leaving those friends behind and heading for the big cities, like all the youth of Zambia. Off to the Copperbelt, where jobs were abundant! Soon he was working in an accounting firm, with a wife and three children, but no church that he could call "home."

God gave me a dream where I was walking along the road and came to a beautiful church. But in the dream I walked straight on. I passed a second church and a third, just walking down the road. Finally I came to the worst-looking church in the world, at the very end of the road, no decorations, only one beautiful cross. The voice said, "Go in there."

That dream came true when I discovered Emmanuel Pentecostal Church in Ndeke, meeting in a primary school at the end of the road. As always in those early days of Pentecost, the Pentecostals were to be found at the end of the road—in the worst-looking church! These were revival days in Kitwe, and the place was packed—with mostly young people! That same voice came back so strong: "This is where I want you to be.' It turned out that Pentecost was in the air with a lot of fervour.

"God is calling you! What are you ready to sacrifice for a truly Spirit-filled and dedicated life?" A young preacher named Chachi Chongo was talking about getting rid of idols.

"You!" he said, before he even knew me. "Your idol is football!" He had that part right. "You need to put that on the altar and let God fill every corner of your life with the Holy Spirit!" So that was what I did. I knelt down and released *my team*, the Power Dynamos, to God—and right away the Holy Spirit just took over in my life.

The amazing thing was that my love for football was gone just like that. I never watched football again, even on TV. The only time I was back to a football match was ten years later—when I came back with the chaplain to pray with the players!

Oliver speaks of very inspiring days of crusades and evangelism in the Zambia Copperbelt, his new home, and of great revival among the youth. Reinhard Bonnke Crusades were breaking out across Zambia, huge soccer stadiums filled with searching people, and brought a special dimension of the power of the Spirit to Zambia.

"What a move of the Spirit we enjoyed!" recalls Oliver. "That uplifting of the Spirit and the joy—it was just irreplaceable. Our Emmanuel Church was a drawing place for people from all over the Copperbelt. We had overnight prayers. We impacted a lot of young men and women who are spiritual leaders today." Frederick Chachi Chongo was part of that mix.

Harrison Sakala. Enula Chibale. Young lives being transformed who would become shapers of the Pentecostal movement in Zambia for years to come.

"One night I was thrown into the fire and had to interpret for Ernest Angley," says Oliver. "He was having a crusade in Wusakile! What a night it was! I received a call from Nwaka about an hour before the service. 'The stadium is packed! Kafwimbe has lost his voice! We need you to interpret for the evangelist!'

"What a night it was! Even the president showed up unannounced! And there I was interpreting for this man I had never met! It was unforgettable. I tell you, deaf ears were being opened. And the dumb went speaking and hearing!"

So that was the start of a lot of interpreting for Oliver Mulenga. And in the process, he got to see God working in powerful ways on a nation that was ready for the move of the Spirit. "It was raining cats and dogs at Buchi for Pretorius," he says. "No one went away."

Revival was in the air! Bonnke crusades were bringing thousands into God's kingdom, one attracting a record audience of 10,000 people every day to the big yellow tent pitched in Buchi (Kitwe). The Matero Stadium crusades in Lusaka and other crusades in the agriculture showgrounds drew tens of thousands to hear the gospel. God was moving upon Zambia in most powerful ways.

One of our students—whose ancestors lived in Ngoniland!—came to Christ at the great Matero Stadium Crusade in Lusaka, 1985:

> I was in the crowd that filled the playing field. The power of God was so strong in the stadium...Rev. Bonnke often shouted, "Zambia shall be saved!" as he preached. At one point as he was preaching, it was like the power of God fell upon the place and everyone, on the whole playing field,

fell to the ground. It was wonderful. When I rose up, I knew the only thing that mattered to me was to serve God.

And what a transformation! Today, thirty years later, Tembo is a very active evangelist and church planter, very much in the Bonnke stream, specializing in those who have never heard, preaching deliverance, planting churches, holding crusades, all over the rural stretches of Zambia.

One of Bonnke's interpreters during those revival days was Nevers Mumba, who at twenty-one had mastered the skill. After a season of studies, he established Victory Ministries in Zambia, with TV and crusade exposure on the theme "Zambia Shall be Saved." It was a great loss to evangelism, so we hear, when Nevers opted for politics over preaching, even though he met with some success along the way. When he was appointed vice president by the late president Levi Manawasa in 2001, even the BBC took note:

> Never in the history of Zambian politics has someone's rise to power been so meteoric as that of Nevers Mumba. Almost overnight, Mr. Mumba moved from being an unimpressive opposition leader to holding the country's second most prestigious political job. But who is he? He is perceived as a man who is driven as much by his deep religious conviction as his boundless ambition...In his own words, he heard God telling him to save Zambia through the ballot box. His vision is to cleanse the country of corruption and improve the living standards of ordinary Zambians (BBC News, June 2, 2003).

## Local Church Revivals

While great crusades filled the land, local churches were also enjoying days of spectacular revival. Not only was the Emmanuel

Church in Ndeke pulsating with young life and raising up the future leaders of the Pentecostal movement in Zambia, but to the north, in Mufilira, God was doing amazing things. Missionary pastor David Way used to bring out his accordion, and as he played, God's Spirit began to move. South African George Holloway was working in the mine workshops and evangelized most of the workforce. One of his co-workers was George Mbulo, good friend and sometime member of the Sky Banda Rock Band, which was quite a force at social occasions in town. Sky was the leader of the band and considered himself invited at most any social event in the city. But George Mbulo was so deeply changed that the other band members took notice. He invited them to join him at Eastlea Church and hear David Way play his accordion— it surely was not the music that reached them!—and one by one all the members of that band, future preachers and revivalists all, bowed their knees before the Lord.

Sky Banda may have been the hardest to wave the flag of surrender, because God had to visit him in a dream and tell him that this could be his last opportunity to get right. So vivid was that dream that Sky was down on his knees beside his bed before morning, turning his life over to the Lord. Such was the power of those revival days in Mufilira that a half dozen outstanding Zambian leaders emerged to have a wide and lasting impact upon the spiritual life of the nation, leading evangelistic thrusts and building major churches. Sky Banda went to Trinidad for early training and ministry, then returned to Zambia to assume the pastorate of the Maranatha Church at the centre of the Copperbelt, with his great gifting for evangelism. Hundreds of people responded to the call to salvation under his ministry. George Mbulo, Green Phiri, Sky Banda—these were the pioneers of Pentecost in Zambia, all emerging from one Mufilira church, under a wave of revival. A rock band playing a new tune!

Canadian Don Schellenberg held a powerful crusade at Kitwe's Freedom Park, today mostly taken over by a gigantic mall. Back in the eighties, malls were unknown in Zambia, but the gospel filled Freedom Park! Harrison Sakala stepped forward at that crusade and committed his life to Christ. After a season with the youth movement of Emmanuel Church, Harrison trained for ministry and went to plant the outstanding Peniel Church in Kasama, 1989. He tells of sleeping at the bus stop when he first came to town, looking for a place to live and start up his church. It wasn't long until the revival fires that were burning elsewhere started up in Kasama and the Peniel church really took off. Again, these were days of targeting the young. My colleagues Victor Chanda and Gabriel Mumba, now leaders of our Christian University in Kitwe, were among the converts and youth leaders at Peniel. They tell of how they were launched into street-corner evangelism and church planting almost immediately, young Christians preaching on the streets of Kasama, winning more youth to Christ, starting up cell groups in various parts of the city. Revival days! Large crusades for evangelism! As with the products of their sister churches, today the young people of Peniel Assembly, Kasama, are academic and pastoral leaders all over Zambia. One church, blowing seeds of blessing all over the nation.

So Oliver Mulenga, director of Advocates For Life, has seen it all in the Zambian Pentecostal movement. Small beginnings, amazing growth. I can't resist the urge to ask him what he thinks of the "Christian Nation" declaration.

"This is not man's scheme," he says. "God ordained this." He tells of prayer movements around the time of the declaration in 1991, prayer that was going on globally, people sharing prayer chain material from Canada and New Zealand, all praying for Zambia.

"Many people joined us for inter-church prayers at the YMCA—noon-hour prayer times. At the Anglican Hall, we gathered and prayed for the nation. This was a critical time...the end of the Kaunda era. No one could talk against Kaunda, even though he had become very dictatorial in imposing some strange humanistic doctrines and gotten into eastern religions...with a lot of demonic associations. We used to pray and bind those powers, especially just before the elections."

*"So you believe the Declaration was an answer to prayer?"*

"One hundred percent answer to prayer," says Oliver. "A prophecy came from New Zealand saying that God was going to bring wealth into this nation and that it was going to be a new season, people whose languages you have never heard. Another prophecy spoke of mineral wealth...stones that you don't even know you have. We knew good things were coming. So when Chiluba declared a Christian nation, we felt it was a confirmation of what God had already been saying."

More recently, Oliver had a gratifying moment when he heard the aged Kaunda, much-loved ex-president, now in his mid-nineties, strongly affirming his Christian faith and endorsing the declaration of Zambia as a Christian nation.

"He even prayed for the nation!" says Oliver. "He said, 'No one will change Zambia from being a Christian nation...I pray against those negative forces that are arrayed against our declaration.' It was wonderful to hear!"

*"So what does the Christian nation declaration mean to you?"*

"It means privilege to worship God at any time, with no fear, no interference. It is a blessing. An answer to prayer. When you declare something, it is a prospect for good. Things will happen as you have prophesied. *One Zambia, one nation.* The prophecy itself wings unity. Whatever is declared shall be. It is the power of the Word."

226

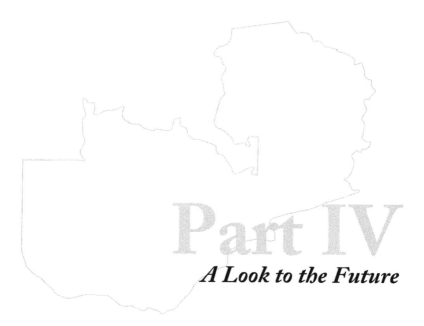

# Part IV

## *A Look to the Future*

# Chapter 11

## *The Butterfly Is Endangered*

We have dedicated a few pages to admiring our butterfly nation. It has emerged from a pretty unpromising chrysalis, that is for sure. Like the beautiful butterfly that breaks out of a moulted caterpillar larva, hanging for dear life to a leaf, it is a miracle birth. Like the Messiah, it sprung "like a root out of dry ground." And it has some incredible, dynamic vital signs—of that there is no doubt. The church of Zambia is officially part of the new "centre of global Christianity." That much we have attempted to note.

All that remains are a few parting glances into the future, which even the best of prophets do not see clearly. We are dealing here with "impressions." If we register some levels of concern, under "The Butterfly Is Endangered," they may be classified as personal concerns from some who are mostly on the ground.

And of course, we must affirm grounds for optimism, related to those things that always enable a church to thrive. These we classify under our heading, "Butterflies In Flight." We suggest here that the Zambian butterfly is poised for flight. The gospel has come to her at much too high a price and flourished too miraculously to be misspent on in-house promises of quick-fix prosperity. The reason for Zambia to have been given the faith is surely for it to shine brightly—and share the light of the world with others. The best way to keep the faith, as they say, is to give it away.

Then we close with a reflection on the new birth, "The Ultimate Metamorphosis."

## Trickle-Down Christianity

It seems the main issue, when people talk of the depth of Zambia's faith, is whether it filters down into people's daily lives. Or is it more like a layer of film that floats on the surface of the sea? Is there genuine, lifestyle transformation taking place, *"old things pass away, all things become new"* sort of thing? People speak of "trickle-down economics," which advocates reducing taxes on the wealthy as a means to stimulate business investment in the short term and benefit society at large in the long term. The people at the top invest and build businesses; those at the bottom receive the benefit as jobs are created. Sometimes it might even work! But can we have "trickle-down Christianity"?

Occasionally a visitor will run into corruption in Zambia and will share the impression that the Christian faith has not trickled down very deep in the Christian nation. Where are the ethics and integrity? Such posts, like the visitors, come and they go. Many times it's "in one ear and out the other."

But these days, it's not only visitors who are saying such things. It is people like Minister of Labour and Social Security Joyce Simukoko, who is developing a national productivity policy to promote a positive work culture and increase employee productivity: "The Zambian workforce," she says, "has generally been associated with poor attitudes toward work, manifested through poor time-keeping, poor quality of work and dishonesty, among others." As a result, "the country's overall productivity has only been increasing at an average rate of 4.6 percent per year against a target of 7 percent while productivity in the formal sector declined by an average of 3 percent per year."[1]

It is people like Maureen Munachonga, whose very high-end Masters dissertation for the University of Zambia chronicles examination malpractice in a thorough study of Lusaka schools:

> Examination malpractices were a big problem in Lusaka as they tended to virtually destroy the moral integrity of the persons involved. This results in a society with a corrupt and incompetent future workforce. By distorting the very essence of education, society tended to be more at a loss than a gain in terms of socio-economic performance because, most often, the certificates achieved did not reflect the actual capabilities of the holder.[2]

It is people like the Honourable Brown C.K. Kapika, President for Adedo-Zamucano Political Party, who writes:

> Since corruption is not new and since it is a global phenomenon, it is not peculiar to Zambia. However, corruption is pandemic in Zambia...the political leaders as well as the followers are corrupt. Consequently, it has defied all the necessary medicines. If there is a lack of control of corruption in every sphere in the nation, it is then like the old saying, when water chokes you, what do you take to wash it down?[3]

It is people like the church elder in the Seventh-Day Adventist Church (SDA) in Nakonde district in Zambia's Northern Province, who says exposure to internet and pornography has contributed greatly to the moral decay and unbecoming behaviour among the youths in the border town. Elder

Musukwa says there is a need "to regulate what information or material is exposed to the youths so as to have decent youths who would grow up into responsible citizens of the country."

> He also charged that some parents have contributed to the diminishing moral fibre in society because of their failure to promote decent dressing among their children. Elder Musukwa said a good parent ensures that a child is well dressed before leaving home, adding that poor dressing that exposes essential parts of the body has resulted into a number of rape and defilement cases.
>
> Elder Musukwa also said broken homes are a source of social problems affecting the community. He said there is need to promote strong marriages that will be responsible for the good upbringing of the children. Elder Musukwa said there is need for couples to be faithful to each other, saying there should be no sex outside marriage as it is a recipe for social ills in the community.
>
> The church elder called on the Christian community to be prayerful in order for them not to be tempted into sinning, saying Zambia is a Christian nation and therefore, there is need to promote good morals among its citizens.[4]

In short, there are a host of Zambians from all sectors of society bemoaning the fact that there is no such thing as trickle-down Christianity. The declaration does not mean transformation. It does not mean consistent strength in areas of morality and ethics.

## Declaration Without Transformation

Indeed, it is the president himself who raises such concerns. In March 19, 2017, the Zambia *Daily Mail* recorded:

> During his address to the nation through Parliament on Friday, President Edgar Lungu expressed displeasure at

the degrading morals and the poor ethics by many Zambians.

President Lungu, who was giving a State of the Nation address, said the ever increasing symptoms of moral decay such as examination malpractices, absenteeism at places of work, child defilement and gender-based violence are worrisome and an indication of the erosion of morals.

In making the constitution, the minds behind it were alive to the moral and ethical values of our society and incorporated them into law as a way of preserving the nation's wellbeing. The underlying principle in upholding morality is that we are social beings who depend on the other. Morals and ethics help us in our relationships with those around us. It is unimaginable what life would be without morals.

This is why we respect people, wish them well, or want to see the best for them merely due to the fact the other is also a human being who deserves what we deserve. It is said ethics are important in guiding us in the choices we make every day. Ethical values and one's views of right and wrong will determine most of the decisions one makes throughout life. We choose to do the right thing because we want things to be well and benefit us all.

At a national level, the laws aid us in upholding morals when they bar us from denying others what rightfully belongs to them. For example, taking away someone's life is not permissible. Furthermore, a nation that does not uphold any moral or ethical values is bound to lose its national identity and is devoid of what it stands for in the eyes of its neighbours.

While these are doing their part, there should be a willingness on the part of individuals to uphold morality and ethical behaviour. For example, the high levels of lawlessness, drunkenness, and laziness that we see on a daily basis can be avoided if individuals have high morals and ethics. Among the youth in the community, we see some of them

233

indulging in underage drinking, watching pornographic material, and other activities that erode morals. What do we expect from such a cadre?

The lack of moral and ethical behaviour is detrimental to the development of a nation. Vices like corruption and theft of national resources are bound to be the norm in the absence of morals and ethics. It is sad to see the levels of corruption in some quarters, where individuals do not just carry out their tasks without being given some money to do so. We have a number of projects that have not reached completion or they have been badly done, all because of a lack of ethics.[5]

On the political side, President Lungu pointed out the lack of morals and ethics as manifesting itself in intolerance and disrespect for one another in Parliament. "Let us seek the unity of the nation at all times. The upholding of morals and ethics begins at the individual level. They should begin with each one of us." The president went on to urge parents, teachers, and religious leaders to be in the lead in inculcating moral and ethical values in Zambians, calling on citizens to "seek God, who changes lives…When we seek the ways of God, we become changed and seek to do good for all the people. The word of God has power to change anyone who wants that change and they will be able to live for the benefit of the nation."

It was a sobering presidential report. In the Christian nation, the president himself was reminding the church of its responsibilities! And no doubt he had it right. Only the church can protect "the Christian nation." It is the only sanctuary that can preserve the butterfly! If the church loses sight of its responsibilities, how can a Christian nation survive? The church is like the habitat of the butterfly Christian nation.

## Loss of Habitat Means Loss of Butterfly

People worry about butterflies because they go extinct—and they're much too beautiful for that. The awesome Mission Blue is one of three rare butterflies that coexist in one place, and one only, on the planet: California's San Bruno Mountain. These butterflies have very specific habitat requirements. They only lay their eggs on one plant species. They are "host-specific butterflies." They rely solely on one plant species for their entire existence, to lay their eggs, to feed the larvae. So the host plant is very essential at all stages of butterfly life: (1) the egg, where life begins; (2) the larva (caterpillar), which emerges from the egg; (3) the "chrysalis" or "cocoon" after the full-grown caterpillar has shed its skin for the last time; (4) the adult, the beautiful butterfly we see filling the sky, which must mate and lay eggs for the next generation.

South Africa's Wolkberg *(Alaena margaritacea)* was so endangered the Lepidopterists Society had pretty much given up on it, scouring its native town of Haenertsburg during one tiny three-week window per year, the flying period of the Wolkberg—in the rainy season! When they finally found it, they were able to help restore the butterfly by rebuilding its habitat.

> There are more than twenty butterflies and moths listed as endangered by the US Fish and Wildlife Service. Most of these species are found in the United States and may become extinct due to loss of their habitat. Some butterflies from other countries, such as some rare birdwing butterflies from New Guinea, are endangered by loss of habitat and by collection of specimens for international trade.[6]

Loss of habitat. If the safe places for breeding are removed by deforestation, plantations, pollution, or development, the butterflies are lost. They need that sanctuary to survive. They need their hallowed forests deep in the heart of Mexico, they need lichens, they need milkweed. Remove their sanctuary, you remove the butterfly.

# 1. Strengthening the Habitat

The church is the habitat for Zambian Christianity. It is only the church that will foster the reproduction, growth, and longevity of the faith. Thus the question posed by a recent guest is a searching one. Is the church calling people to repentance and holy living? Is it, as the president put it, "teaching people how to live"? Or is it engaged in something closer to entertainment?

Femi Adeleye of the Lausanne Commission bemoans the effect of the prosperity preaching in Africa:

> The "prosperity gospel," which is also variously referred to as the "health and wealth gospel," "Name it, claim it gospel," or "Gospel of greed," is one of the fastest growing emphases within the contemporary church. Initially prominent in Pentecostal and Charismatic churches, it has now spread across various denominations and church traditions. This gospel focuses primarily on material possessions, physical well-being, and success in this life, which mostly includes abundant financial resources, good health, clothes, housing, cars, promotion at work, and success in business as well as other endeavours of life. This gospel asserts that believers have the right to the blessings of health and wealth and that they can obtain these blessings through positive confessions of faith and the "sowing of seeds" through the faithful payments of tithes and offerings. The extent of material acquisition and well-being is often equated with God's approval. Although the Bible affirms that God cares enough to bless his people and provide for their needs—and although there are legitimate ways to work for such needs to be met—this gospel often makes the

pursuit of material things and physical well-being ends in themselves. Scripture is always applied and sometimes mis-interpreted or manipulated to promote the main emphasis of the "prosperity gospel."[7]

On a similar note, our colleague Dr. Victor Chanda wants to know where Word Faith preachers find their hermeneutics:

It is difficult to establish a fully developed hermeneutic in the word of faith movement. The problem is compounded by the fact that in the word of faith movement, emphasis is placed on the *rhema* (a direct revelation from God) and not so much on the written word...This direct revelation of God's will and mind through his word and prayer is seen as a purer form of knowledge and source of scriptural meaning than that which can be attained through the intellect in formal training and study in biblical exegesis and hermeneutics. This attitude [means that]...revelation comes from the Bible. The Bible is packaged in letters. But behind the letters is *rhema*.

This view of the Bible is highly subjective to such an extent that the discipline of hermeneutics is effectively ren-dered redundant...Simply put, [the word of faith movement] defines *logos* to be the written word of God and *rhema* is the living word or "now" word of God. The major premise of *rhema* doctrine is that whatever is spoken by faith becomes immediately inspired and therefore dynamic in the particular situation or event to which it is addressed.[8]

In his thoroughly researched doctoral dissertation, "The Word and the Spirit," Chanda takes a long look at the word of faith movement, which Africa has "received with both hands." While he recognizes the positives, he underlines the negatives, particularly in the rather cavalier use of scripture:

What motivates hermeneutics in the word of faith move-ment is the underlying desire for every Christian to prosper materially. This naturally results in selective application of biblical texts. Any hint from the Bible on material prosperity becomes indicative that every Christian should become economically successful. They support their arguments by way of proof-texting. Asamoah-Gyadu...in this case argues that "the problem with the prosperity gospel...is its 'proof-texting' method...A key principle in biblical interpretation is that theology must be based on the Bible's total teaching on a subject and not on selective hermeneutics."

It is also important for us to observe that the word of faith hermeneutics is born out of the quest to address certain existential problems that human beings encounter; more especially in a context of poverty and disease. Of course this is not unique to the word of faith movement. As Thomas notes, "The new hermeneutics arises out of the existential interpretation that primarily is concerned with questions of human existence. Thus, it finds its starting point in human beings. The result of trying to understand a text in relation to how it applies to people is that truth is easily relativized."

The main concern is how the passage of scripture applies to the individual. The major challenge in the word of faith movement is how the scriptures can help an individual escape the shackles of poverty. This begs another idea: the role that "men of God" play in mediating the word of God and subsequently material blessings to the faithful. Believers are encouraged to hear what God is saying through such persons. The Bible almost takes a secondary role to the "Man of God"...If the Bible is no longer the clearest or most complete revelation of the mind of God, then the random, often contradictory, and failed "prophecies" and "divine utterances" of many preachers cannot be checked. Adherents, in order to maintain membership in the church community and to find another source of authority, vest the preacher or "prophet" with a kind of authority once reserved for the scriptures.

In my own exposure to Zambian preaching, which is frequent, given three college chapels per week plus an occasional Sunday in the church pew (when I myself am not the preacher under review!) it is not so much that it is bent out of shape by far-fetched, prosperity-oriented interpretation as that it is not *grave*. In other words, it does not recognize the gravity of the day.

All of us as preachers face the temptation to hang onto a word from our devotional reading and then "preach that word"! One of my recent favourites was, "And Herod added this to all his sins, that he threw John the Baptist in prison." What a text! said I. *That* could preach! Why not the title, "Add Yet One More Sin!" I'm sure that it had a lot of imaginative potential! And what we preachers can do with a simple text by applying a little imagination! But no one would connect that, however inspired I may have felt, with "the whole counsel of God."

This is about majoring on minors. When a spiritual leader consistently majors on minors, it is dangerous to butterfly habitat. Rather than building up the lichens and milkweed upon which butterflies thrive, it litters the landscape with imaginative plantations that cannot sustain life. And where are people to run for a safe haven? Where do they turn when their world is breaking down in a society of rapid and revolutionary change? What refuge for the soul is to be found in a church that is consistently majoring on minors? They need that safe and strong habitat for the soul furnished by consistent expository preaching.

We Pentecostals are especially prone to whimsical preaching, I suppose, inclined as we are to being sensitive to what we hear the Spirit saying as we read the word and pray; strongly believing, as we profess, in the "verbal, plenary inspiration of scripture." But just because every word may be equally inspired, every word can hardly have equal *weight!* This would make a mockery of hermeneutics, that most helpful science of biblical interpretation, which proclaims loudly that there is such a thing as "progressive revelation"—by which we mean that the light of truth gets brighter as you move through the scriptures. In other words, the great truths of Romans and Galatians would be something like the brightest light in the Bible, where new life in Christ is most fully explained.

Included in the salutary "whole counsel of God," which is the great task of the pulpit, is preaching on holiness. Holiness preaching has transformed the church radically in days gone by. Pentecostals are especially indebted to holiness preaching, springing as we do from holiness movements. How is it now possible that its preachers would bypass holiness—"without which no one shall see the Lord?"

This is fundamental. It is great holiness preaching that brings people to their knees. It is great holiness preaching that kick-starts revival. It was great holiness preaching by Jonathan Edwards in one single church that ushered in *The Great Awakening* of 1740, which thoroughly Christianized America. America became, at that time, "a Christian nation," not by declaration, but by revival, a revival that was birthed in holiness preaching. When Edwards stood to preach his famous sermon of 1741, "Sinners in the Hands of an Angry God," there were no dramatics. The man was professorial and used to read his sermons with small reading glasses. Yet as he preached, people started falling out from their benches. Such was the power of Edwards' preaching, that his entire profligate town of Northampton came under immense conviction. Walking the street, people were arrested by the Holy Spirit and fell to their knees. The fear of God gripped an entire community out of one church! From that community revival spread to the next, and soon across a region until it engulfed the entire eastern seaboard. The result was America's *Great Awakening,* which ushered some 300,000 people into the kingdom of God over two decades and birthed many of America's major church bodies and institutions. Ultimately, of course, the Great Awakening greatly impacted the whole world.

Perhaps Zambia, the "butterfly Christian nation," needs a revival of something similar as we enter the twenty-first century. If Edwards' town of Northampton was overrun by drunkenness and immorality, what has overrun Zambia? If Zambia faces a moral crisis and if those who are charged to preach holy living were to slide into quick-fix theology, the foundations would be destroyed, as the psalmist said, and "what shall the righteous do?" The moral gatekeepers of Zambia need to hold to their primary calling. Somehow the voice of a Jonathan Edwards needs to be heard again throughout the land, raising the call for holiness.

## 2. Dealing with Ground Level Pollution

Mexico hosts about 100 million Monarch butterflies during the cool winter months, and these beauties create as much elation when they arrive as when they emerge from the forests the following year to migrate north, into the US and Canada. But scientists are very concerned about the diminishing number of dazzling monarchs in the air. They need milkweed in order to survive. And the milkweed plant is dying along its migration routes. But what is killing the milkweed?

> Development has wiped out much of the natural habitat for this species. The monarch requires the milkweed plant, on which its caterpillars feed, to survive. But the amount of milkweed is diminishing as cities expand. Ground level ozone, the major component in smog, kills milkweed. Even when thriving, milkweed is purposely destroyed because it

is considered a noxious weed. In rural areas where crops are sprayed, milkweed can absorb pesticides that are fatal to butterflies.[9]

Perhaps a layer of moral smog has settled over the Christian nation in recent years, and its effects can be just as deadly. Evangelist Herbert Shabula smells it in the air:

> The escalating moral decay amongst the youth and children is resulting from the immorality some parents and guardians are exhibiting in homes.
>
> What you see is what you become. It is what you are and it is what you will do. So the issue here is that pictures or certain literatures will determine the kind of life that you are going to live. That is why we have ratings for TV; there is PG13, PG18, which is called parental guidance. You are told that a child of this age should not read or watch this in order to control their viewing.
>
> Those pictures are immoral. They are sent to corrupt the minds of a human being. Just by looking at a picture, that picture will set you in a certain position whereby you begin thinking in reverse; you don't do things correctly because of the influence of the picture.[10]

The evangelist urges parents to embrace and stick to their roles of educating and positively impacting their children's lives and to be cautious of their actions if they were to raise their children into responsible citizens.

### *How to Withstand the Waves of Contaminants*

How to withstand the waves of ungodly junk that fill the airwaves in the modern world is a challenge to Christian people worldwide. It's no wonder that the Christian nation is sharing the blight. We might even wonder if the Christian nation is not a particular target. Why not sully the airwaves of the Christian nation so that it's almost impossible for the "glory of the Lord to be revealed"?

Fortunately, the Lord puts a protective shield around his people so that they are not choked up by the smog of our daily environment. *"Thou, O Lord, art a shield for me,"* said the psalmist. *"My glory and the lifter up of mine head"* (Psalm 3:3 KJV). We can claim such expressions as our own. At the same time, it is kind of presumptuous to continually walk into unclean environments. And here is where the church and the homes of the Christian nation need to help their members, by talking about "no-go" zones.

Unfortunately, we are welcoming no-go zones *into our homes* when we give free reign to television and the media. These are "a very present hurt" in the average Christian home worldwide. The Christian community needs to be aware and proactive in terms of restriction and controls. We asked Google the question, "How do we keep TV filth out of our homes?" and sure enough came up with a lot of interesting comments. One that stood out was "13 Ways Pornography Leaks into your Home and How to Stop It."[11] Among other things, the article alerts the reader to:

- mobile devices needing a software filter;

- YouTube ads and related videos;

- previews and deleted scenes on DVDs;

- Netflix and Hulu accounts;

- TV commercials; and

- rock videos.

Then there is the internet, which gives so much access to a lot of data, good and bad. "While the internet can be such a helpful and useful tool, everyone knows it has a dangerous side. With efficient search engines...accessing pornography is easier than ever and accidentally seeing pornography is just as common."

At the end of the day, this article concludes, "There is no perfect way to protect our families completely from the growing pornographic content found on the internet and through all the channels...The most important thing you can do is to teach your family important values and biblical principles they can use to make wise decisions."

It seems that the Christian nation is no exception to the level of moral contamination in the air. Just as in the rest of our global village, parents must work hard to live out the gospel of Jesus Christ, love each other, and make their home a place where the Spirit of God can dwell. And we can pray the prayer of the old hymn:

> Bless this house, O Lord we pray,
> Make it safe by night and day.
> Bless these walls so firm and stout,
> Keeping want and trouble out.[12]

## 3. Rising Up on Spirit Wings

Maybe the best news on this topic comes from the world of the butterfly. Of course the wings of a butterfly are fragile! If you capture one, it's important to handle it with care. Some have even said that once you touch a butterfly wing, it can never fly again.

But this is not the case. In fact, there is good news from the world of butterfly research. *Butterfly wings are built to resist contaminants!*

> The wings of a butterfly are so fragile that even the weight of specks of dust or drops of moisture should make flying difficult. Nevertheless, the wings stay clean and dry. What is the butterfly's secret? The butterfly's wing has minute overlapping scales.

Researchers at Ohio State University studying the Giant Blue Morpho butterfly (*Morpho didius*) found that although the insect's wings look smooth to the naked eye, the surfaces are covered with minute overlapping scales that resemble tiles on a roof. Even tinier parallel grooves on the surface of these scales cause dirt or drops of water to roll off with ease. Engineers are seeking to copy the wings' texture in order to make high-tech coatings for industry and medical equipment that are resistant to dirt and water.[13]

## Butterflies Are Tougher Than They Look

Debbie Hadley, a butterfly expert, says,

If you've ever handled a butterfly, you probably noticed the powdery residue left behind on your fingers. A butterfly's wings are covered with scales, which may rub off on your fingers when you touch them. That's the powder you see on your fingers. But will this prevent the butterfly from flying? Will the butterfly die if you touch its wings? *Butterfly wings aren't as fragile as they look!* The idea that simply touching a butterfly's wings may prevent it from flying is more fiction than fact.

Although their wings appear fragile, they have very hard construction: the longest documented flight by a migrating monarch butterfly was 2,750 miles, from Grand Manan Island, Canada to the overwintering grounds in Mexico. Painted Lady butterflies are known to fly even farther, covering 4,000 miles from North Africa to Iceland. A butterfly found only in Nepal, the Paralasa nepalica, lives and flies at an altitude of nearly 15,000 feet.

Researchers studying the flight of Painted Ladies using high speed cameras reported they flap their wings twenty times per second. The conclusion: if a simple touch could render a butterfly's wings useless, butterflies could never manage such feats of flight. *Butterflies are tougher than they look.*[14]

So that's our good news for the day from the world of butter-flies. Even though the airwaves are full of contaminants, butter-flies still fill the skies.

Obviously, our great Creator has put even more dirt-proof capacity for flight in his people. They are not going to be brought down by rock-bottom, ground-level ozone. "They shall rise up with wings!" That is His promise to us. The scriptures even carry something like a guarantee on this: "Walk in the Spirit and you will not fulfil the desires of the sinful nature" (see Galatians 5:16). As the Michael Forster song says:

Spirit wings, You lift me
Over all the earthbound things,
And like a bird
My heart is flying free.
I'm soaring on the song
Your Spirit brings.
O Lord of all, You let me see
A vision of Your majesty,
You lift me up, You carry me
On Your Spirit wings.

## Ten Great Quotes on Spirit-Filled Living

Fortunately, God supplies us with the Holy Spirit, who often pro-vides "thermals" on which to rise to the heights!

- The Gospel comes in power and the Holy Spirit, with much assurance. If you call upon the name of the Lord, God will transform you on the inside, give you the shock of your life, and give you everlasting life on top of that (Ray Comfort).

- O Holy Spirit, descend plentifully into my heart. Enlighten the dark corners of this neglected dwelling and scatter there Thy cheerful beams (Saint Augustine).

246

- The story of Christian reformation, revival, and renaissance underscores that the darkest hour is often just before the dawn, so we should always be people of hope and prayer, not gloom and defeatism. God the Holy Spirit can turn the situation around in five minutes (Os Guinness).

- We are 100 percent responsible for the pursuit of holiness, but at the same time we are 100 percent dependent upon the Holy Spirit to enable us in that pursuit. The pursuit of holiness is not a pull-yourself-up-by-your-own-bootstraps approach to the Christian life (Jerry Bridges).

- When you read the New Testament, you see the Holy Spirit was supposed to change everything so that this gathering of people who called themselves Christians had this supernatural element about them (Francis Chan).

- My point is simply this: I believe I have a calling. Do you know what that calling is? To stand up in a new and hard-core, radical way for the Lord. In the process, if I insult a couple of people, if I offend a couple of people, and if I got to shake it up a little bit, as long as it is led by the Holy Spirit, amen (Stephen Baldwin).

- God will never direct us to be prideful, arrogant and unforgiving, immoral, or slothful or full of fear. We step into these things because we are insensitive to the leadership of the Holy Spirit within us (Charles Stanley).

- In our friendships we have to be wise that we choose godly people to be our friends. Somebody might say, well does that mean that you should never have a lost person as your friend? No, I wouldn't say that. But you can't have the same intimacy with a lost person that you can with a godly person in whom the Holy Spirit is living (Charles Stanley).

- Human nature must be changed if we are ever to have an end to war or to correct the wrong situations that make our lives sore. Now Christianity, the power of Jesus Christ, the Holy Spirit of God, is the only force that can change people for good (Peter Marshall).

- The Spirit-filled life is not a special, deluxe edition of Christianity. It is part and parcel of the total plan of God for His people (A.W. Tozer).

## What If There Were No Butterflies?

I asked Google the question, "What if there were no butterflies?" What I discovered is that there is a lot of interest in that question! Among other things, butterflies are "quality of life indicators" and "indicators of biodiversity." They "improve our whole environment" and "enrich the lives of people." This should make any of us who are identified with the butterfly species in any way feel pretty special!

## Why Butterflies Are Important

One butterfly website points out many reasons why butterflies are important, both in their own right but also as quality of life indicators. Here are the main reasons provided for conserving butterflies in the UK and around the world:

1. *Intrinsic value:* butterflies and moths are intrinsically valuable and are worthy of conservation in their own right. They are part of life on Earth and an important component of its rich biodiversity, flagship species for conservation in general.

2. *Aesthetic value:* butterflies and moths are part of our natural heritage and have been studied for over 300 years. They are

beautiful. Many are iconic and popular. People like butter-flies. Butterflies are often portrayed as the essence of nature or as representing freedom, beauty or peace.

3. *Educational value:* butterflies and moths have fascinating life cycles that are used in many countries to teach children about the natural world. The transformation from egg to caterpillar to chrysalis is one of the wonders of nature. Other educational aspects include the intricate wing patterns and iridescence and as examples of insect migration.

4. *Scientific value:* butterflies are an extremely important group of "model" organisms used, for centuries, to investigate many areas of biological research, including such diverse fields as navigation, embryology, genetics, and biodiversity.

5. *Ecosystem value:* butterflies and moths are indicators of a healthy environment and healthy ecosystems. Areas rich in butterflies and moths are rich in other invertebrates. Butterflies have been widely used by ecologists as model organisms to study the impact of habitat loss and fragmentation, and climate change.

6. *Health value:* people enjoy seeing butterflies both around their homes and in the countryside. Over 10,000 people record butterflies and moths in the UK alone, involving getting outside and walking considerable distances.

7. *Economic value:* Thousands of people travel abroad each year looking for butterflies and moths. Eco-tours bring valuable income to many European countries and developing countries around the world.[15]

I find it interesting to apply all of the above to the presence of the great young church of Zambia, the church of the butterfly

Christian nation on the world stage. It is very much needed because of its life and beauty, because of its joy and its spirit—it simply must not be excluded from our great global village.

Thus we may have an answer for the question of *why*. Why must the Zambian church be found among the great throng of Christian emissaries worldwide in the twenty-first century? Why must they not be excluded? I think it must be for similar reasons! Because of its intrinsic value; because of its aesthetic value—such headings give us a hint about the value of all nations in our great calling to share the gospel!

When it comes to *intrinsic value*, there must be a reason why the church of Southern Africa is perhaps the fastest growing in the world. Whatever those intrinsic values are, and we have noted many of them above, the world desperately needs them now.

Under *aesthetic values*, we discussed in chapter six how one young "cheetah" with a cellphone can change a whole society. This is so partly because of music and the arts, which are such a big part of Zambian Christianity's contribution to the world.

*Educational value*: just as the butterfly is one of the wonders of nature in its transformation from egg to caterpillar to chrysalis, we maintain that the transformation of Zambia's Christian nation over 100-plus years is one of the wonders of the world of Christian missions.

*Scientific value*: just as butterfly studies are important indicators of the environmental health of the globe, the nations of Southern Africa are indicators of the ethical and moral health of the earth. Just as the world is trying to find ways to save butterfly populations, the Christian nation has a role in helping the world find ways of levelling the economic playing field for all people, of eliminating grotesque disparity and levels of severe poverty. Just as butterflies are important for scientific research on climate change, the Christian nation points to a changing world in global alignment and Christian theology.

*Ecosystem value*: just as butterflies bring rich benefits to their environment, in terms of pollination and nature pest control, the Zambian church is a case study and model of "pollination and pest control" in the realm of theology and church growth!

*Health value*: the butterfly Christian nation's church is important because people like to see it in action, to enjoy its vibrancy—and hope that it is contagious. How will the world be saved from its tired and desacralized secularism without exposure to a people that is decidedly *not* secular? This is critically important for the overall moral health of the planet.

*Economic value*: the Christian nation is definitely involved in "the best use of resources" for world missions. Why would the wealthy half of the Christian church invest huge resources in less promising ventures? Why not invest in a flourishing church of the global south and let it help "crack the window" of unreached people groups wide open! It just makes sense.

In short, a world without butterflies is not a world anybody wants to contemplate. How much less our twenty-first-century world of great need, spiritual, social, and environmental, without the presence of God's people from the butterfly Christian nation? It is just so vital.

So this is not a season for withdrawal into the dark forests of our own habitat. This is a season for the Christian church of Zambia to carry its vibrant faith far and wide, like the myriad butterflies of the earth, to fill the sky with dazzling colour and irresistible grace—to testify to the wide-as-the-world love of our heavenly Father.

# Chapter 12

## *Butterflies In Flight*

### From Walter Fisher to Barry Ilunga

When Dr. Walter Fisher entered Africa in 1889, he came in from the west, landing on the Angolan coast with two parties whose aim it was to penetrate the interior of the continent where no missionaries had worked before. They came in the spirit of the Plymouth Brethren who came out of the British Prayer Revivals of 1859, along with the Keswick movement and the Salvation Army, fuelled by the preaching of D.L. Moody and others. The Brethren were strong premillennialists in their convictions, highly motivated to reach the world with the gospel before the imminent return of Christ—hence some very zealous missionaries all over the world at the turn of the twentieth century. To follow in the steps of Livingstone captured the vision of young missionaries coming out of The Hall on King George Street, Greenwich, which commended and sent forth Walter Fisher and others.[1]

The Fishers were destined for the Kalene Hill Mission Station and Hospital in Northern Zambia, which would become such a strong centre for Christian witness that all of Zambia and especially the Lunda people would be deeply impacted. But they would not claim the hill for their ministry centre, near the headwaters of the Zambezi, until 1906. In the meantime, there were seventeen years of hard labour on the Angola side of the border: burying colleagues and friends and even their own children, struck down by malarial fever or other infections; trekking unbelievable distances through modern Angola with "carriers" of one hundred men along narrow paths; building schools and outreach centres in very primitive, illiterate communities that had never heard the gospel. All of this, at one time, with four children under five!

By the end of 1905, the need for a sanatorium was acute. Dr. Fisher was treating many patients and performing delicate eye surgery in all kinds of less than ideal settings. He found Zambia's Kalene Hill in his exploratory surveys, fifteen miles from Congo to the north and fifteen miles from Angola to the west, and sensed at once that this was their new ministry centre. This hill had been named "Border Craig" by Fred Arnot some years earlier. But Fisher laid claim to it with a new name: "Kalene Hill," named after a local chief. Its primary attraction was that it stood 4,850 feet above sea level, far above malarial valleys. There was a spring of pure water and a mountain stream for power. There were no white ants. What else was needed? This was in British territory. According to the doctor, it was the "best site in Central Africa." And truly, its illustrious history says he was right!

It was out of Kalene Hill that Barry Ilunga's great-grandparents heard the gospel. It may have been through Walter Fisher's translation of the gospel of John into Lovale, before the turn of the century. It may have been through Fisher's son, Singleton, who returned to the mission in 1914, with his sister May, and conducted regular evangelistic circuits to surrounding villages. It may have been through the growing schools around Kalene Hill, which invited promising students from bush schools to come to the mission station for further instruction in history, geography, sewing, carpentry, and agriculture—all part of the curriculum—accompanied the teaching of the Bible. "Education is not an end in itself," said the Fishers. Nor, for that matter, was the great ministry of the hospital. Indeed, the Ilunga forbears may have first heard the Gospel through the medical work of Dr. Fisher, who was in high demand as a doctor, removing cataracts and supplying a full range of medical care, including surgeries. In 1915, the hospital had thirty inpatients and hundreds of outpatients. And few of the patients were discharged without hearing the good news of Jesus Christ.

Kalene Hill! This mission centre had such a full range of ministries and such powerful seasons of revival where hundreds were brought to faith—it is hard to determine just when and how Kirio Ilunga, great-grandfather to Barry Ilunga, came to Christ. Their village was *ikelenge*, and somehow through God's faithful servants, it was thoroughly evangelized.

"My great-grandfather, Kirio, became a well-known evangelist all over northern province," says Barry. Kirio was followed by Barry's uncle, Gene Kahona, who became bishop of the United Methodist Church in Zambia and was also well known among the Lunda people as a pastor and evangelist.

And now the line continues with Barry and his brothers, many preachers and pastors all over Zambia. Nothing pleases Barry more than to see one of his six sons, Kyembe, training for ministry at our Trans-Africa Christian University. Missionary calling is contagious, says Barry Ilunga. "The future will trace all my boys, Kyembe, Mundemba, Nkuuli, Makonga, Barry, and Kuwaha, involved in meaningful service to Jesus Christ the Lord."

When Barry founded WOTA, it was with the intention of sending missionaries from the Christian nation. That is beginning to happen. Zambia is mobilizing and recruiting workers to cross borders for evangelism and church planting. As Barry puts it,

> This is our window of opportunity!...This is the appointed time, a season in the purpose of God for Zambia! Who knows how long we will live under the blessing of the declaration and the gospel receive such a strong support within our borders? God has given us this special moment in time! I do not believe it is for nothing. We need to be sharing our blessings with the nations around us—especially those who have no light of the gospel!

So Barry Ilunga interacts with ministries to North Africa, the Middle East, and restricted access nations. Most recently he has found that the doors are wide open to Zambians in North Africa.

> There will be three months of cultural sensitization. The following six months, our Zambian missionaries will be working in conjunction with a small church already established. These Zambian missionaries will assist with a medical centre, teaching English, Bible studies with youths, ministry to refugees from Syria, Palestine and Iraq—the needs and opportunities are many. And Zambians are the best equipped to fill them...We are very much equal to the task.

## Butterfly Nation Taking Flight

You could almost say we have come full circle. Created out of chaos by the breath of the Spirit, a Christian nation radiating so much gospel light! But this circle is far from full. The reality is that there is so much gospel light in Zambia that it has plenty to share with the world. So "why not now?"

"Missions is not about money," says Barry Ilunga. I get the

feeling he has proven that to be true! "It's about obedience. We do not have a money problem: we have an obedience problem. Once we obey, the needs will be met."

*"What about partnering with international friends to make Zambian missions happen?"*

"Yes, very important and helpful. But we do not want the Zambian church to miss the blessing! We need to assume responsibility for the Great Commission. We can do a lot just by rallying our resources."

*"What about the notion that we need to get our own house in order first?"*

"We cannot think like that. If we do, we will never go. There will always be in-house matters to be set in order. But God blesses a sending church! Once we are obedient, we will find that everything falls into place."

I cannot ask Barry Ilunga about what some call the lack of Zambian role models. He *is* one! As was his spiritual father, Dr. Walter Fisher, who answered the call of God over a century ago, along with a host of very promising, young Plymouth Brethren.

## The Tembo Principles

If the early Ngoni converts could speak today, they might say, "If God could save us, surely God can save anyone!" We could call it the "First Tembo Principle," Mawalera Tembo having been the first convert among the Ngoni people, young son of the witch doctor, who came to pray at night. The Ngoni were so bound by the forces of darkness! Their redemption testifies that *anyone* can be redeemed. No one is excluded—no matter their culture, their environment, their struggles, their bondage, their failings, no matter how far they have wandered or how deep they have fallen—no one is excluded from the reach of God's love.

Nor is anyone excluded from our Great Commission: "Go therefore and teach *all nations,* baptizing them...." The Great Commission excludes no one. This is such an important message for our time, faced as we are with that ominous 10/40 window. Painted like a black cloud on our prayer maps of the world, looking so impregnable—how will the Christian church ever reach those 4.9 billion people who have never heard the good news? This challenge looks just too overwhelming. That's why we need the Ngoni message: "If God can save us, he can save anyone."

According to the Joshua Project,

> The 10/40 Window is the rectangular area of North Africa, the Middle East and Asia approximately between 10 degrees north and 40 degrees north latitude. The 10/40 Window is often called *The Resistant Belt* and includes the majority of the world's Muslims, Hindus, and Buddhists.
>
> Approximately 4.95 billion individuals residing in approximately 8,587 distinct people groups are in the revised 10/40 Window. 5,894 (68.6%) of these people groups are considered unreached and have a population of 3.05 billion. This means approximately 62% of the individuals in the 10/40 Window live in an unreached people group. The 10/40 Window is home to some of the largest unreached people groups in the world such as the Shaikh, Yadava, Turks, Moroccan Arabs, Pashtun, Jat and Burmese.
>
> Thus, the 10/40 Window is home to the majority of the world's unevangelized countries. The "unevangelized" are people who have a minimal knowledge of the gospel, but have no valid opportunity to respond to it. While it constitutes only one-third of earth's total land area, nearly two-thirds of the world's people reside in the 10/40 Window.
>
> An estimated 3.05 billion individuals live in approximately 5,894 unreached people groups in the 10/40 Window. The 10/40 Window also contains the largest

unreached peoples over one million in population. In addition, the 10/40 Window contains the overwhelming majority of the world's least evangelized megacities—that is, those with a population of more than one million. The top 50 least evangelized megacities are all in the 10/40 Window! That fact alone underscores the need for prioritizing 10/40 Window Great Commission efforts.[2]

Can this overwhelming bloc be included in the "Tembo Principle?" Is God limited by size of tribe? Our answer would have to be, "Yes, even these are included!" If God provided a way to evangelize Chief Mombera and his people in 1900, surely he can provide the way to evangelize our 10/40 window! God's methods and power, his infinite resources—these do not change. All it takes is the right people carrying the right message to the right places. As Paul says, "How shall they hear without a preacher?" Even our infinite God cannot work without human agents. Nor does the message change. The gospel of Christ remains *the power of God for the salvation of everyone who believes*" (Romans 1:16). Our concern here is not with the message, nor with the Lord of the harvest, but with "right people" carrying it to the "right places."

## Even the Large 10/40 Tribe Can Be Reached

I went online and asked, "Are we making inroads in the 10/40 window?" For starters I got a list of the nations—4.95 billion people. This is a very large tribe! But then I found signs of progress. There are developments that all Christians should be celebrating. Plenty of lost sheep are being found. And there is a great mobilization of world-wide prayer.

Moreover, according to many, the key player in this great missionary enterprise is "the global south." So says Mike

259

Petengill, for example, in his article, "Crawling Through the 10/40 Window,"

> In the current geo-political environment [westerners] are not favourably viewed by a majority of the governments in the 10/40 Window countries. Of the ten countries in the world that are classified as hardest for US citizens to receive visas for, seven of those are located in that area. In much of the 10/40 Window, missionary visas are simply not granted to foreigners.
>
> The [west] and its missionaries are simply not welcome in much of the 10/40 regions. But this doesn't mean [North] Americans [and Europeans] should fold up their missions tents...There may be a better approach.
>
> Already missionaries are going out from the Global South. But why not send more?...Missionaries originating from the Global South can gain easier access to countries in the 10/40 Window. It may be time for [western] churches to embrace the shifting landscape. Rather than sending missionaries from our home country, we can send...our brothers and sisters from the Global South.[3]

Currently, Barry Ilunga is recruiting Zambians for a Middle Eastern nation where a large community of Zambians already live, involved in various businesses, associated with a church that is registered. From that centre, they minister to people from Syria (refugees) and North Africa. They live among the people, show Christ's love, and practice the incarnational ministry that reached their forefathers. For Barry Ilunga, this looks like a launching pad to put many Zambian missionaries among the unreached peoples of the 10/40 Window.

No doubt this is just the beginning. Zambia has the potential to be a major missionary-sending nation. The butterfly Christian nation must take wings! The Ngoni spirit is alive and well and already making great strides in various parts of the world. These young cheetahs for the gospel are spilling across borders and making good things happen! Why should such wings not spread far and wide? Why should the world not see a vast array of Zambian missionaries carrying the Good News to the world?

## Second Tembo Principle

Another key which those early Ngoni converts would put in our hand today would surely be, "Come, live in our village." How would the Ngoni ever have been reached with the liberating good news if a band of highly motivated young people from the UK had not resolved to move in with them and build clinics and schools? "Come live in our village!" Incarnational missions. There is no other way.

Larry Sharp is a long-term "global worker" who explains in an article, "Why I Am No Longer A Missionary." It seems, for Sharp, that building bridges of friendship and communication is number one in modern missions. He calls for a different kind of missionary involvement to meet the challenges of the new millenium, people who share "faith as a lifestyle and principles to live by." In much of the world of the unreached, "intrusiveness" is rejected, whereas bridge-building and friendship evangelism are welcome. Sharp says, "The bottom line is that Jesus asked us to follow him, be his witnesses, and help others to follow him. *Disciple-making is all about trusted relationships with people.*"

Sharp continues,

> Muslims do not understand Christian proselytizing. While we might understand very well that one who preaches the gospel is giving their hearers a choice, Muslims do not see it that way. They perceive this as *forcible conversion*...That message of having a choice does not reach the Muslim world at all. Muslims understand conversion to be linked

to imperialism…they hear the 10-40 window as the obliteration of the Islamic world…Thus evangelism becomes a very sensitive topic, tied to the idea of Western imperialism. The two are the same to Muslims; they appear to be deliberate attempts to undermine their power and individual and collective identity, to wipe Islam off the world map. They believe Christian proselytizing to be cultural genocide…and that's why they respond so aggressively to it. We know that…missionaries did not understand themselves as agents of imperial powers, and many times they understood themselves to be working against those forces. But that message has never reached Muslims. They see the Christian West as a monolith.[4]

So Larry Sharp and his Business as Missions (BAM) group call for a new kind of missionary for a new kind of world!

Jesus said, "Be my witnesses." He did not say, "Go and be missionaries." A witness has to be credible (i.e., have the ability or power to inspire belief). Perhaps then the starting point in building relationships is to not identify ourselves as "missionaries" or professional clergy. Even in places where it is legal to have such an identity, people often put us in a box and expect us to have religious answers and live the life of a cleric.…

When we look at the Gospels, we see that Jesus met people at their point of need or context—he fed the hungry, healed the blind, taught lessons and parables, and provided wine at a wedding. These were starting points to conversations that linked him to deeper spiritual matters.

The issue, says our writer, is overcoming the age-old division between the sacred and the secular. It may be that the best way to crack open the 10/40 Window is to do it through the workplace, the service sector, and the marketplace.

Consider the great value that medical training brought to Zambia through doctors Elmslie, Laws, Fisher, Chisholm, and others. In many cases, it was missionary clinics that broke the hold of the witch doctors over communities.

> Historically, the gospel has spread because persecution scattered believers...[who] took their skills in order to survive as they dispersed...William Carey easily connected making disciples in India with medicine, steam engines, savings banks, and education. Surely, we [are not] going to get the job done with professional "missionaries" alone.

> How then is it possible to transform our world in a manner similar to how it happened in the first century? In the twenty-first century it is likely to be similar—through the spreading out of all people to the whole world taking their primary skills to less-inviting places. These workers have a valid identity and a credible answer for why they are there. Only then will the gospel be present in dark places.

And so, in his call for a new kind of "missionary," Larry Sharp calls for something like the mobilization of the entire church. It is those who take their skills with them to unreached people groups who have the most credible witness.

> Their jobs grant them access to people and places most religious professionals will never encounter. The new rule of engagement is that *one hundred percent of all believers can and should be involved in mission.* Such people may be considered "missionaries" by the mission committee of their home churches, but...they are just friends and professionals with a skill. They are simply *people being witnesses and making disciples of Jesus* in countries where few people know our Saviour. Each live in countries that will not grant missionary visas.

It all amounts to very exciting opportunities in the world of missions! These are days that call for maximum involvement from the body of Christ, when all kinds of different skills and professions are welcome! None of us should disqualify ourselves from this very high calling. As Larry Sharp, the ex-missionary says, "Kingdom professionals can live in some of the highest-risk countries because they honestly bring their skill to the country. Simultaneously, they can live out the gospel and testify to the grace of God."

### Sending the Right People

So the vast challenge before us calls for all kinds of skills. Probably all of us should consider ourselves "the right people" for certain situations. After all, *who are the right people?*

When I think about the "right people" for missions, I think back to those great hearts that streamed out of England to central Africa to close out the nineteenth century. Amazing and intrepid people like Dr. Robert Laws, Dr. William Elmslie, Donald Fraser, Frederick Stanley Arnot, Dr. Walter Fisher— these were radical and sold-out Christian emissaries, building educational and medical centres for vast regions of Africa, elevating communities wherever they went. Truly it seems that mother Britain sent to Central Africa its absolutely best people.

These were people who had some skills, some credentials, who could enhance a whole community just by their presence.

These were people who were tough, almost beyond comprehension. They suffered sustained deprivation and great personal losses "for the Lord's sake."

These people were spiritual, taking "everything to God in prayer" at every turn, from critical impasses to daily bread. They relied on divine guidance to direct their steps.

These emissaries of the good news also showed respect and care for all people, finding "image-bearers of the Creator" wherever they went. Regardless of status or race—they were sent to work among lost people whom God loves. They carried the heart of God for Africa.

They embodied love, this crowd, that primary gift of Christian character. Such love attracted interest and loyalty wherever it manifested.

They were peacemakers among people who didn't even have a word for peace! As such, "they shall be called the children of God."

These were people of ethics, uncompromising integrity, deep commitment to truth, without which there is no progress. These people had credibility.

They were people of sensitivity, who respected the natural beauty of God's green earth and truly believed that "the earth is the Lord's."

They were people of ingenuity, who knew how to build basic tools, create irrigation canals, do whatever needed to be done when and where needed, devising solutions to meet the challenges of the day.

They were people of simplicity, who like Livingstone or Arnot, knew how to travel light. Or like Dr. Walter Fisher, even ready to be buried in a small ceremony at Kalene Hill, without a coffin.

These early missionaries were people who found joy in all circumstances in that their joy, of course, was "in the Lord."

They were indefatigable, that is for sure. One foot in front of another without giving up—that was Frederick Stanley Arnot, who just kept walking, 29,000 miles through the heart of Africa before he was done, opening up vast stretches for Christian schools and mission stations from the royal palace of the Barotse people to Katanga, Congo, and King Msidi's Garenganze.

These were people who made friends and influenced people, be they African chiefs who held sway over entire tribes or women and children they encountered along the way.

Maybe in the final analysis, God looks for a surrendered life, for obedience and dedication more than anything else. And who would question that *Christlikeness* might be the quality to be most looked for in missions. "Let the beauty of Jesus be seen in me." What else would it have been that drew a most pagan chief like Mombera of the Ngoni to missionaries like Koyi and Laws? Was it not that he detected Christ?

In our enlightened days, we teach cross-cultural communication to help people cross borders and share the Good News with different cultures. Indeed, our lecturers might wonder, how is it possible that the Ngoni people were won without their course in cross-cultural communication! Can it be that our "study of communication in and between different cultural contexts" was missing in 1900? What about the influence of "thinking processes and world view?" We almost have to believe that as people carry Jesus, be it in 1918 or 2018, cross-cultural communication comes naturally! It might even be that the principles of our cross-cultural communication *emerged from the experiences* of those early pioneers in the craft. What cross-cultural communication teaches is that most *any* of us can acquire the skills that will enable us to engage other cultures positively and become great emissaries of the Good News. And that is good news in itself!

Yet one can acquire all those skills and still come up short. This is because of the obvious: nothing happens without our *presence!* The question becomes, How can they be reached if not by the same *incarnational method* that brought Dr. William Elmslie to live in an Ngoni village until hearts opened up to Jesus? The Good News was incarnated in human flesh again. This is always God's method. "A body you have prepared me."

Ehud Garcia, in his course on cross-cultural communication, says, "The message we are called to proclaim is incarnational. It must become flesh for those who are going to hear it. The message is never absent from the ones who will carry it on...Always the Christian message will accompany the messenger, and as such, both message and messenger must *become flesh* wherever they go." In other words, the communicator's personality and experiences shape the form of the message. Thus the "vessel" that carries the Christian Good News is most important. To understand the message, people need to understand the messenger.[5]

In short, we are left with the Tembo principle, which says, *Come live in our village.* There is no getting around this call. To reach the most unreached people on the planet, it all starts with befriending them. And the Christian nation definitely is a part in the harvest. *The David Livingstone legacy in Zambia is world missions!*

Thinking back to Mawalera Tembo, the original Ngoni convert: he was won to Christ by missionaries Elmslie and Koyi. They in turn were won over to missions by the life and death of David Livingstone. Thus, the Zambian church has missions *stamped upon its DNA.* It was the same story all over the Zambian butterfly—great preachers like Kirio Ilunga being evangelized out of Dr. Fisher's ministry centre at Kalene Hill; Kirio Ilunga passing the great legacy down to succeeding generations. Yes, Zambian Christianity has missions *stamped upon its DNA!* It is virtually inevitable that it will produce great missionaries, by whatever title, for the twenty-first century.

The David Livingstone legacy in Zambia lives on.

## Jacob Ntuntu's Story

### *Incarnational Missions in Chief Nsokolo's Area of the Mambwe People*

From my personal experience, incarnational missions played a major role in the conversion of my family to Christ. I was born on 11th November,

1982, a few years after my father had retired from the Zambia police force to take up his traditional position as sub chief of the Mambwe people in a Chief Ntuntu's village. Being born after twins (Ya Mpundu) they named me Chola; later I came to learn that I was first male child born after my father's installation as chief, therefore I carried the title Chisola (heir to the throne).

The Christian missions had already reached the Mambwe people more than century earlier through the Livingstonia Mission, the London Missionary Society, and the Jesuit fathers who had established mission centres at Kayambi, Mambwe, and Kawimbe. Our grandfather had been a convert to the faith, and he died the year I was born. The missionaries had given him the name Jacob, as such that name was transferred to me. As if to authenticate the name transfer, they also called me Lombe at birth, the name I later dropped after converting to Pentecostalism and replaced with the name Palo. Of course at one time, the Pentecostals were very strong about rejecting the names of our ancestors that had hereditary implications as it was felt they could have been carrying demonic affiliations with them.

But by 1890, the Jesuits and the Livingstonia Mission had already penetrated the Mambwe land. Mission centres had been established at Kawimbe by the Jesuits. The Kayambi Mission was on the east of the chiefdom while Mambwe Mission was established in the centre of the chiefdom.

By the 1980s, all the Mambwe land had been Christianized, although it must be admitted that the people remained highly syncretized. They practiced both Christianity and African traditional religion. They went to church on Sundays but when faced with hard times during the week they consulted witch doctors. The message of the missionaries had brought schools and hospitals but did not emphasize the kind of power of God that the Pentecostal movement would later emphasize.

## Chief Ntuntu—the Hard Nut to Crack

My father, Mr. Alfred Jacob Sichula Ntuntu, had a great exposure to civilization. He was born in approximately 1930 and had the blessing of receiving formal education at the Roman Catholic Mambwe Mission School. His exposure to education provided for by the mission school helped him move from the northern village into the Copperbelt where he enrolled in the police service, then known as Zambia Police Force. He rose in ranks to the position of chief inspector and was privileged to travel into Europe, through the United Kingdom and West Germany.

In 1979 he retired and was to become chief in 1982. However, he had no interest in religion or church activity. My mother, Rodah Namfukwe, was a strong member of the United Church of Zambia (UCZ), a church that had been formed soon after independence as a unification of the Free Church of the Copperbelt, the London Missionary Society, the Methodist churches and others to form one church under Kenneth Kaunda's quest for one Zambia, one nation. To date the UCZ is among Zambia's most influential and biggest denominations. My mother prayed earnestly every day and always aimed to be at church every Sunday. She introduced us to the faith as soon as we were born. But the chief, my father, was far from the faith. He was not interested in either God or religion. He believed in work. You needed to work and work hard to touch his heart. He was a difficult person, strong willed, and difficult to convince. He simply was a hard nut to crack. He always praised himself as having no reverse gears. "*Nshawelela ichisila wakwe lorry,*" he would say, meaning "I have no reverse gears like a lorry truck." Once he is decided, it is done. This would be a great tool in God's work of salvation on his life later on.

In 1989, a Reformed Church missionary from Ngoniland, named Rev. Nyemba, came to Mambweland with World Vision. Rev. Nyemba's tenacious efforts helped convert my father to the Christian faith. He joined the Reformed Church in Zambia, and my mother later moved from UCZ in submission to her husband. We as a family became committed members of the Reformed Church. My mother became an active RCZ evangelist, and my father later became an elder and a preacher at the local church. It was from there that I developed passion for God's work. As a little boy, we trekked to villages to spread the gospel, plant churches, and strengthen them. Finally, the gospel had touched the chief and Jesus had cracked the hard nut—Chief Ntuntu was now the leading elder at the local RCZ church and was the chairman of the World Vision projects in the area.

### *Pentecostal Missions, Emmanuel Silwamba*

Pentecostal missions were introduced in the land by a retired soldier named Emmanuel Silwamba. He had his own Pentecostal encounter in Lusaka at a Reinhard Bonnke crusade and joined the Pentecostal Assemblies of God at Lilanda under Rev. Kampinde. He, along with others, including the late Rev. Chirambo, was exposed to the School of Ministry run by Morris Cerullo. He retired early from the army to respond to God's call and moved to his home-land, Mbala, to spread the good news he had received. He settled in Chief Nsokolo's area, near a stream called Mwala. There he estab-lished a Pentecostal mission called Rehoboth Ministries and embarked on a passionate evangelization of Mambweland, planting churches in Mbala, Nakonde, and as far as Tanzania.

Emmanuel Silwamba was a tool in God's hands to transform the Christian landscape of Mbala rural. His Rehoboth church was a centre of healing, revival, and salvation. Many came to faith in the power of God and the Holy Spirit through him. Silwamba, preached the "born again" Pentecostal message, emphasized baptism in the Holy Spirit with the evidence of speaking in tongues, prayed against witchcraft powers, cast out demons from people, and had a rare combined gift of music and oratory. He was also a gifted faith healer. His son, Paul, took after him, but Silwamba had a rare choleric trait of courage, which Paul lacked. His daughter Victoria was to later marry my brother, Alfred, who had become a committed follower of Silwamba. It was Silwamba who preached the Pentecostal message to my family. The already cracked hard nut, my father, Chief Ntuntu, gladly opened the doors of his palace for Silwamba. Silwamba held services in my father's house with villagers coming from all over in search of an encounter with Christ. We witnessed the deliverance of many from demon possession and witchcraft powers. Many received instant healings from God through the ministry of Silwamba. My brothers Alfred and Salmon were among the people who experienced instant healings through the prayers of Emmanuel Silwamba. Later my father attended a Benny Hinn crusade in Lusaka in the mid-1990s and came back a completely transformed person. He remained strong in the faith until his death in September 2011.

Silwamba was also a Puritan preacher. He emphasized holiness and purity. He taught against involvement in all worldly activities, including watching football and listening to secular music. He helped stop the abusive practices conducted at the initiation ceremonies of girls at puberty. He also had access to various chiefs in the area, including Senior Chief Nsokolo. He was instrumental in eliminating idolatrous practices conducted in chiefs' palaces. His efforts helped the church in the area to believe in the God who has the power to save, heal, and deliver. This message was well received by the villagers, who needed a religion that would provide solutions to the spiritual problems they encountered in their daily lives.

Pentecostalism has touched a lot of churches in Mbala. The UCZ and RCZ have embraced a lot of Pentecostal beliefs, and several Pentecostal churches have been established in the area, such as the PAOG-Z, the Pentecostal Holiness, Bread of Life Church, the ZAOGA, just to name a few. It cannot be denied that the Pentecostal seed was planted in the area by Emmanuel Silwamba. One of the major benefits of Pentecostalism, not only in Mbala, but to Christianity generally in Zambia, is that it has eliminated the tendency of syncretism. It is now clear that Christians can turn to God for healing, deliverance, and salvation.

### *My Journey to Christian Ministry*

I gained a lot of inspiration for Christian ministry from the Reformed Church in Zambia pastors who did mission work in our village and other surrounding villages. RCZ ministers like Rev. Nyemba, Rev. Kaziya, Rev. Simutunda and others served as my primary inspiration for Christian ministry. On several occasions, missionaries came from Eastern Province, Lusaka, and South Africa into our village. Their dedication triggered a passion in me to serve God. A specific event was during a mini village crusade held at Kawala village around 1994, along the Mbala Nakonde road. Ministering was a young evangelist named Phiri. He was preaching from Daniel 4 about the turning of Nebuchadnezzar into a beast. He delivered his homily in Chi Chewa as one of the local pastors translated into Mambwe. The message touched my heart in a very special way, and I desired to be a minister some day. On several occasions, my mother would tell me, as if prophesying, "You are destined to be a pastor." Our exposure to the ministry of Pentecostal minister Silwamba increased the passion.

Qualifying to grade eight was a great blessing in our time. It meant two things: escaping the painful labour of the village and pride for the family. I was among the five who made it to grade eight from Chipoka Primary School (now Secondary) in 1997. This made my parents proud, but for me it was a relief from village life. Anyway, like my other brothers, I had great passion for school from my preschool days at a World Vision Preschool. But an additional blessing of escaping farm labour just made going to Isoka Boys Secondary boarding school even more wonderful. At this time Pentecostalism was booming. The Scripture Union patron, Mr. Manga, was also a pastor of an emerging Pentecostal Holiness Church at Isoka Town. Pastor Mubanga of Pentecostal Assemblies of God at Isoka was another inspiration. The bald-headed prolific Pentecostal preacher delivered homilies with a passion. In my heart, I desired to be like him. My stay at Isoka Boys was not long. It only lasted two years. I had to shift to the nation's capital, Lusaka, and in 1999 enrolled at Nyenyezi High School where I was to complete my secondary education. Having had a brief stay in Matero and a long stay in Emmasdale, I became an active member of Bread of Life Church International at the invitation of my brother, Timothy.

It was at Bread of Life where I had a real Pentecostal encounter in a very personal way. During the 1999 Word Explosion Conference, I experienced the baptism of the Holy Spirit during the ministry of Ghanaian pastor, Bishop Charles Agyin-Asare, who had been invited by Bishop Joe Imakando. Bishop Imakando was raising a thriving missionary church with a very clear missionary mandate of "Bringing Thousands into the Kingdom, Possessing the Land and Feeding People with the Bread of Life." To date, Bread of Life Church has a vigorous missionary passion, sending young cheetahs across the nation and to other nations of the world, such as neighbouring Malawi, Zimbabwe, Namibia, Tanzania, South Africa, and overseas to Australia, New Zealand, America, and England. Friday Fumbilwa, who founded El-Shaddai Church in

New Zealand, has grown it to be one of the biggest churches on the island. Meanwhile, young cheetahs like Luckson Ngozo, Noah Chibamba, Austin Makota, Lewis Shikapwasha, Gideon Kapafu, Stanley Lyatumba, and several others have been sent to America, Europe, and the neighbouring nations to spread the gospel. There is need for new missionary strategy in Bread of Life Church to send young cheetahs to the 10/40 Window region.

It was from Bread of Life Church International that my zeal for Christian ministry grew even greater. I was sure of my calling in my secondary school days where I led the Scripture Union, and soon after completing secondary school, I enrolled at Trans-Africa Theological College, now Trans-Africa Christian University. The ingenuity, dedication, and passion of my professors, especially, Dr. Victor Chanda, Dr. John Kerr, Dr. Adrian Chalwe, and other visiting professors, triggered a strong desire for the books. From there I have believed that Africa must raise its own theologians who will provide biblical answers to African challenges.

### *From TACU to the Ends of the Earth*

Trans-Africa Christian University, like other institutions in Africa has become a missionary sending institution. I am privileged to be a 2008 degree graduate of TACU, and by God's grace, my colleagues and I have seen the faithfulness of God on the mission field. Chomba Kalyati, one of the 2008 graduates, has gone to Tanzania where he is spearheading Christian missions in some Islamic-dominated areas. Other graduates are spread across Zambia, propagating and defending the gospel. Andrew Chapuma has been ministering among poor communities in Kasama and Mpika districts, while Morgan Mukumbuta, Abraham Chitambi, and a few others are labouring for the Lord in Eastern Zambia.

In February 2009, my presiding bishop, Dr. Joe Imakando, assigned me to pastor a church in Chimwemwe, one of Zambia's large townships. Located in the heart of Kitwe, just a few miles from TACU, we were to continue interactions with college professors and fellow graduates. Chimwemwe Bread of Life Church was not only my first pastoral assignment, it was also a place of meeting the love of my life, Loved. Loved and I got married in May 2010, and God has blessed us with two daughters, Temwika and Wankuzya (Rehoboth). We are believing God for the third one—a son. Our three-year-long Christian ministry was a great learning experience. Ministry was exciting, lives were being transformed, we hoped for a great revival, we hosted a Seven Days of Revival Conference, and we always aimed to raise believers with a strong knowledge of the Bible and a solid relationship with God. The church, which I had taken over from Rev. Simon Phiri, continued in stable growth. We were favoured to get land and started building a church auditorium in the big township. It is not so hard to get church land in the butterfly shaped Christian nation. Most people in government offices are either born again or at least have some fear of God or are simply scared of God. However, the mushrooming of many churches over the past twenty years has made land access a bit difficult. God made a way, and we started raising a structure for worship. When a church owns land in an area, it signifies stability and longevity.

### *An Evening Phone Call from My Regional Overseer*

One Tuesday evening, I received a phone call from my Regional Overseer, Rev. Kangwa Mumba. He asked to meet me at his office the following day. He was to break the news that I was being transferred to one of the rural districts in Southern Province. I was to make a choice between Namwala or Ithezhi-thezi. It was a challenging test. I would be going to a land I hardly knew and to a people whose language I could not speak.

I reflected on the sacrifices other missionaries had made in the past. They laid down their lives in order to get a soul saved. My response was, wherever God sends me, I will go. My overseer expressed a bit of surprise, although he never said anything more than "You have spoken well."

It was not easy for me. My wife, daughter, and I were headed for a rural district. It was a tough one. The hymn "When you walk with Lord in the light of His word…" played in my heart. I sat on my bed holding, then, my only daughter. I sang it with tears. My presiding bishop was to visit Kitwe in a few days. On a Sunday evening, we sat under the ministry of Bishop Imakando, who ministered with great charisma as usual. I was not sure what God had for me in the future. My dreams to expand my theological knowledge and become a great African theologian of our time were on the line. Namwala and Ithezhi-thezi have no theological colleges and obviously internet access would be difficult.

Sunday night, my overseer called me to cancel the appointment to travel to Namwala the following Monday. I was no longer destined to the south. I remain on the Copperbelt, this time to lead a newly established church in a small mining town, Kalulushi, which was meeting at Kalulushi Secondary School. It was a small church with a membership of about 55 people. From 2012 to date, we have been leading the Kalulushi Bread of Life Church. God's grace has been abundant. We have seen great progress, including possessing the land on which we are building a multi-facility blessing centre.

# Epilogue

## *The New Birth: The Ultimate Metamorphosis*

This book is really about miracle births—the birth of the butterfly from a moulting caterpillar, one of the wonders of nature. The birth of a Christian nation out of chaos. The rebirth of the Ngoni people from their war-like ancestry. These are, as we have said, the stuff of wonder. Yet there is a greater wonder. It is the birth we have saved to the end, the new birth that is in store for every one of us who comes in from the night.

If those early Ngoni converts could speak today, Mawalera Tembo and his young friends, no doubt they would want to add that it takes a transformed heart to create a transformed people. To think that the Ngoni could experience transformation with anything less than heart change would be to entertain some very dubious fantasies. Everything begins with the new birth, within the individual human heart, life's greatest miracle. This transcends even the transformation of the Christian nation. It surpasses even the transformation of a caterpillar into a butterfly. In fact, the new birth is *The Ultimate Metamorphosis*, that "change in the form or nature of a thing into a completely different one, by natural or supernatural means."

## Midnight Visitors

Just as Mawalera Tembo came by night, met with Dr. Walter Elmslie, back in 1897, and discovered the new birth—a new heart, a transformed life—another figure came out of the night and found his way to our Lord. Out of that meeting with Nicodemus came our most familiar teaching on the *new birth*, that "implant" of new life into a spiritually dead soul, that spiritual conception in the room of the heart from which a miracle birth takes place, that spiritual resurrection of one who was "dead in trespasses and sin." This beautiful experience remains the highlight of our human existence and life's greatest miracle.[1]

Here's the way that nighttime encounter is portrayed in John's Gospel:

> There was a man of the Pharisees named Nicodemus, a member of the Jewish ruling council. He came to Jesus at night and said, "Rabbi, we know you are a teacher who has come from God. For no one could perform the miraculous signs you are doing if God were not with him."
>
> In reply Jesus declared, "I tell you the truth, no one can see the kingdom of God unless he is born again."
>
> "How can a man be born when he is old?" Nicodemus asked. "Surely he cannot enter a second time into his mother's womb to be born!"
>
> Jesus answered, "I tell you the truth, no one can enter the kingdom of God unless he is born of water and the Spirit. Flesh gives birth to flesh, but the Spirit gives birth to spirit. You should not be surprised at my saying, 'You must be born again.' The wind blows wherever it pleases. You hear its sound,

*but you cannot tell where it comes from or where it is going. So it is with everyone born of the Spirit"* (3:1-8).

Unlike Mawalera Tembo, this was a very enlightened man who came in from the night, one who was known as *the* teacher of Israel. Yet as far as the needs of his soul were concerned, Nicodemus stood on exactly the same level as Tembo.

He needed to receive the *necessary* birth. "I tell you the truth, no  one can see the kingdom of God unless he is born again." The difference between "May I?" and "Can I?" is the difference between permission and *ability*. What Jesus is saying is that it is *not humanly possible* to see, much less enter, God's kingdom without the new birth.

**Second,** to his great surprise, Nicodemus needed a *second* birth. "Born again" means "born a second time," as Nicodemus picks up quite well. There is a physical birth; there must also be a spiritual birth. The one, "born of the flesh," the other, "born of the Spirit." To enter God's kingdom, you have to have two births. The visitor might have asked, "Why? Wasn't my first birth good enough?" The answer would have been, apparently, "Not good enough at all," in that we are all born with a sinful nature.

This nighttime visitor also heard a ***third*** thing about this new birth: by implication it is an *unmerited* birth. There was no credit even he, an illustrious Jewish leader, could build up to step across into God's kingdom. Nothing can commend a person to be born again. The question before him would be, "What did I do to be born the first time?" Obviously, *not one thing*. That's what makes the birth language so stark. Our arrival in this world was entirely out of our hands. Similarly, our new birth must be entirely a work of God's grace.

And this is very good news for all of us who crawl into the realm of light by night! The new birth is not a reward for the righteous. It is a gift for the guilty—for those who know deep down that they need a Saviour.

*Fourth*, once Nicodemus caught the drift, this birth is a *heavenly birth.* The Greek word for *again* can also be translated "from above." In other words, this is an "out of this world birth"—which makes you wonder why anyone in our experience-oriented age would ever want to decline it! It is new life that comes down from the throne of God itself! It does not "well up" within us but comes down upon us. That is to say that if you are going to go to heaven, heaven must *first come to you.* The new birth must come down and flood your soul. This makes the new birth so incredibly inviting. This is what drew Mawalera and Nicodemus and a great host of others out of their spiritual night. This is the most other-worldly experience available to the human soul: to be born from above.

Number *five*, this birth from above is *an illuminating birth!* It brings a level of insight that one has never had before. We could call it revelation, enabling one to "see" spiritual things, to break out of the spell in which "the god of this world has blinded the minds of unbelievers." This is like spiritual cataract surgery and the sudden gift of 20/20 vision. As the hymn says, "Once I was blind, but now I can see!" This means to see with understanding, to have discernment. The new birth gives us spiritual eyes to see what we have never seen before. We can now see *ourselves* as we never have before. Best of all, we have eyes to see the cross of Jesus as God's loving invitation to a fallen world, as the bridge that leads us back to the Father. Without the new birth, we are pretty much blind to all of that.

**Sixth**, and maybe best of all, this is a *cleansing* birth. When Jesus introduces "water and the Spirit," he is referring to the work that God's Spirit does in the human heart. He is taking Nicodemus back to a very familiar passage of restoration, cherished by every Jew:

> For I will take you out of the nations; I will gather you from all the countries and bring you back into your own land. I will sprinkle clean water on you, and you will be clean; I will cleanse you from all your impurities and from all your idols. I will give you a new heart and put a new spirit in you; I will remove from you your heart of stone and give you a heart of flesh. And I will put my Spirit in you and move you to follow my decrees (Ezekiel 36:24-26).

This is the new birth. It's a heart transplant. God takes out a heart of stone and replaces it with a heart of flesh. He implants his law within that heart. He puts his Spirit within. He causes us to walk in his statutes.

What a birth this is, a birth that must have dawned upon Nicodemus like a lightning bolt! First there is the washing, the "sprinkling with clean water," the cleansing "from all your impurities and from all your idols." Then comes the new heart! It's like before God delivers a new heart, he first has to clean house! He cleans you on the inside and washes away your sin. Then he puts in a new heart. This is a cleansing birth. He washes away your past. He cleanses from the inside out.

The same experience was opening up before the nighttime visitors: for the first time in your life, *you can feel clean*. In the words of Isaiah, *"Though your sins are like scarlet, they shall be as white as snow; though they are red as crimson, they shall be like wool"* (Isaiah 1:18). This is what makes the new birth a truly ultimate experience. From the top of your head to the soles of your feet, you are washed clean by the Holy Spirit.

Another remarkable thing about the new birth, by implication, is that, **seventh**, it is an *instantaneous birth*. We're talking about a lightning bolt out of heaven. Implied in the birth metaphor is immediacy. As if to say, no one is progressively born into the family of God. We may be under conviction for a time and, like Augustine, growing ever closer to the ultimate experience. Or we may be searching, like our nighttime visitors Mawalera and Nicodemus. But when the new birth comes, it comes in a moment. We go from being unborn to born in a second, just as we came into the world—a sudden infusion of divine life. There may be an extensive buildup to birth, which all mothers know about, the protracted labour pains and contractions. But when the moment of birth arrives, and the newborn babe gives its first cry, it is immediate—and of course it is celebratory! A new life has been born into the world!

So it is with going from spiritual death to the realms of life. This is not going to be like another day at the office. By implication, this is an *event*. A person will know when this happens! How could you not know the day of your birth? Just as your passport states the day of your physical birth, there is a day and a time when you are born into the kingdom of God. Your spiritual birthday. A day to be remembered and celebrated. Many people can take you to the very place, the exact bench where they knelt, the exact place and time. For all of time and eternity, it remains a sacred place. That's where they were made alive.

As we think some more about this birth metaphor, number **eight** becomes obvious: this is a *comprehensive birth*. It is implied in the idea of birth. Under normal circumstances, no one is born into this world with only half their appendages. Just as we were born physically with two hands and two feet, receiving the whole appendage package at birth, so the new birth is a comprehensive birth. What God delivers is new eyes to see, a new mind to understand, a new heart, new hands to serve, new feet to obey, new affections, new tastes, new priorities, and a new disposition. From the top of your head to the soles of your feet, everything inside is new. No part of you remains unaffected. There is no back room closet that has escaped the new birth. This new creation of his receives the full package at the front end.

And this we certainly need. Such is our natural state, living only in the power of our first birth, that the interior of our lives might as well be under the rule of Chief Mombera, the warrior chief of the Ngoni. The new birth must break his hold. The comprehensive new birth reverses his comprehensive rule, the spread and penetration of sin. The mind that was in the dark can now see; the defiled heart is replaced with a new heart; the will that all too often, according to Donne, "proves weak and untrue" is set free and revitalized. Paul describes it as a whole new creation: *"old things are passed away; behold, all things are become new"* (2 Corinthians 5:17 KJV). New eyes to see, new ears to hear, new heart and mind, new hands to grasp the truth, new lips to sing for the truth—in fact, with the new birth, you are not the same person. You are—lock, stock, and barrel—brand new.

Number *nine*, this is *a radical birth*. The term "birth" is a lot more radical than "correction" or "adjustment." Neither of our nighttime visitors needed a mid-life correction. This is a *birth*. It is the most life-altering change imaginable. There will be no greater transformation than this. Dramatic and radical, from grunge to godliness, from profanity to purity, vulgarity to virtue—a new self has been created in righteousness. With the new birth, you have received a "total makeover."

On American television, they have a "Total Makeover" show where they take a rather unkempt and overweight person and "make them over" in a few months. There are special diets and emollients—and plenty of trips to the hairdresser's. Then when the day of the great unveiling occurs, the curtains are opened and the "made over" person steps out. *Voila*, it is a total makeover! A "new person" emerges and nobody even recognizes her! "Where did you come from?" their friends ask.

With the new birth, we receive something even more than a total makeover. What we receive is a total *takeover* of a life. Old friends may not even recognize "the new you." They might have trouble believing that this is the same person. This is because with the new birth you are really *not* the same person deep down. You have experienced one radical, and total, reorientation.

Another thing about this new birth: **tenth**, this is a *sovereign birth*. Here, Nicodemus has to really expand his mind and grasp a second metaphor: the wind. It "blows where it wishes." No one can start the wind, steer the wind, or stop the wind. The wind has a mind of its own. It is only guided by God's hand. It goes where God directs.

And this is like the new birth. It is a majestic work of God by the Holy Spirit. As we make a turn toward God in repentance and faith, he does the work: he regenerates our dead heart.

This is more good news for our nighttime visitors. Just as we had nothing to do with our physical birth, our new birth is not something we can orchestrate. God creates new life in those who believe and call on him. It's as simple as that. We are born again, "not of human decision," John writes, "but by the will of God" (1:13).

**Eleven**, there is something *inscrutable* about this new birth. "You do not know where it comes from" (v. 8). So it is with everyone born of the Holy Spirit. No one can explain how God works in these matters, bringing some people out of the night and not others. Sometimes it is the last person we would ever expect who comes into the new birth. Our prime candidate misses the moment while the Spirit reaches to bottom of barrel, to the outer perimeters of any interest in spiritual things, and reels another in to the realm of grace. The Spirit comes, inviting and calling, and only God knows where and when. This is all about the wisdom and genius of the will of God.

Finally, by implication, we have number *twelve*: this is a *lasting birth*. It is a profound and enduring birth. Again, we build on the birth metaphor. It just makes sense. In fact, later in the conversation, Jesus said, *"Whoever believes on him shall not perish but have eternal life."* No doubt that is what put the smile on the face of Mawalera Tembo, back in 1897. If you could be born for five years and then unborn, it would not be "eternal life" but "five-year life." But the Lord gives *eternal life* and settles your destiny forever. Infant mortalities are not part of the picture here. This nighttime conversation carries eternal implications.

This is a pretty special assurance that comes with the new birth. When your eternal destiny is settled, there is a certain peace that prevails over all the affairs of this life. This gift of God is not going to be taken back within time. We are not stillborn into the kingdom of God. This gift of life goes on through all ages to come. Eternal life begins now and extends forever. And it is all due to our great new birth.

The only question left is, how? If the new birth offers so much radical life transformation, how do we access it? In fact, Nicodemus asked the right question after all! *"How can a man be born when he is old?...Surely he can not enter a second time into his mother's womb and be born!"*

There is only one way to access it, and that is the way discovered by Malawera Tembo and Nicodemus. They *came in out of the night*. As the hymn puts it,

> Out of my bondage, sorrow, and night,
> Jesus, I come! Jesus, I come!

Into Thy freedom, gladness, and light,
Jesus, I come to Thee!
Out of my sickness into Thy health,
Out of my want and into Thy wealth,
Out of my sin and into Thyself,
Jesus, I come to Thee!

Anyone can do that. Whether they come out of dark corners of an Ngoni village or off the cobblestone streets of Jerusalem—anyone can find their way to the Saviour. They can turn the words of that very old hymn into a prayer.

And be born again.

# Bibliography

Adeleye, Femi, *Preachers of A Different Gospel.* (Grand Rapids: Zondervan, 2011).

Ayittey, George B.N., *Africa Unchained: The Blueprint for Africa's Future* (New York: Palsgrave Macmillan, 2005).

Birkinshaw, Peter, *The Livingstone Touch* (Cape Town: CTR, 1973).

Bishop, Colin, "13 Ways Pornography Leaks into Your Home and How to Stop It," *LDSLiving*, January 1, 2018.

Blaikie, William Garden, *The Personal Life of David Livingstone* (London: Chatto, 1880).

Chanda, Victor, "The Word and the Spirit: Epistemological Issues in the Faith, Health and Wealth Movement in Zambia," Doctoral Dissertation in Theology (Pretoria: UNISA, 2013).

Davidson, Basil, *Black Mother: The Years of the African Slave Trade* (London: Little Brown & Co, 1961).

Dyrness, William A., *Learning About Theology from the Third World* (Grand Rapids: Zondervan Publishing House, 1990).

Elmslie, Walter A., *Among the Wild Ngoni* (London: Clarke, Doble & Brendon, 1899).

Fraser, Agnes Renton Robson, *The Man Who Made Friends: Donald Fraser of Livingstonia* (London: SCM, 1936).

Golding, Vautier, *The Story of David Livingstone* (New York: Yesterday's Classics, 2007).

Greear, J.D., "Only the Word Brings Order out of Chaos," www.jdgreear.com, Feb. 8, 2016.

Hadley, Debbie, "Not That Fragile" www.thoughtco.com

Hinfelaar, Hugo, *Religious Change Among Bemba-Speaking Women of Zambia*. PhD Diss., Northwest University, 2008.

Hodges, Melvin, *The Indigenous Church* (Springfield: Gospel Publishing House, 1953).

Hunter, Scott, "A Case Study" PAOC, 1985.

Jeal, Tim, *Livingstone* (Yale: Nota Bene, 2001).

Jenkins, Philip, "Believing in the Global South," *First Things*, December 2006.

Kraft, Charles, *Worldview for Christian Witness*. (Pasadena, William Casey, 2013).

Livingstone, David, *The Last Journals of David Livingstone*, compiled by Horace Waller (London: John Murray, 1874).

*Missionary Travels and Researches*

*The Zambezi and Its Tributaries*

McAndrews, Brian, *Niagara Parks Butterflies*.

McNair, James, *Livingstone the Liberator: A Study of a Dynamic Personality* (Glasgow: The David Livingstone Trust, 1976).

Mahajan, Vijay, *Africa Rising* (Upper Saddle River, NJ: Wharton Publishing House 2009).

Maluleke, Tinyiko Sam, "Half a Century of African Christian Theologies," *Journal of Theology for Southern Africa* 99, 1997.

Mbiti, John, *Introduction to African Religion* (London: Heinemann Educational Books, 1991).

Northcott, Cecil, *David Livingstone: His Triumph, Decline and Fall* (Guildford: Lutterworth, 1973).

Rob Peters, "Modern Leadership Lessons from Don Quixote," www.standardoftrust.com, March 29, 2015.

Pettengill, Mike, "Crawling Through the 10/40 Window," May 20, 2013.

Pradervand, Pierre, *Listening to Africa* (New York: Praeger, 1989).

Schapaera, Isaac, *Livingstone's African Journal* (London: Chatto & Windus: 1963).

Sharp, Larry, "Why I Am no Longer a Missionary," www.emqonline.com.

Summerton, Pauline, *Fishers of Men* (Tiverton: BAHN, 2003).

Taylor, Charles, *A Secular Age* (Boston: Harvard University Press, 2007).

Taylor, John Vernon, *Christians of the Copperbelt: The Growth of the Church in Northern Rhodesia* (London: SCM Press, 1961).

Endnotes

Introduction

1.  John Vernon Taylor, *Christians of the Copperbelt: The Growth of the Church in Northern Rhodesia.* London: SCM Press, 1961. Taylor provides much helpful information for this section on the original settlement of the region.

2.  Philip Jenkins, "Believing in the Global South." *First Things.* December, 2006.

3.  A growth parallel to a decrease of traditional religions, from 20.5% to 8.7% over the same period, and a slight increase of Muslims (from 40.0 to 41.7%). See Adriaan van Klinken's notes in "On the Growth of Christianity in Africa" *Wordpress.* June 12, 2013: "The Center for the Study of Global Christianity at Gordon Conwell Theological Seminary has just released a new report…The report covers major demographic trends in global Christianity, world religions, and mission over the past 40 year, while tracking potential trends for the next 10 years." Van Klinken notes that "the report is based

on the Word Christian database, which divides Christianity in six traditions (Anglicans, Independents, Marginals, Orthodox, Protestants, and Roman Catholics) but does not look at Pentecostal Christianity as a separate category. Instead we read that Catholics may remain the largest block and that Anglicans have seen the fastest growth. This may partly be explained with a reference to the Charismatic renewalist movements within these denominations. But what about Pentecostal Christians outside the six established categories counted by the WCD, such as those in the new-Pentecostal mega-churches that are booming? ... By sticking to the six WCD categories, the report risks ignoring a major development in African Christianity."

4. Philip Jenkins says, "We must be careful about generalizations concerning the vast and diverse world of southern Christianities, and I stress the plural. There is no single southern Christianity, any more than there is such a thing as European or North American Christianity: Each of these terms involves numerous components, some strongly at odds with the other...Yet we can say that many Global South Christians are more conservative in terms of both beliefs and moral teaching than are the mainstream churches of the Global North, and this is especially true in Africa. The churches that have made most dramatic progress in the Global South have been...evangelical and Pentecostal Protestant sects" ("Believing in the Global South," December 2006). "These newer churches preach deep personal faith and communal orthodoxy, mysticism, and puritanism, all founded on clear scriptural authority...For better or worse, the dominant churches of the future could have much in common with those of medieval or early modern European times."

5. Melvin Hodges, *The Indigenous Church*. Springfield, MO: Gospel Publishing House, 1953, 14.

6. Quoted in "Africa's Burgeoning Evangelicals," *Daily Maverick* 16:09 (December, 2013).

7. Tinyiko Sam Maluleke, "Half a Century of African Christian Theologies," *Journal of Theology for Southern Africa 99*. 1997, 3-4.

8. Joe Imakando is quoted in *Daily Maverick* 16:09.

9. Victor Chanda, "The Word and the Spirit: Epistemological Issues in the Faith, Heath, and Wealth Movement in Zambia." PhD diss., UNISA, 2013.

10. Jenkins, "Belief in the Global South."

11. Mbiti is quoted in Maluleke, "African Christian Theologies."

12. Schapera, Isaac, *Livingstone's African Journal: 1853-1856, Vol. 2*. London: Chatto & Windus: 1963, 303.

13. *The Last Journals of David Livingstone* compiled by Waller. (London: John Murray, 1874). Nov. 8, 1872. Subsequent quotes from this text noted as LJ.

14. Centre for Global Christianity, Gordon Conwell Seminary: Christianity in its Global Context 1970-2020. Society, Religion, and Mission, 2013.

Chapter 1

1. Cecil Northcott, *David Livingstone: His Triumph, Decline and Fall*. Guildford: Lutterworth, 1973. Future references noted as Northcott.

2. James MacNair, *Livingstone the Liberator: A Study of a Dynamic Personality.* Glasgow: The David Livingstone Trust, 1976.

3. Thoreau, Henry David, Jeffrey S. Cramer ed., *Walden.* Yale University Press, 2004, 313.

4. Emerson, Ralph Waldo, Stanley Applebaum ed., *Self-Reliance and Other Essays.* New York: Thomas Nelson, 1993, 35.

5. Rob Peters, "Modern Leadership Lessons from Don Quixote," www.standardoftrust.com, March 29, 2015.

6. Peter Birkinshaw, *The Livingstone Touch.* Cape Town: CTR, 1973, 12. University of Cape Town's Birkinshaw considers Livingstone "the African Corbett" and says that, like the English nature writer, he "places us in the same situation with himself and makes us see all that he does...He belongs at his best...to the oldest and central tradition of English prose, not only the factual prose of ordinary journalism, but that of chronicles and logs, with their transparency and impersonality, and of diaries and letters, with their trust in colloquial directness, their tendency to express on paper exactly what one would say to the same person by word of mouth." As for Livingstone's immersion in the KJV, Birkinshaw says, "this habit formed Livingstone's prose as well as his life...a style of timeless energy, economy and music," 14. All quotations from this text will be noted as LT.

7. David Livingstone, *Missionary Travels and Researches in South Africa.* London: 1857. All references to this text will be noted as MT. *The Last Journals of David Livingstone in Central Africa* (London: John Murray, 1874) will be noted as LJ. *Livingstone's Narrative of an Expedition to the Zambezi and its Tributaries* (London: John Murray, 1865) will be noted as ZT.

8. William Garden Blaikie, *The Personal Life of David Livingstone*. London: Chatto, 1880, 102. Future references noted as WGB.

Chapter 2

1. Birkinshaw, 12.

Chapter 3

1. Birkinshaw, 78.

2. Meriel Bunton, *David Livingstone*. London: Springer, 2001, 127.

3. Northcott, 47.

4. Birkinshaw, 54.

5. Tim Jeal, *Livingstone*. Yale: Nota Bene, 2001.

6. R.N. Campbell, *Livingstone*. London: E. Benn Ltd., 138

7. Northcott, 45.

8. Basil Davidson, *Black Mother: The Years of the African Slave Trade*. London: Little Brown & Co., 1961, 15.

9. Vaultier Golding, *The Story of David Livingstone*. New York: Yesterday's Classics, 2007.

Chapter 5

1. William Dyrness, *Learning About Theology from the Third World*. Grand Rapids: Zondervan Publishing House, 1990, 12.

2. Ikechukwu Anthony Kanu, "J.S. Mbiti's African Concept of Time and the Problem of Development." *International Conference on Humanities, Literature and Management*. Dubai,

ICHLM 15, Jan. 9-10, 2015.

3. Edmond Sanganyado, "Five Reasons You Should Consider Reading African Theologians." www.africatheology.com, Imani, Aug. 7, 2017.

4. Victor Chanda, "The Word and the Spirit: Epistemological Issues in the Faith, Health and Wealth Movement in Zambia." PhD diss., Pretoria: UNISA, 2013.

5. Pierre Pradervand, *Listening To Africa*. New York: Praeger, 1989, 212.

6. Ibid 212.


Chapter 6

1. Adam Clarke's commentary on the Bible was published by London: Thomas Tegg and Son, 1830 and was forty years in the writing.

2. This quote by James K.A. Smith is from his 2007 Regent College lecture, "Thinking In Tongues."

3. Charles Taylor, *A Secular Age*. Boston: Harvard University Press, 2007.


Chapter 7

1. George B.N. Ayittey, Africa *Unchained: the Blueprint for Africa's Future*. New York: Palgrave Macmillan, 2005. So quoted in Vijay Mahanjan's *Africa Rising*. Upper Saddle River, NJ: Wharton Publishing House 2009, 130.

2. Vichy Mahanjan, Africa Rising, 130.

3. Ibid, 130.

4. Ibid, 130.

5. Ibid, 131.

6. Ibid, 132.

7. Ibid, 132.

Chapter 8

1. The Mother Bodies are quoted in www.lusakatimes.com, June 17, 2017.

2. Zambia's Mother Bodies are quoted to this effect in www.lusakatimes.com, May 15, 2013.

3. World Vision's initiatives against child marriage are covered in www.lusakatimes.com, Dec. 19, 2017.

Chapter 9

1. J.D. Greear, "Only the Word Brings Order out of Chaos," www.jdgreear.com, Feb. 8, 2018.

2. Walter A. Elmslie, *Among the Wild Ngoni.* London: Clarke, Doble & Brendon, 1899, 79. All citations from this text will be noted as "Elmslie."

3. Elmslie, 35ff. The missionary is often mindful of the Ngoni beliefs in the spirit world and the recurring need for something like propitiation.

4. Ibid, 69. Elmslie's reflections on philosophical arguments for the existence of God remind me of my classes in philosophy and our section on "Grounds for Belief" with Pascal and Thomas Aquinas. For Elmslie in his new field of labour, laying such grounds is quite unnecessary: "In preaching, we have not first to prove the existence of God. He never dreams

of questioning that. We have in our instruction merely to unfold His character as Creator, Preserver, Governor, and Father to us all. As He is revealed to them, they do not question his sovereignty but bow to it. While we meet with many obstacles in their life and thought, yet as they are, we have in them much that is a help—a basis on which we may operate. However dim their spiritual light may be, we have but to unfold truth to them and it is self-evident to their minds. No preparation by civilization is required, as their spiritual instincts find in the truth of God what they are crying out for. The cry is inarticulate an unuttered, save in their unrest and blind gropings after spiritual things."

5. Elmslie, 93. Doctor Elmslie speaks about Hora Mountain "where now on of our Ngoniland stations is situated." It must have been especially meaningful for the missionaries to plant a mission station on the very site of the horrible massacres of former days.

6. Quoted in Agnes Renton Robson Fraser, The Man Who Made Friends: Donald Fraser of Livingstonia. London: SCM, 1936, 186.

7. Agnes Fraser, The Man Who Made Fraser, 198.

Chapter 10

1. Hugo Hinfelaar, "Religious Change Among Bemba-Speaking Women of Zambia," PhD diss., University of London, 1989.

2. John Vernon Taylor, 47.

3. Adriano Chalwe, "An Evaluation of the Mission History of the Pentecostal Assemblies of God Zambia," PhD thesis, North-West University, 2008.

4. Scott Hunter, "A Success Strategy in Zambian Missions: A Case Study," PAOC, 1985.

5. Chalwe, "Evaluation."

Chapter 11

1. www.zambiadailymail.co.zm, Aug. 17, 2017.

2. Maureen Munachonga, "An Ethical Evaluation of the Causes and Effects of Examination Malpractices in Zambia: A Case Study of Selected Schools in Lusaka District." MA diss., University of Zambia, May 2014.

3. Brown C.K. Kapika, "The Evil Spirits of Corruption in Zambia," www.lusakavoice.com, Jan. 19, 2016.

4. Quoted in www.lusakatimes.com, May 9, 2011.

5. President Edgar Lungu's speech was carried by the Times of Zambia, March 18, 2017.

6. US Fish and Wildlife Ecological Services, Jan. 6, 2016.

7. Femi Adeleye, www.christianitytoday.com, Apr. 11, 2014.

8. Victor Chanda, "The Word and the Spirit: Epistemological Issues in the Faith, Health and Wealth Movement in Zambia." PhD diss., UNISA, 2013.

9. Brian McAndrews, *Niagara Parks Butterflies.* Toronto: James Lorrimer 2000, 69.

10. Shabula is quoted in *The Post*, October, 2016.

11. Colin Bishop, "13 Ways Pornography Leaks into your Home and How to Stop It." www.ldsliving.com, Jan. 1, 2018.

12. Words and music by Helen Taylor & May H. Morgan, 1927.

13. Quote from www.wol.jw.org/en/wol 2014, 16.

14. Debbie Hadley, "Not That Fragile." www.thoughtco.com, Jun. 19, 2017.

15. "Why Butterflies Are Important" www.butterflyconservation.org

Chapter 12

1. Pauline Summerton's book, *Fishers of Men*, (Tiverton: BAHN, 2003) is a rich source of information on Walter Fisher and his multi-generational family ministry in Zambia.

2. The Joshua Project, www.thejoshuaproject.net

3. Mike Penttengill, "Crawling Through the 10/40 Window." www.thegospelcoalition.org, May 20, 2013.

4. Larry Sharp, "Why I Am Not A Missionary Any More!" www.emqonline.com, Oct. 2016.

5. Ehud Garcia's Cross Cultural Anthropology notes are carried by ICI/Global U.

Epilogue

1. I was inspired by Dr. Steve Lawson of OnePassion Ministries as he preached along these lines at Kitwe church, early in 2018.

Ingram Content Group UK Ltd.
Milton Keynes UK
UKHW011816170323
418736UK00001B/188

9 781460 009420